Olya's Story

This book tells a true story of events
that happened in our time. Its heroes
and heroines were ordinary people
living ordinary lives until the course
of events brought them face to face
with choices that few of us are asked
to make. The choices they made
changed the course of their lives,
and the lives of countless others who
have heard their story.

Olya's Story

A SURVIVOR'S DRAMATIC ACCOUNT OF THE PERSECUTION OF BAHÁ'ÍS IN REVOLUTIONARY IRAN

by

Olya Roohizadegan

ONEWORLD

OXFORD

Olya's Story

Oneworld Publications
(Sales and Editorial)
185 Banbury Road
Oxford OX2 7AR
England

Oneworld Publications
(U.S. Sales Office)
County Route 9, P.O. Box 357
Chatham, N.Y. 12037
USA

ISBN 1-85168-073-X

Printed and bound by
Werner Söderström Osakeyhtiö, Finland

This book is dedicated to the memory of Akhtar, 'Izzat, Mahshíd, Mona, Nusrat, Roya, Shírín, Símín, Ṭáhirih, Ṭúbá and Zarrín.

Contents

Acknowledgements

The events described in this book are those that I have personally experienced and been a part of. Many other atrocities not mentioned in these pages took place in other parts of Iran, affecting both Bahá'ís and other groups. Nor is the book complete in describing all the events that took place in Shíráz. Lack of space has forced me to exclude details of the fate of many individuals whose lives were affected in those difficult years. I also wish to state at the outset that I bear no grudges against the government of Iran and that my dearest wish is to return one day to its fair land and live in my own country as a free citizen.

I wish to record my warm appreciation of the sincere efforts of Saghi Jayhoon for her draft translation of the original text from Persian to English. My deepest thanks go to my son Fazlu'lláh for reviewing and completing the translation, and for the enormous time and effort he put into helping me with this project, and also to my eldest son Behnam for his continued encouragement and support for the publication of this book.

I am also sincerely grateful and indebted to Juliet Mabey for her editing and sheer hard work on the book, and to Novin Doostdar, Mark Jolly, Jan Nikolic, Linda Lloyd and Michael Sours of Oneworld Publications, without whose dedication it would not have been possible to publish this book in the short space of a few months. My special gratitude goes to the many friends and relatives who have sent me numerous photos and letters, which have helped enormously in the preparation of this book and in ensuring its accuracy. I am also grateful to Dr Faramarz Ettehadieh for his support of the film project and to Mr Abu'l-Qásim Afnán for his encouragement.

Last but not least I wish especially to thank and acknowledge the role of my husband Alláh-Morad for his love and devotion, for being instrumental in my release from prison at the cost of sacrificing everything, for sharing with me in my suffering and pain and for unstintingly giving me his support. Also to my youngest son Payam who, as a three-year-old child, was a witness to and a victim of my imprisonment in those turbulent years. Who knows how much a small child, forcibly separated from his mother, has suffered? Who can feel the pain and anguish of the families of those dear souls who were killed, and who knows what they are still going through now?

O. R.

Prologue

It was 10.30 a.m., 19 January 1983 when I heard the sound of my name echo throughout the prison. They were calling me for release over the loudspeakers. Or at least, I hoped they were.

I wouldn't be the only one to be put through their cruel game. It was a familiar trick. Bails had been paid in vain and false promises made on other occasions. Friends and relatives of prisoners would be forced to surrender their homes in the hope of being reunited with their loved ones, only to discover that the prisoners had been led to execution.

The day before, the prosecutor had offered to set me free – so long as my husband Morad could come up with 800,000 tuman. There was no way of telling if the order for my release was genuine, but I had to believe it was.

At the announcement of my name, everyone rushed out of their cells and gathered round. In the excitement each began to talk over the other's voices. 'Take this with you,' said Ṭáhirih, handing me a bar of soap. 'If you *are* released, give it to the guard and tell him it belongs to me. If not –'

'Then you can be sure I am dead.'

She tightened her grip on my hand. I looked at her and at the others – Mona was there and so was S͟hírín and Roya and Nusrat and Túbá and Zarrín and Mahs͟híd and A͟khtar and Símín and 'Izzat. Every face wore a smile that whispered: 'Remember us.'

My name was announced for a second time.

I had rehearsed this moment a thousand times in my head and now I was barely able to speak a word. These women were my dearest sisters. We had shared the same food, the same cell, the same air, the same pain.

And now I was leaving them.

But there was a purpose in my going. I had often sworn to them – as they had to me – that if I was ever to get out of Adelabad Prison I would tell the world their story, our story.

Nusrat threw her arms around me. 'If only I could sneak into your pocket and come with you,' she said, tears streaming down her face. I couldn't bear to look into her eyes; I was scared I might not be able to tear my gaze away from them. But how could I turn away from those eyes? I had to keep this moment with me.

She was still embracing me when I heard my name called for a third and final time. If you failed to show up after the third call, your release was cancelled. Fakhrí, one of the political prisoners who had come out from the cell opposite, tried to loosen Nusrat's hold. 'Let her go. Olya will be too late for her release,' she urged. In the end Fakhrí practically bundled me down the stairs.

I mechanically descended the steps, but at the same time I felt myself being pulled back towards my friends. The conflicting emotions were almost paralysing. Remember this, I kept telling myself. Remember this. My feet became rooted to the spot as though in a dream. By now the women above me were all imploring me to go. 'Run. Before it's too late,' they cried.

I took one last look at them from the foot of the stairs. Oh God, would I ever see those dear faces again? Would they ever be free?

PART I

PERSECUTION

Trial by Fire

CHAPTER 1

A tank was stationed at the school gate, the barrel of its gun pointing directly into the school yard – martial law had been imposed. Fazlu'lláh, our fourteen-year-old son, left school early that day. The principal had no choice but to send the children home when the older boys started a riot and demanded the teachers go on strike. They were protesting against the killing of hundreds of demonstrators the week before in Jaleh Square in Tehran. We were living in troubled times.

Faz had to walk through the centre of S̲h̲íráz to get home. Tanks and truckloads of soldiers were stationed everywhere. Approaching Zand Street, he found himself caught up in a public demonstration against the Shah; the army was out in force, and began to fire tear gas and live bullets into the crowd. Ducking into a side alley, Faz managed to escape. It was not long before all the schools were closed for the children's safety, but Faz and his older brother Behnam didn't complain. Instead of sitting at a school desk, they spent much of their time engrossed in making model aircraft and flying them around the house or in the parks – keeping well away from the tanks.

All through that long, hot summer of 1978, the riots and demonstrations against the government of Iran had escalated. Trouble had begun in January with a religious march in Qum protesting at an official newspaper article critical of the exiled Islamic leader, Áyatu'lláh Khomeini. The police opened fire, a number of seminary students were killed, and the government was promptly denounced as anti-Islamic by one of the leading Áyatu'lláhs in Iran. The revolution was under way.

First there were a few small demonstrations in Qum, Tabríz and my parents' home town of Jahrum. People marched in the street, shops were looted, banks burned. The Shah called in the army, more people were killed, and further demonstrations were held to protest against the deaths. Each new clash with the security forces added fresh momentum, and the riots and strikes spread like wildfire throughout the country.

By the autumn the whole nation seemed to be mobilized against the Shah. Civil disorder and public protests had become daily occurrences, factories and offices were out on strike, public transport ground to a halt, and now even the children were being dragged into it.

In the uprising against the Pahlaví regime, the Bahá'ís, as the largest religious minority in Iran, were vulnerable to persecution from all sides. The army and police, so quick to crush demonstrations against the Shah, did nothing to protect them. Since the start of disturbances there had been an increasing number of attacks on Bahá'ís in rural areas and small towns. Houses were looted, livestock stolen, shops attacked.

My own family had suffered. In August my brother-in-law, Zíyá Ḥaqíqat, had been mown down by a motor cycle on a foot-path outside his office in Jahrum. After the accident a crowd of people had gathered around – eyewitnesses agreed it had looked deliberate; Zíyá lay face down in the street, until my brother happened to be passing and spotted him. He was taken to the nearest hospital only to be refused medical treatment. He was a Bahá'í.

His wife Laqá, my eldest sister, hurriedly arranged for him to be transferred to the Namází Hospital in Shíráz with the help of a Bahá'í doctor. In the ambulance she kept asking Zíyá how the accident happened, but Zíyá didn't know. By the time they reached the second hospital, which was 120 miles away, he had fallen into a coma. He never regained consciousness.

Laqá contacted the judge at the criminal court and told him all the facts, but he refused to investigate the case or press charges. The matter was closed, she was told.

As the wave of religious fundamentalism began to sweep the country, news of other such isolated incidents began to reach us in Shíráz. Living in the relative safety of a large town, however, we were not expecting serious outbreaks of violence – certainly nothing on the scale of the events that followed.

It started on 9 December of that year, three months after martial law was declared. Áyatu'lláh Misbáhí and Áyatu'lláh Dastghayb, the most prominent clergymen in Shíráz, incited a crowd of their followers to join them on an expedition against the Bahá'ís of Sarvistán, a small town about fifty miles from Shíráz.

Several hundred people descended on the small town, looting Bahá'í shops and attacking Bahá'í homes; men, women and children were dragged out by force. Many, including the sick and the elderly, were bundled into large sacks and then carried to the mosques – in order to be forced to 'accept Islam' by those who believed the Bahá'í Faith was a heretical sect.

Some Bahá'ís bowed to the pressure, others took advantage of the darkness and slipped away in the night towards Shíráz, travelling across mountains and valleys on foot with only the clothes they were wearing. Meanwhile their properties were confiscated, their possessions stolen, and their homes burned. Within two days, 300 Bahá'ís had been made homeless. Many had to be accommodated in the Shíráz Bahá'í Centre, and others moved on to seek refuge with friends and relatives in other towns.

A couple of days later my husband Morad and I, with Behnam and Faz, set off to spend the day with my parents, brothers and sisters and Laqá's five children. They had all just moved from Jahrum to Bábákúhí on the outskirts of Shíráz for safety, following a recent outbreak of violence. They were staying in the house of one of the local Bahá'ís, which was situated at the foot of a mountain. It was a lovely, bright December day, and Behnam and Faz decided, since this was their first visit, to go mountain-climbing.

Half an hour later they came rushing back to the house out of breath. At first I thought they'd simply been racing each other, but their expressions were serious. They were clearly worried about something, and the mood of the afternoon suddenly changed.

'We had only managed to get half-way up the mountain', Behnam panted, 'when we heard helicopters overhead and the sound of fire-engines from the direction of the city . . .'

'So we looked back,' interrupted Faz, 'and saw thick columns of smoke rising up all over the place.'

Perhaps there was some sort of demonstration going on, the boys said, and some of the people were burning paper in the streets. By now we were all quite used to the fact that our country was in turmoil – marches and demonstrations against the government were everyday occurrences, even in Shíráz. But despite events in Sarvistán, it never occurred to them that it could be people's houses that were being attacked this time. My mother immediately phoned some friends. She rushed back into the room and confirmed my deepest fears: the smoke was indeed coming from the burning houses of Bahá'ís, and the authorities, desperately clinging on to office, were unable or unwilling to protect them.

The smoke, according to Behnam and Faz, was coming from the direction of the Sa'adi district of the city, so my first concern was to get over there to the Reyhánís' house, where many of the documents belonging to the Bahá'í community of Shíráz were kept. The widowed Mrs Reyhání had gone on holiday to Germany two days previously. The home would be empty, but her neighbour Sattár Khushkhú might still be there and in need of help.

My father, Morad and the two boys climbed into the car. For anonymity, I quickly slipped on a chador – the all-encompassing veil that was favoured dress for Islamic women – and then snatched up a spare one. I thought that when we got to Mr Khushkhú's we could perhaps disguise him with the chador and discreetly lead him out of his house and away from the area to safety.

As we approached the Sa'adi district, we ran into a mass of people wielding shovels and pickaxes, and heading in the direction of the street where Mrs Reyhání and the Khushkhús lived. The din of shouting voices became louder and louder.

We turned the corner that led into their street; there was a crowd of over 2,000 people, headed by mullahs, and they were already destroying Mrs Reyhání's house. Men were running out with furniture and electrical appliances, while others ripped out wall tiles, light fittings, toilets, taps – everything they could reach. Mrs Reyhání owned a very large Persian carpet, and to our surprise we saw several men carrying sections of it rolled up on their shoulders; they had obviously divided the spoils between them. In a few minutes the entire house had been stripped and then they threw firebombs into it and burned all that was left to a charred shell.

The mob moved on to the Khushkhús' house opposite. Mr Khushkhú had already left the area with his wife and daughter, leaving their house to suffer the same fate at the hands of the crowd.

When they were finished with this and the other Bahá'í houses in the area, the mob moved east, towards the Pepsi bottling factory, located near the airport just outside the city. With Morad in the driving seat and the two boys in the back, we edged along carefully behind the crowd, monitoring their every movement to see what would happen next, keeping a safe distance of some fifty yards between the mob and ourselves.

It took two hours before all of the mob reached the factory. The crowd was clearing out crate upon crate of Pepsi. I persuaded Morad to drive closer so we could see exactly what they were doing. Then, having emptied the warehouse of all they could get their hands on, and instructed the workmen to leave the premises, the mob moved in with firebombs and other explosives. A few minutes later the whole structure burst into flames and a thick plume of black smoke curled into the sky.

Morad wanted to turn back at this point as the road had become jammed with people; it was too dangerous to go any nearer. The boys were too young to be witnessing this sort of mob violence, he argued, and I should be more careful – I was four months pregnant. I was scared too, but my curiosity got the better of me. Why were they doing this? What gave these people their urge for destruction?

I wound down the car window to ask one of the men in the crowd why they were all so intent on destroying the factory. The man was perhaps in his mid-sixties and wore a stained shirt – from all appearances he was from a peasant background. He replied, in answer to my question, that the owner of the Pepsi factory was a Bahá'í.

Without a thought, I decided there and then to try and reason with him. 'Don't you realize you're ruining the livelihoods of more Muslims than Bahá'ís? All kinds of people work here. You're destroying your own property.'

'Why are you defending the Bahá'ís?' he asked suspiciously.

'Bahá'í, Muslim, we are all human beings. We have to learn to live together,' I replied impulsively.

Behnam and Faz were growing restless in the back of the car. 'You want to get us all killed Mama?' they whispered desperately. More and more people were milling round the car, and we began to feel very vulnerable.

'Are you Bahá'ís?' the man demanded, suddenly suspicious. He turned as if looking for reinforcements, and my father quickly leant forward to touch my shoulder, warning me to keep quiet.

At that moment, the man spotted some others he knew and began to beckon them over. Morad had had enough. He quickly slid the car into reverse and sped out of sight.

We headed back to the city. Wherever we turned we saw the blackened skeletons of houses. Bahá'ís who had been forced to abandon their homes and everything in them stood gazing at the smouldering rubble. In one of the side streets we saw a pile of broken furniture dumped in the middle of the road, and beside it an old woman stood weeping. We went to comfort her. She was a Muslim, she said, but her heart went out to her Bahá'í neighbours whose home had just been attacked. They were a poor family, she told us, and their life's work had gone up in flames. 'They are human beings too – it's not right,' she sobbed.

The army and security forces, who were constantly called out these days to halt demonstrations against the Shah's regime, were nowhere to be seen. A helicopter flew overhead to monitor the movements of the crowd, and the fire brigade stood by just to make sure none of the fires spread to any adjoining properties belonging to Muslims.

These destructive mobs, and the authorities who stood by and did nothing, were the same Iranian people who had always been respected for their humanity; the descendants of those who had built one of the world's most advanced civilizations and set the highest standards for the treatment of their fellow citizens, including the first charter of human rights. Now, as I looked on in disbelief, they were erasing centuries of their own work, their own achievements, and their own dignity.

That evening I went back to Bábákúhí to ensure that my parents and the rest of my relatives were safe. As I drove into their street, dusk was beginning to fall and I saw a large throng of people gathering around the entrance to their house. Quietly, I parked my car at a distance and worked my way into the crowd to hear what they were saying.

Since my relatives had just moved to the area, they were unknown to the local people. No one had any idea who they were or what beliefs they held. All that was known was that the house belonged to a Bahá'í and that he had now moved elsewhere. After much heated debate, the crowd decided to wait until morning and then return to the house with a copy of the Qur'án and ask the people staying there to swear upon it that they were Muslims. If they were found to be Bahá'ís, the crowd would first plunder the house and then set it on fire.

As soon as they had scattered, I slipped into the house to tell my relatives what I'd heard. We waited until dark and then I drove a group of them to my house, on the other side of Shíráz, some three miles away. Since there were around sixteen people in all, I would have to go back twice in order to transport them all.

On the second trip, we were approaching the city centre on the way back to my house when a group of soldiers suddenly barred our way. We had broken the curfew. Because of the burning of Bahá'í homes, the curfew had been brought forward by an hour that night, so instead of 10 p.m. it came into force at 9 p.m. We had been so involved in our attempt to rescue everyone from Bábákúhí that we'd completely forgotten the time.

Through the thick darkness, the soldiers shone their arc lights on us and ordered us to stop. My husband, who was driving on this trip, brought the car to a halt. Ten soldiers appeared, aiming their guns at our car. One of the officers yelled: 'Driver, come out of the vehicle with your hands on your head.' Morad immediately got out of the car.

They asked us what we were doing outside at this time of night and why we were not complying with curfew orders. We

told them the truth, that our relatives were Bahá'ís living in
Bábákúhí and a mob was planning to attack them in the
morning.

'Are you Bahá'ís?' one of the soldiers asked, and I admitted
that we were. The directness of my response impressed them;
they seemed genuinely to respect our honesty.

A man who introduced himself as Ja'farí, the officer in
charge, wanted to know what we were going to do next. I
explained we would have to go back once more to move everyone – unless, of course, they were able to help us. To my
surprise, Ja'farí said he was happy to help, and immediately
ordered an army jeep to accompany us back to Bábákúhí.

They escorted us close to the house where my relatives were
staying and told us to wait until the time came for them to
change shifts, because they couldn't leave their posts for the
moment. So we stood in the cold with Ja'farí and a dozen or so
other soldiers, chatting to them about our faith.

'I remember when I was young,' Ja'farí mused, rolling a ciga-
rette, 'the mullah used to lecture us endlessly on different verses
from the Qur'án. Not once did he ever teach us anything about
the Bahá'ís, even though some of the class would often ask him
about this new religion.'

'That doesn't surprise me,' I answered.

'He insisted that the Bahá'ís did not believe in the holy
book of Muhammad and that they were heretics and atheists.'

I explained to Ja'farí that as Bahá'ís we did believe in God,
we accepted all previous religions as teaching essential truths
and that Bahá'u'lláh, the founder of our Faith, teaches that the
Qur'án is the 'surest testimony of God unto men'. Bahá'u'lláh
was simply the new messenger of God for our time, as foretold
by previous prophets, including Muhammad.

We continued our friendly discussion with Ja'farí and the
other soldiers until 1.30 in the morning.

It was from Ja'farí that I first learned the army had been
ordered not to interfere with the recent attempts to burn Bahá'í
homes. The clergy's influence had become so great that even
the military now appeared to be under their control.

Ja'farí added: 'I am only helping you because it is the
humane thing to do. I can't afford to get involved. Nobody

knows what happened here tonight – it's best if we keep it that way.' He was doing all he could for us, which was more than most would have done in the same situation.

While it was still dark, Ja'farí provided an army car with more than fifteen soldiers and a jeep, and with their help we managed to move everyone out to safety.

In a period of twenty-four hours, our lives had been turned completely upside down. One night we were sleeping in peace and quiet, and the next our home was bursting at the seams with family and friends who had fled the mob. We didn't know if we ourselves would have a home to sleep in the next night. Our time from then on was totally taken up with caring for refugees, always wondering whose home would be attacked next.

The looting and burning continued to spread, and for the next two days the mobs swept through the city. Although martial law had been imposed, the authorities maintained a low profile throughout. One Bahá'í family after another were evicted and their home emptied of all its contents before being burned. The mob even went so far as to douse in petrol any pets or domestic animals they found, and immediately set light to them.

Around 8.30 on the morning following the Bábákúhí episode, I called Yadu'lláh Vahdat, who was a retired colonel and one of the most well-known Bahá'ís in Shíráz. I described the dramatic rescue of the night before and repeated what Ja'farí had told me – that the government wasn't prepared to protect the Bahá'ís.

Mr Vahdat, who was holding a meeting for some of the local Bahá'ís when I called, said he had already consulted certain senior army officers and they had promised to put a stop to the attacks.

As I spoke to him over the phone, I could see houses burning in the distance. I insisted, 'But even while we are standing here talking, I can see Bahá'í homes on fire. It looks like the mob is on 'Abírámíz Street, going from house to house.'

Mr Vahdat immediately brought the meeting to a close because of the danger – the mob was not far from his own street.

Two hours later, they reached his house. Like locusts, they consumed everything in sight, right down to the window frames. Doors were removed, and sinks, bath tubs, furniture and appliances. In less than an hour only the shell of his house remained.

In those few days, several hundred Bahá'í homes in the city and surrounding area were gutted and burned, and many more were looted and vandalized; more than 1,000 Bahá'ís were made homeless. Some were squeezed into the Shíráz Bahá'í Centre along with the refugees from Sarvistán, but a large number had been taken in by Muslim friends and neighbours.

There were, of course, many Muslims who sympathized with the plight of the Bahá'ís, and who immediately offered to help. My boss at the National Iranian Oil Company of Shíráz was typical. He was a very religious man, and felt deeply ashamed of the events that were taking place in the name of Islam. He sheltered a Bahá'í family of seven in his home for some time, offering protection from the mobs in a wonderful spirit of hospitality and love.

Other Bahá'ís abandoned their houses and fled to the relative safety of cities like Iṣfahán and Tehran, which so far had not suffered Shíráz's fate; some had reluctantly left the country.

The day after the rescue of my relatives, we took them to the safety of a hotel in the city, since our own house was not safe. We decided to take refuge with Morad's sister and her family in Ábádán on the Persian Gulf, where we stayed for a few days waiting for the situation to calm down.

Just before we left Ábádán, we took the car to the garage for a service. When Morad went to collect it, however, he noticed that the mechanics were not as polite as before; if anything they were surly. He was puzzled, and when he got back to his sister's, he checked the car thoroughly. His suspicions were confirmed. A few white granules were scattered around the oil cap. It turned out to be sugar, intended to burn the engine as soon as it got hot. The men had obviously noticed our Shírází number plate, heard about the attacks on Bahá'ís in Shíráz and put two and two together. This was their little contribution to the persecution!

Quickly, Morad and the boys drained the oil as best they could, replaced it, and we set off on the long journey home.

They evidently hadn't managed to flush out all the sugar, however – the engine seized when we were driving trough the mountains. Eventually we succeeded in flagging down a passing truck, and the driver kindly towed us all the way back to Shíráz. It was a long journey and we arrived home very late that night.

On our return, we found all was quiet in Shíráz once more. But we discovered that the only reason the mob violence had been checked was because Mr Mu'íní, the Governor General of the Province of Fars, of which Shíráz is the capital, had intervened. He had worked with Mr Hassan Afnán, a well-known Bahá'í, and they had become good friends. At Mr Afnán's urgent request he had used his influence with Áyatu'lláh Mahallátí, one of the prominent clergy in the city, to persuade the mobs to return to their homes. Reluctantly, they had obeyed.

Although the mob's attacks on Bahá'í homes had stopped, however, they promptly switched their attention to the Bahá'í cemetery just outside the city, which was renowned for its beautiful, peaceful gardens. The crowd vandalized and destroyed the tombs, then they bulldozed the area, burning the trees and setting the cemetery hall on fire. They had even stolen the flowers from the graves. They maintained that pillaging from the Bahá'ís was legitimate: they were infidels, so their possessions and money belonged to everyone.

I felt so sad to think of human beings doing such things in the name of Islam, defiling their own unique heritage. What took place on that December afternoon at the cemetery surpassed even our worst fears: people in that crowd even stooped to the vile act of opening the graves of the dead and exhuming the corpses of men and women who had been hastily buried the night before under the supervision of the army.

As soon as we had settled in to our home again, I rushed round to the Bahá'í Centre to see if help was needed. There was much to be done. Bahá'ís have no clergy or religious hierarchy, and our community affairs are organized under the guidance of elected local and national assemblies. Along with the international body, the Universal House of Justice, these institutions function solely on the principle of service rather than individual power or authority. It was largely on the shoul-

ders of the Local Spiritual Assembly of Sh̲íráz, therefore, that
the burden of caring for so many refugees now fell.

The assembly immediately set up a committee called the
'Protection Committee', which was responsible for looking after
the Bahá'ís who had been forced by the mobs to recant their
faith. Mr K̲hush̲k̲hú and I became members of this committee.

Many Bahá'ís had been badly hurt. Some relatives of ours in
Sarvistán had been among those attacked and dragged to the
mosque – even their disabled son had been manhandled in this
way. For propaganda purposes, the people who had organized
these attacks wanted to publish the names and photographs of
Bahá'ís who had recanted. However, to make the list look more
impressive, they had included the names of Bahá'ís who were
dead or had left the country, so one of our jobs was to sort out
who had indeed been forced into recanting, and to check newspaper reports against our community lists to determine the
truth. It was heartbreaking work.

Another committee set up by the assembly was the
Samaritan Committee to organize relief efforts, and Mr
K̲hush̲k̲hú and I were members of this one too. Our first task was
to find somewhere for all the homeless Bahá'ís to stay, and
decide who needed other kinds of help such as financial support.

The scale of the destruction was staggering, not just in
Sh̲íráz but in the outlying districts. Rural Bahá'ís had been
attacked too, and many had their land and livestock taken from
them and given to Muslim families. Accurate news was hard to
come by, so we set out to try and see what was happening in the
surrounding areas, to find out how many Bahá'ís were affected
and how widespread the suffering was.

We visited some of the refugees from Sarvistán, among
them whole families sleeping rough in the desert where nights
were freezing cold, or in cars, or hiding in the homes of Muslim
friends. I had to wear a chador to visit them, so that I would be
inconspicuous.

Meanwhile, Bahá'ís from all over the country were rallying
to the aid of their fellow Bahá'ís in the Sh̲íráz area. Cash, blankets, clothes and other necessities poured in. The rooms in the
Bahá'í Centre began to fill with sacks of rice, drums of cooking
oil, furniture, carpets, stoves and crockery. The centre began to

feel like a commune. Everyone bedded down on the floor of the meeting hall, cooked together, and ate together – there was a tremendous spirit of love and friendship.

Mr Khushkhú was a wonderful, kind man, and a joy to work with. He had been very amused when I told him that I had gone to his house to try to rescue him carrying a spare chador for his disguise.

'I'm a seventy-five-year-old man, and you want to turn me into a woman?' he laughed.

Poor Mr Khushkhú had recently bought the plot of land for his home from Mrs Reyhání, and he had only just finished building the house when it was attacked. 'Don't worry, Olya,' he smiled. 'I'm used to this. It's the third time I've lost my home.'

He was a very patient, tolerant man. Although he had become homeless himself, he set about devoting all his time and energy to helping other homeless Bahá'ís. When I asked him why he hadn't tried to find new accommodation for himself, he replied: 'How can I think about my own problems, knowing there are others who still don't have a place to stay? To be a Bahá'í is to serve others. If we are to commit ourselves to being good Bahá'ís we must serve with all our heart and soul.'

One Bahá'í from Marvdasht had fled his house with only slippers on his feet, having lost everything he owned. When he came to the centre he was taken to the room where all the clothes were kept. He picked out a pair of shoes for himself and offered fifty tuman for them, saying: 'I know these shoes are worth a lot more, but all I have left is the eighty tuman I had in my pocket.'

Mr Khushkhú tried to make him understand that not only was there no need for him to pay for the shoes, but that he should accept some money from the emergency funds. The man politely declined. 'It is true', he said, 'that all my belongings have been taken away, but I have trust in God, I will work again and start a new life.' There were many Bahá'ís like him.

Meanwhile, my parents, brothers, sisters and all Laqá's children were once more staying with us. For about a month the twenty of us lived in that one house, and then we managed to find my parents and brothers somewhere else to stay in Shíráz.

Laqá desperately wanted to return to her home town of Jahrum with her children, but she was not sure whether the situation there had settled down and whether the children would be allowed to go back to school. She rang up the Religious Magistrate in the Jahrum court and pretended to work at the local school.

'I'm a teacher and I have a few Bahá'í children in my class,' she fibbed. 'I wonder what I should do about them. Should I admit them to the school?'

'Yes, you can,' the Áyatu'lláh assured her. 'We already have plans for the Bahá'í children. First we must make them feel welcome at school, and then we'll ensure they give up their religion and return to the holy religion of Islam.'

Laqá nevertheless returned to Jahrum with her family and put her children back in school. A few months later, however, their teacher suddenly made them sit at the back of the class and told their classmates, 'These children are unclean because they're Bahá'ís. No one must touch them or talk to them.' So it wasn't long before the family came back to Shíráz.

A few weeks after the mob attacks on Shíráz, the Bahá'ís began to come out of hiding and set about repairing their homes and settling back into normal life. Some houses had been damaged beyond repair, others had simply been looted and ransacked, while yet others had been confiscated. Despite all the fear and upheaval, and despite the fact that many had lost their homes and all their possessions, there was a tremendous feeling of love and unity among the Bahá'ís.

After the attacks in Shíráz, a series of allegations and counter-allegations began about who was responsible. Áyatu'lláh Mahallátí, in discouraging Muslims from vandalizing and attacking Bahá'í property, not only publicly condemned these assaults, he went so far as to claim they were all part of a malicious plot by SAVAK – the Shah's secret police – to discredit the mullahs. The government, however, vehemently denied any involvement in the violence, firmly blaming the mullahs for the attacks.

Why would anyone want to bother us? We were obedient to the government, and our religion did not allow us to take part in politics. In Sh̲íráz there were less than 4,000 of us; yet there were some 450,000 Bahá'ís in Iran, which made us larger than the Christian, Jewish and Zoroastrian communities combined. We were regarded, whether we liked it or not, as a threat.

There had been phases of intense persecution previous to this, in the 1950s, the 1920s and of course in the last century when 20,000 early believers were massacred. But that seemed so distant now. This was 1978, and we were living in civilized times, or so we thought. It didn't even occur to us that the Shah's regime, until then supported by western governments, could be under threat and a new leadership with less liberal attitudes to Bahá'ís would take over the country.

As the popular uprising gathered momentum, the Pahlavís were soon being strongly advised to flee the country for their own safety – not only by the mullahs, but also by many western diplomats – and expectations rose about a new future for Iran. Attention began to focus on one man in particular who, according to rumour, was preparing for re-emergence after fifteen years of obscurity.

In 1964, this notorious Religious Judge of exceptional influence had been banished from Iran for his outspoken anti-government views. He had become so popular that people would travel long distances just to attend his lectures and hear his interpretations of the Qur'án. Among his more well-known theories was the importance he attached to the need for an Islamic figure-head who could inspire all mullahs under one theocratic republic – a supreme Guardian or Áyatu'lláh to lead all other Áyatu'lláhs. Also of vital importance to him was the view that the Bahá'í Faith was anathema to Islam.

In a matter of weeks, Áyatu'lláh Khomeini would be returning to the nation that once exiled him, to establish and head an Islamic Republic.

Revolution

CHAPTER 2

The streets of S͟híráz exploded in jubilation the day the Pahlavís left Iran. Drivers were hooting their horns and flashing their lights, people were dancing in the streets and on rooftops. On television I saw the Shah weeping as he waved goodbye to some of his staff on the airport runway. It was a sad portrait of loneliness, that single image of him bending down to scoop some of his country's soil into his pocket.

Just over a fortnight later, on 1 February 1979, Áyatu'lláh Khomeini left Paris on a flight bound for Tehran. In a few hours he would be proclaiming the birth of a new state in front of a throng of three million people.

On the Air France plane, in a televized interview relayed to Iran, the Áyatu'lláh announced that all Iranians were to be free under the Islamic regime. As I watched, I wondered what was in store for the Bahá'ís now. During the Shah's reign we had sometimes been left to ourselves, sometimes used as political pawns and at other times openly persecuted. Perhaps we were destined to be like the chicken, whose head, as we say in Iran, is cut off for both weddings and funerals!

What were the Áyatu'lláh's feelings, asked the interviewer, now that he was returning to his homeland after such a long absence? Looking straight into the lens of the camera, Khomeini replied: '*Hitchi* – Nothing.'

For ten days, the armed forces still desperately clung to power. There was fighting on the streets of S͟híráz, and in Tehran the people surrounded the barracks and demanded that the army surrender. The whole country came to a standstill. By 11 February the airforce and the army had both capitulated and Iran was under Khomeini's control. Khomeini called for order to be restored and told the country to return to work. Everyone hoped that the dust of 1978's civil unrest would soon settle, and the many political factions and cultural and religious groups that made up modern Iran would be able to put their differences aside and work together to rebuild their country.

When the new constitution was drawn up by the Islamic Republic of Iran, its articles guaranteed 'justice and fairness to all' and equal rights for everyone under the law. Article 21 stated: 'Interrogating people about their beliefs is forbidden. No one can be persecuted or punished purely for holding certain beliefs.'

The Bahá'ís were very happy to hear this, though some expressed concern that the Bahá'í Faith had not been specifically mentioned in the constitution. Official recognition, we noticed, was extended to the Christians, Jews and Zoroastrians, who were allowed to practise their religion, educate their children in their faith and be represented in the parliament.

Our concern, of course, proved to be well founded; the protection ostensibly offered by this new constitution was not to be extended to the Bahá'ís. The official view, reflected in law, was that we were a heretical sect of Islam and not a separate religion (even though we were recognized as such by the United Nations). This was a crucial legal distinction, as we were to discover to our cost.

The mullahs were now running the country. It was quite obvious that they had been patiently waiting for this moment for many years, and now that they were in control one of their priorities would be a serious assault against the Bahá'ís. The eradication of the Bahá'í Faith, they believed, was their sacred responsibility and duty towards God and Islam. Exterminating or converting the followers of Bahá'u'lláh had always been their aim, and with the fall of the Shah's more liberal regime there was nothing to stand in the clergy's way. It wouldn't be long before the pogrom began.

Meanwhile, our concern for Behnam and Faz's safety was growing. The country was gradually beginning to settle down and people had started presenting themselves for work, but the schools were still closed; there was little prospect of the boys continuing their education in Iran. Moreover, Behnam, already seventeen, would be liable for conscription into the army in a few months, so we had to get the boys out of the country urgently.

Morad and I decided to send them to England where they could continue their education in safety, and after weeks of uncertainty, we finally received the necessary letters of acceptance from an English school, and exit visas. On their last evening in S͟híráz, I arranged a special visit for the boys to the Bahá'ís most holy place in Iran, the House of the Báb.

S͟híráz had always occupied a pre-eminent place in Iran's history. Nestling in the Zagros mountains of south-west Iran, this was the city whose famed nightingales and roses inspired Háfiz and Sa'dí, two of Persia's greatest poets. Persepolis was founded near here by Cyrus the Great, two and a half thousand years ago, as the capital of the Persian Empire. And it was here that the Bahá'í Faith began 140 years ago.

✳ One May night in 1844, a man called Mírzá 'Alí Muhammad and known to his followers as the Báb (meaning the Gate) declared He was the dawn of a new age. He had, He claimed, come to prepare the way for another, even greater figure, foretold in the scriptures of every religion of the past, a man who would revive the hearts of all people and usher in a new era of universal peace: Bahá'u'lláh.

✳ From that simple house, in the middle of the nineteenth century, the Bahá'í Faith has spread to 200 countries around the globe. It has become the second most geographically widespread religion in the world (after Christianity), and is embraced by some five million people from over 2,000 different ethnic backgrounds.

But from the earliest ordeals faced by the followers of the Báb to the present-day upheavals, the Bahá'í Faith had met with fierce opposition. The belief that a new Messenger of God had come to herald the long-awaited regeneration of humanity was, to many mullahs, a wicked heresy – just as Christ's proclamation had been to the Jews 2,000 years ago.

While ordinary people the world over were celebrating its visionary ideals, the religion of Bahá'u'lláh was being denounced by Islamic fundamentalists as a degenerate sect. In the months after the revolution, their animosity would refocus

on the town of Shíráz, and more significantly, on this sacred
house. For the moment though, perhaps for the last time with
all our family together, the House of the Báb was open to us.

Fourteen-year-old Fazlu'lláh captured his feelings about the
visit in these words:

> My last night in Shíráz was one of the most memorable
> times of my life. We were given the great privilege of
> visiting the House of the Báb and saying goodbye to this
> beautiful and most holy place. Although we had come
> here many times before, it had always been in the
> daytime. The house was normally closed after dark, and
> so we had to ask special permission from Mr Abu'l-
> Qásim Afnán, the custodian of the House of the Báb, to
> be allowed in. It was like a pilgrimage for us.
>
> Mrs Fátimih Ḥaqiqatjú (who everyone called
> Naniyyih Aqá Rizá), the caretaker, took us up the stairs
> by candlelight to the room where the Báb had declared
> His mission for the first time. There could not be too
> much light or too many visitors at the house for fear of
> attracting attention in the tense atmosphere that pre-
> vailed in Shíráz at that time. But despite this fear, there
> was the most wonderful spiritual atmosphere in the
> room as we stood in the light of a single candle and
> gazed out at the horizon, where the last traces of the
> sun's orange glow were fading in the west. We each said
> our prayers quietly in the half-light and remained
> immersed in our own thoughts. For my part, I was
> thinking, 'When will I be privileged enough to come
> here again?'

We came down the stairs with heavy hearts, and after
thanking Naniyyih Aqá Rizá we left. On our way out my
brother and I stopped to pick up two oranges that had fallen
from a tree in the outer courtyard of the house. We took them
with us on our long journey to England as small reminders of
our beloved and holy home town of Shíráz.

Next day, on 13 March, Morad and the boys boarded a
jumbo jet in Tehran and flew to England, where Behnam and

Faz were to begin their new lives. Exactly a month later to the day, an order from the Revolutionary Guards of the Province of Fars was presented to Abu'l-Qásim Afnán. It stated that the house had been confiscated and would be occupied 'in trust' by the government to protect it from destruction. For the moment, the Bahá'ís living in the adjoining buildings were allowed to stay.

A month later, on 18 May, my third son Payam was born, bringing Morad and myself much comfort in the absence of our elder boys. Every day I wrote some lines to Behnam and Faz, and at the end of each week I would send off the collected news together in one letter.

The Muslim clergy tried all kinds of tricks in their offensive against the Bahá'ís. At the end of May 1979 a group of mullahs approached the Bahá'ís claiming to be our friends; they said they wanted to prove they could live with us side by side. They started coming to the Bahá'í Centre where we held our community meetings, and where Mr Khushkhú, among others, worked for the Shíráz community. He was working for the Local Spiritual Assembly of Shíráz by this time, and with 4,000 Bahá'ís in Shíráz the assembly's heavy workload kept him very busy.

These visitors first asked for the use of storage space at the centre, then little by little they began confiscating our property until finally, at the end of June, they seized all the buildings owned by the Umaná Company, a Bahá'í co-operative. Its properties included Bahá'í Centres all over Iran, houses of special historical importance to the Bahá'ís and the Bahá'í hospital in Tehran which was funded by Bahá'ís but open to all. In the process of expropriating the Shíráz Bahá'í Centre, they managed to get their hands on some documents and letters, giving the names and addresses of local Bahá'ís, which was later to create many problems for the Bahá'ís of Shíráz.

For the next three weeks we tried to carry on with our normal work at the centre, and continued to hold our assembly and committee meetings and large Bahá'í gatherings there. We were hoping that when they witnessed the spiritual nature of the Faith with their own eyes, it might clear up any misunderstandings they might have about the Bahá'ís. However, on 18

July the centre was declared to be the new headquarters of Shíráz's *Komiteh*, the Revolutionary Council, and the Bahá'ís were no longer allowed to use it.

At the beginning of June, just after the guards had first begun their gradual expropriation of the Bahá'í Centre, the assembly had asked my parents to move into the house adjoining the House of the Báb. They had known, as soon as the trusteeship was claimed by the government, that it would only be a matter of time before the Revolutionary Guards turned their attention to the House of the Báb. It had been attacked twice before.

The first time was in 1942 when it was raided and damaged by fire, after which the Bahá'ís raised funds to restore it to its original condition. The second was in 1955 when 'uncontrollable mobs' stormed the building, looting anything of value and reducing part of it to rubble. That day my grandfather had taken me to visit the house, and as we were walking back down the alley towards the main street, we heard a great commotion behind us. A large crowd was swarming towards the house armed with guns, pickaxes and shovels, bursting into the Bahá'í shops and houses in the alley. I was very frightened and we hurried away, but not before we had seen the first pickaxe fall on that beautiful house.

The mullahs were well aware of the historical and religious significance of this building to the Bahá'ís in Iran. Indeed, it was a place of pilgrimage for Bahá'ís from all over the world, although all too often it was not safe for them to visit.

The assembly was equally aware that for this reason it would always be a target whenever one was needed. My parents, along with my three brothers, were asked to stay next door to the house in case there was trouble. Perhaps, it was hoped, their presence and that of the other Bahá'ís already living in the alley would act as a deterrent to anyone planning an attack on the house. They were encouraged to stay, if they could, regardless of the pressure that might be put on them.

Every morning I used to drop Payam off at my parents' on my way to work. One evening towards the end of June, just after we heard that the Umaná Company had been confiscated, I was arriving to collect Payam as usual when I saw my mother rushing towards the end of the alley to warn me not to come any further.

She told me that a large group of Revolutionary Guards with machine guns had just stormed the House of the Báb. Some had climbed onto the roof of the house and its surrounding buildings. They had evidently expected armed resistance from the Bahá'ís.

The guards told Naniyyih Aqá Rizá and my parents that they had been instructed to take over the House of the Báb and the surrounding area for its protection. They swarmed over the building, searching for valuables and photographing each room.

Then the guards evicted Naniyyih Aqá Rizá and her family and burst into my parents' house, ordering them to leave. My brother Mas'úd had flu and was asleep in one of the rooms. They hit him and told him to get out.

'I can't,' he told them; 'I'm feeling too ill. Even if you kill me, I'm not going.'

'Don't worry,' the guards replied with a smile, 'we're going to kill you as well!' And four of the guards picked up the mattress he was lying on, dumping it and him in the alley. They threw a few personal belongings out of the door, along with the soup my mother had been making for Mas'úd, and slammed it shut. My mother banged on the door and begged them to let her at least collect some of their things and the medicine for her son, but they wouldn't let her back in.

Naniyyih Aqá Rizá, her family and all my relatives moved into a large house on the opposite side of the alley. Despite their forced eviction and the continued presence of armed guards in the alley, they were determined to stay put.

A month later another attempt was made to evict them. This time Áyatu'lláh Maḥallátí arrived in the alley demanding that all the Bahá'ís – then numbering about 100 – leave their houses. Again the Bahá'ís refused.

It was August when the influential Áyatu'lláh Rabbání Shírází visited the alley to remove any valuables from the House of the Báb – for safekeeping, he explained. He told the Bahá'ís that their houses had been allocated to homeless Muslims, and they would be forcibly evicted if they didn't leave immediately.

He had also brought an order for the arrest of Abu'l-Qásim Afnán, the house's caretaker. Mr Afnán, however, had flown to England with his brother Hassan and sister Firdaws just half an hour before, to arrange for Firdaws' heart operation. Mr Afnán stayed in England, and from that time on I began to document all the circumstances where Bahá'ís were dismissed from work, robbed, arrested or killed, and send the information to him in letters. In helping to inform the outside world in this way, I felt that at least I was doing something constructive.

It was not until September that the attack on the House of the Báb started in earnest. It had been locked since June, and although the guards had left months ago, a watchful eye was kept on it from the mosque opposite. The night of the seventh, armed guards surrounded the building again, stationing themselves on the roof, their machine guns trained on the alley.

In the morning, by the order of Áyatu'lláh Ṭálaqání of Tehran and Áyatu'lláh Dastg̲h̲ayb of S̲h̲íráz, a large group of people armed with pickaxes and shovels descended on the alley and started to destroy the holy house and some of the houses in the alley. Immediately, the National Spiritual Assembly urged all the assemblies in Iran to contact the government authorities of their area and register their protests.

But then the most extraordinary thing happened. The very next day, Áyatu'lláh Ṭálaqání suddenly died. A three-day public holiday was immediately announced in his honour, but some of the mob defied the order and continued the work of destruction on the holy house. Their defiant mood was short-lived, however; within a matter of hours, two men had fallen from the roof, and one had been killed. These deaths raised an interesting question for the Muslims: was it possible that these ill-fated people had somehow been punished for their actions against the Bahá'ís? Whatever the reason for these events, they halted any further destruction for the time being.

The next day I visited the damaged house. The doors and windows of the room where the Báb had declared His mission all those years ago had been smashed, and the room itself was badly damaged.

The temporary lull provided an opportunity for my three brothers and Naniyyih Aqá Rizá's son, D̲h̲abíhu'lláh, to erect a

cover over the area that been attacked, saving it from further
damage by exposure to the elements. In addition, my parents
and Naniyyih Aqá Rizá moved back into the houses adjoining
the House of the Báb in the hope that their presence might
offer additional protection.

Meanwhile, the authorities were still trying to evict Bahá'ís
from their homes in the alley. To encourage them to leave, they
first began charging a monthly rent, and then they disconnected the water and electricity supplies. The Bahá'í youth,
however, rose to the challenge and organized the delivery of
water to each house. They installed a large water container for
each family and filled it daily using buckets. In the evenings
they took responsibility for the protection of the houses, and
they would gather nightly in the courtyard of the House of the
Báb to pray and read from Bahá'í scriptures.

Many Bahá'ís were by now living in houses where doors and
walls had been missing for months, yet they kept on going
about their normal lives. One family, the Mihdízádihs, lived in
what was basically a shell for over two years. Mobs repeatedly
looted the house, until all that was left were stone walls, cheap
chairs and a table.

Whenever a house was completely demolished, the family
living there would move on to the next one in the alley, to the
point where at one time there were five or six families living in
each house. They patiently tolerated a year and a half under
constant harassment, living without water or electricity, and
their courage was astonishing.

On 10 October some men had returned for a day to complete the destruction of the Báb's declaration room on the
upper storey of the house. A month later another group
returned, but a wall collapsed on them as they were trying to
pull it down, killing one of the workers. Again the demolition
work was stopped. Each time the attackers left we held our
breath, hoping the project would finally be abandoned.

But the end came at one o'clock one morning. As the
Bahá'ís were sleeping, the mob came not only with picks and
shovels, but with cranes, arc lights and bulldozers, and this time
they completely tore apart the House of the Báb and some of
the buildings beside it. Only rubble remained.

Next morning I went to see the destruction with my own eyes. In front of me were the ruins of a once beautiful house, thousands of pieces scattered across the ground as if discarded from some giant jigsaw puzzle. I couldn't believe that this tragedy could happen, despite all the protest telegrams sent from the international Bahá'í community to the government of Iran, drawing their attention to the fact that the House of the Báb is one of the most holy places for Bahá'ís all over the world.

In 1981 the government began building a major road through Shíráz, which provided the authorities with a belated excuse for destroying the holy house. It was quite clear, however, that the road had been deliberately re-routed so that the site of the House of the Báb fell conveniently in its path. And to ensure that any traces of the original site, with its historic alley of simple stone houses, were completely obliterated, a public square was laid out beside the new road.

The First Arrests

CHAPTER 3

By the end of 1979, fourteen Bahá'ís, including my brother-in-law Zíyá, had been killed by individuals or mobs, or had been executed by the authorities, often after prolonged torture. Hundreds more were homeless, jobless and penniless, their houses looted and vandalized, their shops, offices and farms seized and their valuables stolen. All over Iran, Bahá'í Centres, cemeteries and holy places had been confiscated by the authorities, and the House of the Báb, the most cherished Bahá'í property in the country, had been levelled to the ground.

At the beginning of 1980, a new stage in the repression of the Bahá'í community was initiated by the government. A proclamation was made banning Bahá'ís from government and teaching jobs, and Bahá'í children were suspended first from universities, then from schools. Of course, the order was not immediately enforced on everyone, but it gave the Bahá'ís of Iran advance warning of what lay ahead.

It was not long before news began to reach us in Shíráz of raids on the homes of several prominent Bahá'ís in Tehran, including members of the National Spiritual Assembly. Arrests soon followed.

Meanwhile in Shíráz, since the commandeering of the local Bahá'í Centre, the assembly had been forced to find another suitable place for their archives and meetings. They chose a house belonging to a local Bahá'í, and Mr Khushkhú, still homeless, continued with his daily duties there, looking after refugees and managing the affairs of the community. All our meetings were also held there under the utmost secrecy.

One morning, when I had gone to see Mr Khushkhú to report on some committee matter, as I frequently did, he told me that he had just received a call from one of the members of the local assembly saying that, since he was overloaded with work, he was to hand over some of his duties to Muhammad Rizá Hisámí, who had just returned to the city having been in hiding for the past nine months. Neither Mr Khushkhú nor myself could understand this decision.

The next day, 3 May 1980, Mr Hisámí went to the assembly's new office to receive instructions. The moment he entered, six armed guards burst into the house and arrested him, together with Mr Khushkhú and several other Bahá'ís, including Ihsán Mihdízádih, and took them to the old Bahá'í Centre for questioning.

Both Yadu'lláh Vahdat and I narrowly escaped arrest – we could easily have been in the office at the time. In each area a few individuals are appointed for a fixed term to encourage and support the Bahá'ís, offer advice and counsel them on any problems they wish to raise, and at that time Mr Vahdat was one of these Auxiliary Board Members. As such, his name might well be on the list for arrest. I wasn't so worried for myself, since I was only his assistant, but when I saw Mr Vahdat that evening, I pleaded with him to be very careful, as the guards were evidently seeking prominent Bahá'ís.

He replied by asking: 'Is it possible for me to leave the scene of battle and hide for my own safety?'

But my concern for him increased the more I thought about the situation, and the next morning I went to his house to beg him to leave home for a few days. He refused, saying: 'My dear daughter, put your whole trust in God.' The following day I went to his house yet again, this time to invite him to come and stay with us for a while. I had made up my mind that I was not going to take 'no' for an answer.

The front door was ajar when I called on him, so I went straight in and closed it behind me. In the living room sat Mr Vahdat in his best clothes, calm and with a luminous smile on his face that I shall never forget. His wife Qudsíyyih was also relaxing in her armchair, chatting to her daughter. I asked Mr Vahdat if he was planning to go out anywhere.

'No, my dear,' he replied, still smiling. 'I am waiting; I am waiting for the guards.' He and his wife were completely resigned to whatever was destined to happen, and were prepared for the Revolutionary Guards to walk in at any moment.

Nevertheless, I continued to plead with Mr Vaḥdat: 'Please give us the honour of being our guests, even if for only two days.'

'Olya, think for a moment,' he chided me gently. 'If I hide myself, what will happen to others? A soldier [he was a retired colonel] never abandons the battle front.' He then added: 'Don't worry about us. Everything will happen according to God's will.' I left without saying another word.

The next afternoon, minutes after his arrival home from a meeting, four armed guards rang at Mr Vaḥdat's door. Qudsíyyih saw them from the window and told her husband there was still time to escape to their neighbours' house, but Mr Vaḥdat just got up and went to the door. He greeted each one of the guards and welcomed them to the house. 'I am Yadu'lláh Vaḥdat and this is my wife, Qudsíyyih; we were waiting for you. Welcome.'

The guards searched the house and then took both him and Qudsíyyih to the old Bahá'í Centre to join the other prisoners. At 10.30 that same night they released Qudsíyyih on a conditional security bond, giving her twelve hours to find the other six members of the Local Spiritual Assembly of S͟híráz who were not yet in custody, and to turn them in.

Qudsíyyih and the remaining assembly members immediately formed a meeting in which they agreed they would all turn themselves in to the Revolutionary Court in the morning, unless the National Spiritual Assembly advised otherwise. The National Spiritual Assembly, hastily consulted, suggested that the six members should go into hiding, and that Qudsíyyih alone should go back at the appointed time to turn herself in. Courageously, she did so.

When I found out what had happened I went straight to the Vaḥdats' house to invite their daughter Mahvas͟h to stay with us, but the young woman was as firm as her parents. 'I have to learn to stand on my own two feet,' she said. 'If I am afraid of being alone now they have taken my parents into custody, how can I prepare for future tests?'

Five days after the arrest of the Vaḥdats, my sister-in-law Nusrat Yaldá'í and I went to the Bahá'í Centre to visit them. They were held in the same room where the assembly meetings used to convene. When the guards opened the door, we saw the cheerful faces of our friends.

The men were sitting on one side and Qudsíyyih on the other. Even though the weather was hot, Qudsíyyih had to wear a chador, now compulsory dress for women, wrapped tightly around her. Despite everything, she looked totally composed, without the least trace of fear or grief on her face. I remember that her husband was reading the papers and Mr Ḥisámí was eating fruit as we entered.

For the first few minutes the guards stood over us, watching our every move, but it wasn't long before they left and we were alone with the prisoners. We talked for about two hours. I was amazed to find how happy they all seemed, especially Iḥsán Mihdízádih, the youngest at thirty-one, whose wonderful sense of humour kept everyone laughing.

Three days later I went to visit them again, and what caught my attention this time was the marked difference in the way the guards treated the prisoners. Their captors seemed to have been genuinely touched by the behaviour of the Bahá'ís, and regard themselves as the prisoners' servants rather than their jailers. The ten-year-old son of one of the guards came into the room while I was there holding a tall glass of iced water which he gave to Qudsíyyih, saying, 'I brought this especially for you.' It was obvious the prisoners had shown much love and affection to the guards, and that they were beginning to respond in kind.

On one side of the room there was a large bowl of fruit and a plate heaped with cookies that the Bahá'í families had sent for the prisoners. Every day one family would accept the responsibility of providing meals for them. Their captivity continued in these civilized conditions for about three weeks.

Then the authorities at the Revolutionary Court announced they would trade the prisoners for valuables from the House of the Báb. The local assembly immediately agreed that some of the valuables should be handed over, and it was duly promised that the Vaḥdats would be released at noon, followed by the other prisoners. We were all so happy; we

prepared a special lunch and waited for them. We waited and
waited, but there was no word.

After some hours, we were told that they were waiting for
the formal approval of the Religious Magistrate, and it would
shortly be forthcoming. But days later the authorities were still
promising to release the prisoners.

They then began to come up with new excuses, first saying
they had not received all the valuables of the house, and secondly, that the carpets were marked 'gift to the holy house' and
were unsaleable. Therefore, they explained, the prisoners would
not be released unless a bail of 24,000,000 tuman in cash (at
that time about £350,000) was raised. Of course, we simply did
not have access to that sort of money. We were in despair
when, some days later, they moved the prisoners to Adelabad
Prison and arrested more Bahá'ís, including Dr Mihdí Anvarí
and Hidáyat Dihqání, taking them straight to Adelabad.

Our visits to Adelabad were a world away from those in the
Bahá'í Centre. Here the prisoners were separated from us by
two thick panes of glass, and we had to talk to them via a telephone link. Some were soon released; some were not yet
informed of their sentences; Muḥammad Riẓá Ḥisámí was given
four years in prison; and Qudsíyyih Vaḥdat was sentenced to a
hundred lashes and life imprisonment. Her husband was condemned to death. We were stunned, not only by the severity,
but by the arbitrariness of the sentences.

When Qudsíyyih was flogged, the force of the whipping was
so intense that she became paralysed down one side and one of
her eyes was badly damaged. She was transferred to the prison
clinic, and by God's grace, the head of the clinic turned out to
be a Bahá'í. He was not publicly known as a Bahá'í, but nevertheless he had always been one in his heart and was extremely
helpful to both Bahá'í and Muslim prisoners. The
Revolutionary Court, not knowing he was a Bahá'í, had given
him his position because of the great respect in which he was
held in S̲h̲íráz. Through his efforts, Qudsíyyih's prison sentence
was reduced from life to two and a half years.

On 21 August 1980, all nine members of the National Spiritual
Assembly and two other prominent Bahá'ís were kidnapped by

Revolutionary Guards in Tehran. This was a terrible blow to us, not least because the clergy quickly disclaimed all knowledge of their arrest and of their whereabouts. To this day it is not known what happened to these people. Despite early rumours of sightings, they are almost certainly dead. The Bahá'í community, however, demonstrated its resilience. Nine new members were immediately elected, and the government was duly informed that a new National Spiritual Assembly had been established.

That same month, I went with Morad and Payam to visit our elder sons in Abingdon, near Oxford, England. We had not seen Behnam and Faz for a year and a half now, and so this was their first opportunity to meet their baby brother.

I had told little Payam many times that he was going to see his brothers soon, and somehow – even though he couldn't really understand what having a brother entailed – this became an exciting prospect for him. But when he saw Morad and I embrace our sons at the airport, he began to cry – perhaps he had thought a brother was something to eat!

Our visit was one of the happiest periods of my life: picnicking beside the river, taking long walks in the park and sight-seeing in London. But our stay came swiftly to an end and it was time for the family to part once more.

On the flight home I felt emotionally and physically drained and soon fell asleep. It was then that I had a strange dream about Mr Khushkhú. I dreamed that the Báb had given me a letter written in red ink and had asked me to go to Shíráz and give it to Mr Khushkhú. I thought about the significance of this dream when I woke up, but the more I thought about it the less I could understand its meaning.

At my first opportunity on our return to Shíráz, I went to visit the prisoners in Adelabad. I told Mr Khushkhú about my dream straight away, and he appeared to understand its meaning at once. He held the receiver through which we were speaking with one hand and slapped his forehead with the other. 'Am I worthy of such a station?' he kept repeating.

Although he had recently been informed he would be executed, I discovered later, Mr Khushkhú had not told a soul. He began to comfort me, saying, 'Olya, don't ever lose hope; try to always do your best, just as you did when we were working together. Let's hope I'll be released soon and we will work together once again.'

I was very close to this dear man, and loved him like a father. Although he was well over seventy, he had amazing energy and an incredible capacity for hard work. His name, Khushkhú, was truly appropriate: it means good natured.

A few months earlier, just after the May arrests in Shíráz, news had reached us of the execution of Bahá'í prisoners in various parts of Iran. Three in Tehran were killed that same month, followed by two assembly members in Tabríz, a Bahá'í in Rasht, and then two more in Tehran.

One night in early September, not long after we had returned from England, I received a phone call from a Bahá'í in Tehran. He had just heard that seven Bahá'ís in Yazd had been executed, including three Auxiliary Board Members and two members of the assembly. We immediately called a meeting in our house that night to share the news.

One of those killed, we discovered, was 'Azíz Dhabíhíyán, a close friend of Mr Vahdat's. He had been visiting Shíráz when the guards had raided the Bahá'í homes in Yazd, so had initially escaped arrest. However, he was later picked up in the street and taken back to Yazd. Several times on the way they stopped the car and hauled him out, saying it was too much trouble to take him to Yazd and they would kill him on the spot unless he recanted his faith. Once they even blindfolded him, tied him to a tree and then shot into the air.

By the time he reached the prison, Mr Dhabíhíyán was in a weakened state. His cell-mate, 'Abdu'l-Vahháb Kázimí, arrived in an even poorer condition. An old man in his eighties, his house had been raided twice. The first time he had been beaten very badly and his wife had died shortly afterwards from the shock. The second time the guards came he was beaten up again and thrown into a car, which set off from his village towards Yazd. The guards considered shoving him out of the car and running him over, but in the end they decided that at his age, and with his injuries, it would be enough just to dump him in the desert. So they left him in the cold and dark, confident that he would die. Mr Kázimí managed to pick himself up and struggle back to his home in Man<u>sh</u>ád, but he was discovered next day and rearrested.

This large-scale, official persecution of Bahá'ís was prominently reported in the newspapers and on television, along with the explanation that the victims had been arrested and executed in 'compensation' for the many Muslim lives lost in the revolution.

The news of these executions caused a great deal of anxiety among Bahá'ís. Most of us had resigned ourselves to the fact that the situation was very serious, but this was the first time we realized that *all* our lives were in danger. In <u>Sh</u>íráz we were particularly concerned about the Bahá'ís already in prison. I was in constant contact with their families and frequently visited the prisoners, so I was able to keep abreast of events. Although we were worried, the periodic promises of freedom kept our hopes up.

However, the local authorities had executed 'A*̣*zimat Fahandi<u>zh</u> in <u>Sh</u>íráz in December 1979 on trumped-up charges, so it was with great sadness and grief, but little real surprise, that we heard that Dr Mihdí Anvarí and Hidáyat Dihqání had been shot on 17 March 1981.

The following month, Ihsán Mihdízádih's wife, his little daughter Ilhám and I visited him, Mr <u>Kh</u>u<u>sh</u>khú and Mr Vahdat for what turned out to be the last time. As usual we waited for hours, and had to listen to the insults of the guards until they decided they were ready to bring out the prisoners. The three of them had now been imprisoned in Adelabad for ten months, but as soon as we caught a glimpse of Ihsán coming towards us, we could tell he was in good spirits. The first thing he said when he picked up the receiver was, 'Take care of my wife, Olya – now that I'm not around she's putting on weight!'

I told him, 'You are so lucky to be in prison for your faith.'

'If you want to join us you are welcome!'

Since time was very limited I moved to another booth to speak to Mr Vahdat. There was a special glow about him and he was speaking as if addressing a meeting. 'My dearest Olya,' he said, 'there is a lot to be done and very little time to do it. Try to serve even more if you can.'

That day the guards allowed us three separate visits with Mr Vaḥdat. Every time we left they announced over the loudspeakers that visitors for Mr Vaḥdat could return to the visiting room. We wondered why – did they want to arrest us, or just get to know our faces? Or were they about to execute Mr Vaḥdat? Every time we were called, there he was, alone on the other side of the glass, waiting to talk to us again.

Mr Vaḥdat asked for the receiver to be passed to me once more. I looked closely into his eyes and I knew the moment of separation was near. His face was calm and radiant; it was reflecting a different world. He kissed his finger and put his hand to the glass, and I did the same.

When visiting time was finally over and we had to leave, he wouldn't take his eyes off us. As he was leaving the room he repeatedly turned his face towards us and waved his hand. Now, years later, I can still recall that scene as clearly as if it had happened yesterday. Mr Vaḥdat was in his mid-seventies.

On 30 April, 1981, at six in the evening, he and Sattár Khushkhú and Iḥsán Mihdízádih were led to the execution ground. A Muslim whose car had just broken down in the area watched the scene with curiosity. The guards spotted him and told him to make himself scarce, but he only became even more curious, and crept back to witness what was happening. He later investigated the background to the executions, and recounted to a local Bahá'í what he had seen that day. This is his story of the last moments of those three dear men.

They were only a few steps away from death when the guards tried for the last time to get them to recant their faith. They were told that if they denied being Bahá'ís they would be allowed to go back to their families at once. Their reaction was incredible. Mr Mihdízádih, who seemed perfectly composed, said: 'Now that I'm captive and you know I don't have a weapon with which to defend myself, please uncover my eyes and tell me who is the person among you chosen to give me the drink from the water of eternal life.'

One of the guards uncovered his eyes and introduced himself as the soldier who was about to kill him.

Mr Mihdízádih held the guard's hand and kissed it, then with indescribable excitement he looked at the sky and said: 'I praise God that I can, in the last moments of my life, be obedient and carry out what He has asked me to do – to kiss the hand of my killer.'

Mr Vaḥdat also asked the guards to remove his blindfold so that he could watch the bullets as they flew towards him. 'My only request', he said, 'is that you aim at any part of my body but my heart, because my heart is where the love of Bahá'u'lláh resides.' He raised his hands to his chest the moment they fired, but those murderers deliberately aimed for his heart, killing him, Mihdízádih and <u>Kh</u>u<u>shkh</u>ú: three men of truth.

Eight days before her father's execution, Mahva<u>sh</u> Vaḥdat had been arrested and taken to Sepah Prison, and the family home was confiscated.

An hour before Mr Vaḥdat was executed they transferred Mahva<u>sh</u> to Adelabad, where both her parents were held, and at the same time allowed Qudsíyyih to see her husband. The couple had been separated during their entire imprisonment. The guards lied to Qudsíyyih, saying that they were to take her husband to Tehran, but Mr Vaḥdat knew very well what they had planned for him.

Mahva<u>sh</u> was released three days after her father's execution. This is what she told me:

I saw my father in the prison hallway one hour before his execution. I could barely contain my emotions. 'You are not my daughter if you tremble in front of the guards. You must be firm in your love for Bahá'u'lláh,' he said.

'Be certain, Father, that I am your child and my path is the same as yours,' I reassured him.

The guards who were waiting to take him to the execution site knew him from the army, and as soon as they recognized him they gave him the army salute. In that moment I felt as if my father was the commander and they were his soldiers, as if he were passing them in review as he proceeded to his death.

Shortly afterwards one of the guards brought the news to my mother and me in the prison cell. My mother started crying, but the guard, who had himself seen the executions, said to her: 'Why are you sad? If you only knew how happy your husband was, and how at the last moment, he stepped forward towards the bullets.'

The guards transferred the three bodies to the Bahá'í cemetery. The news of their execution spread like lightning among the Bahá'ís, and they began to make their way in large groups to the cemetery. But the guards would not let them enter. They stood in front of the gates, allowing in only a few close relatives of the dead; the others continued to pray quietly outside.

On her release from prison, Mahva<u>sh</u> discovered that she had no home to go to. Áyatu'lláh Burújirdí, the Religious Magistrate who ordered the execution of the three men, had confiscated it and moved in. Without knowing where she was going to sleep that night or how she was going to survive, she went directly to her father's grave and joined the other relatives of the dead and prayed for their souls. The strength and courage of those families was astounding.

A number of Muslims had come to say how sorry they were. Two of them, who were crying and distraught, said they had been in the same prison with the three Bahá'ís. I also spotted a colleague of mine from work who was holding a newspaper in his hand, saying: 'I swear to God I am a Muslim, but the things they write about the Bahá'ís are simply lies. It says here that three Bahá'í *spies* were found guilty and were executed by order of the Revolutionary Court.'

He then added:

A few years ago my son was in the army and Mr Vaḥdat was his commander. One day my son had a big problem, and Mr Vaḥdat helped him out. I put a cheque for 30,000 tuman into an envelope and took it to him the next day. Mr Vaḥdat was very upset and refused to take the cheque. 'I'm a Bahá'í', he said. 'I don't accept bribery. I only helped your son out because it is my responsibility as a human being to help others in time of need. It would have been enough for you to have just called me and told me your problem had been solved. That would have made me very happy.'

Coming on top of the demolition of the House of the Báb, the confiscation of our Bahá'í Centre and a spate of raids on Bahá'í homes in Shíráz that left over twenty Bahá'ís in prison, these executions were a bitter blow to us all. We also began to suspect that membership of Bahá'í assemblies was regarded – in itself – as a crime punishable by death.

The Eye of the Storm

CHAPTER 4

Following the funerals of our friends Iḥsán Mihdízádih, Sattár Khushkhú and Yadu'lláh Vaḥdat, restrictions on Bahá'í burials became even more severe. The authorities couldn't risk allowing any further gatherings on this scale. Such public demonstrations of sympathy for the Bahá'ís – particularly from Muslims – were becoming embarrassing.

Now, whenever there was a death in a Bahá'í family, the body had to stay in the Revolutionary Court morgue for three or four days until permission was given for the burial, and then it would only go ahead if 10,000 tuman in cash (about £150) was received from the family of the deceased.

To make life even more difficult, the water supply to the Bahá'í cemetery had been disconnected and so barrels of water had to be taken in trucks to the cemetery for washing the corpses.

About that time the National Spiritual Assembly instructed all the Bahá'ís of Iran to write letters to the heads of the Islamic revolutionary regime and plead for clemency towards the Iranian Bahá'í community. We were asked to write directly to the heads of the government, to send the letters by special delivery with our complete names and addresses, and to keep a copy for ourselves.

Soon post offices all over Iran were packed with Bahá'ís, and for three days most of the counters were assigned to take care of Bahá'ís who wished to send their letters to the government. They even wrote letters on behalf of their children. It was an extraordinary time; from the oldest to the youngest, the Bahá'í community was galvanized into action.

The death of a Bahá'í portrayed in a Persian magazine, 1911.

Senior Iranian military officers under the Pahlaví government attacking the National Bahá'í Centre, Tehran, 1955.

The House of the Báb, the birthplace of the Bahá'í Faith and the most sacred spot in Iran for Bahá'ís throughout the world. Top left: the room where the Báb declared His mission in 1844. Top right: the destruction of the House of the Báb begins, 1979. Bottom: workmen using pickaxes to demolish the interior.

Top left and right: Graffiti in the interior of the House of the Báb. Top right states: 'This nest of espionage should be demolished'. Bottom: the House of the Báb levelled, and the site prepared for a new roadway to be built.

The seven members of the Hamadán Spiritual Assembly who were executed on 14 June 1981. From right to left: Ṭarázu'lláh <u>Kh</u>uzayn, Fírúz Na'ímí, Suhráb Ḥabíbí, Náṣir Vafá'í and Ḥusayn <u>Kh</u>ándil; sitting, Ḥusayn Mutlaq and Suhayl Ḥabíbí.

The funeral of three Bahá'í men, Iḥsán Mihdízádih, Sattár <u>Kh</u>u<u>sh</u>khú and Yadu'lláh Vahdat, who were executed on 30 April 1981. Of these, two are pictured on the following page.

Ihsán Mihdízádih

Sattár Khushkhú

جمهوری اسلامی ایران
وزارت نفت

بسمه تعالی

وزارت نفت جمهوری اسلامی ایران

نام : علیا مصلی نژاد

XXXX شماره XXXX ۶۷۲۴۸

۴۲۷۲ کارمند XXX

بر اساس رای هیات بدوی بازسازی نیروی انسانی وزارت نفت بها ستناد بند ۸ ماده ۲۹

قانون بازسازی مصوب ۱۳۶۰/۷/۵ مجلس شورای اسلامی :

به جرم عضویت در فرقه ضاله بهائیت ازتاریخ ۱۳۶۱/۲/۲۸

به مجازات انفصال دائم ازخدمات دولتی ومؤسسات وابسته به دولت محکوم میگردد

این حکم ازتاریخ ابلاغ بعدت پانزده روزقابل پژوهش در رهیئت تجدید نظرمیباشد .

هیئت بدوی

بازسازی نیروی انسانی

The original document informing Olya that her employment at the
National Iranian Oil Company is terminated due to her membership of
'the misleading sect of Bahaism'. Dated 18 May 1982.

(OFFICIAL TRANSLATION)
EMBLEM
ISLAMICREPUBLIC OFIRAN
MINISTRY OF OIL
IN THE NAME OF GOD
MAN-POWER REORGANIZATION
MINISTRY OF OIL
No: 86-3-BH
Date: May 18, 1982
TO:Ms. Olya MOSSALA-NEJAD
    EmployeeNo. 67348
According to the verdict of primary board of man-power reorganization
of Ministry of Oil and by virtue of Para. 8 of Article 29 of Re-organi-
zation Act approved on Sep. 27,1981 by Islamic Consultative Council,
you areadjudged to:
PENALTY: permanent discharge from state services and institutes
affiliated to the state
ON CONVICTION: membership is the misleading sect of BAHAISM
from May 18, 1982.

This verdictis appellable by appeal board within 15 days after
it is communicatedand notified to you.

SGD& SLD:
Primary Board No. 3
MANPOWER RE¢ORGANIZATION

True translation from Persian original certified.HS.
March 14, 1983

كيت امناى آقاى حسين تقنيان متر... زمسيم
كرامى ميشود اداره كى ونلايت واد... ى كا

حـسـين تـقـيـان
مترجم رسمى دادكسترى

HOSEIN S. GHAFIAN
OFFICIAL TRANSLATOR
to
THE MINISTRY
OFJUSTICE

Official English translation of document on preceding page.

Desecrated Bahá'í cemetery, Shíráz, 1979.

A Bahá'í house, attacked by mobs in Shíráz, 1979.

All Bahá'í meetings were now being held with a limited number of people. The government was becoming increasingly concerned about opposition from political factions such as the mujáhidín and communists, as well as the various tribal populations, and had pronounced it illegal for more than two families to gather together in one home under any circumstances. If more than the permitted number of people were found, the guards could take all of them to prison and confiscate the premises. The Bahá'ís complied with this ruling.

All our office equipment including typewriters, copiers and stationery had been taken away, so all correspondence and programmes for gatherings had to be written out by hand. Since only two families were allowed to meet in each house for feasts (our get-togethers where Bahá'ís meet every nineteen days to pray, socialize and discuss the affairs of the community), we had to write out about forty programmes each time in order for everyone to receive a copy on time.

This was one of my jobs. Following the arrests last year of so many assembly members, the National Spiritual Assembly advised against announcing the names of assembly members in 1981. Instead, a few individuals were appointed, myself among them, to liaise between the assembly and the community. Much of my free time after work, therefore, was taken up with visiting the Bahá'ís in my area as an unofficial messenger and post-woman, trying to keep everyone up-to-date with the news.

Delivering the programmes or other essential messages to the 4,000 Bahá'ís in Shíráz was no safe job, because guards were all over the streets and alleys and could challenge or search us at any time. We had to change our outfits several times so we wouldn't be identified. If the messages were short we tried to memorize them and deliver them verbally so that if we were caught there would be no evidence. Many were so lengthy, however, that we had to write them out, hide them, and discreetly deliver them to people's houses, sometimes in the early hours of the morning.

Since the death of Mr Khushkhú, a young man of about twenty-eight by the name of Hidáyat Síyávushí had kept the administrative files and documents at his house. He was a member of the assembly that year and worked at an optician's

shop on Zand Street in central Shíráz. Every day, from morning
till night, this shop was used as a safe meeting place for Bahá'ís.
Along with Farhád Bihmardí, who owned the shop and whose
brother Faríd was a member of the National Spiritual Assembly,
Hidáyat would pass on messages and news.

We used to enter his shop with prescriptions for glasses in
our hands, in case we were stopped by guards, and our two
friends would pass on the precious information. But this neat
system of ours came to an end when, one day in June 1981,
Hidáyat and a friend were stopped while riding a motor cycle
near his house, and they were both arrested and imprisoned.

We were living in dangerous times, so the National Spiritual
Assembly had instructed us to elect two sets of reserve assemblies that year. Although we didn't inform the reserve members
at the time, we chose a second group of people who would be
asked to step in if the elected members were detained, and a
third group to replace them if they too were arrested. On
Hidáyat's arrest, a member of the first reserve assembly was
promptly called up to replace him. He was not the only reserve
member to find himself on the assembly that year.

That summer, the authorities embarked on a renewed offensive. The next two months saw a serious escalation in the
persecution of Bahá'ís all over Iran. On 14 June seven Bahá'ís,
all members of the Local Spiritual Assembly of Hamadán, were
tortured and shot after nearly a year in prison. Their bodies,
bearing the evidence of prolonged torture for all to see –
crushed fingers, broken limbs and ribs, thighs cut open from
knee to hip – were unceremoniously dumped in a pile at the
government hospital in the middle of the night.

An anonymous phone call at 3 a.m. to a Bahá'í nurse
working the night shift there gave the alert, and by daylight a
crowd of Bahá'ís as well as Muslims had gathered at the hospital gates to pay their respects. In fact, Muslims outnumbered
Bahá'ís at the funeral that day.

The news had barely reached us in Shíráz when we heard of
the tragic execution only a week later of another seven Bahá'ís
in Tehran. Towards the end of July, two Bahá'ís were killed in
Mashhad and nine more in Tabríz – eight of them members of
the Local Spiritual Assembly.

The following month, in August, I decided to visit my children in England once more. At that time the Islamic regime had not yet begun to restrict the movement of Bahá'ís, but one still needed to apply for permission to leave the country. The British Embassy in Iran had just closed, so obtaining a visa for England was now impossible; I managed to get the necessary permission to go to Germany, however, which at that time required no visas for Iranian nationals. From there, I hoped to get to England.

In spite of the fact that almost all the Bahá'ís had been fired from their jobs in government offices by then, I was still working at the National Iranian Oil Company. My boss was a Muslim but showed the utmost kindness to Bahá'ís. Often he would look at me with an embarrassed expression on his face and say, 'I'm so sorry for what this country is doing to your people. I hope you don't hold it against us and think that all Muslims are like that!'

When he heard I was planning to take my vacation, my boss came to offer me his advice.

Now that you've finally managed to get permission to leave Iran after all these difficulties, Olya, you'd better stay in England. The government has plans for you Bahá'ís. You know how they have fired your friends from their jobs under false charges! The Public Prosecutor's office has called me a few times to ask about you, but I don't give them any straight answers. I have told them I am very happy with your work in the office, and that seems to pacify them a bit. But one of these days I'm sure they'll manage to dismiss you.

I'll be glad to issue a few months' leave of absence for you, on top of your paid annual vacation, while we wait to see what happens under this terrible government. Maybe things will change!

I thanked him for his consideration, but I told him I intended to return to Iran as planned, after spending two weeks with my children. I couldn't possibly leave my friends, who were already in prison or under extreme pressure.

Before my holiday, it was necessary for me to get some new passport photos. When I took them to the passport office, however, they refused to accept them, saying that too much of my hair was showing under the chador. So I had to get them done again in a more 'modest' pose. When I returned with the second set of photographs, I said to the clerk, 'The chastity of women has nothing to do with the amount of hair showing under their chadors.' He was not amused.

The night before I was to leave with little Payam for Europe, Bahrám Khushkhú came to see me, bringing film of the Bahá'í funerals and a copy of his father's will. The assembly had asked me to take these and other photographs of the victims, their wills and letters out of Iran for safekeeping as it was too dangerous for anyone to hide them any longer. No one knew whose house might be raided next.

Morad took Payam and me to the airport next morning and I asked him to wait fifteen minutes after the plane had taken off just to make quite sure everything was all right.

'How do you mean?' quizzed my husband. He didn't know I had the photos and documents in my handbag.

'Because', I replied lightly, 'I might be taken to prison instead of being allowed to board the flight.'

'Why would they do that? You haven't done anything wrong.'

I could see he was getting worried, so I reassured him that I was just being cautious because of what had happened to so many other Bahá'ís recently. I kissed him goodbye with a smile.

At the customs point where they conducted the searches, I joined the queue and watched anxiously as security officials searched the luggage of the people ahead of me. They seemed to be checking every inch of the hand baggage and conducting thorough body searches, even taking notes from any personal documents and letters they found.

My heart was pounding so hard I thought I would faint from fear – I could see I didn't have a chance of getting through the checkpoint. I stood in that queue for nearly an hour and a half wondering what I was going to do, watching and praying.

As my turn drew near, it suddenly occurred to me that I could use Payam as an excuse to delay going through the checkpoint. I took a bottle of milk for him out of my bag and continued to watch from further back in the line. There were only four or five passengers left now. I noticed that there was one woman responsible letting the female passengers through for a body search after their bags had been checked. She looked kind and helpful. My only chance was with her.

I braced myself, picked up Payam and approached the woman. 'Could you please look in my bag and let me through?' I asked. 'I've been waiting here with my son for some time.'

'Sorry dear, it's not my job. I can only let people through once they've been searched by her,' she said, pointing to a colleague. 'You'll have to wait your turn.'

I returned to my place in the queue. While no one was looking, I took the films and photographs and slipped them into one of Payam's nappies – a clean one, of course. I wrapped them up and then put the bundle back into my bag. After another fifteen minutes of anxiety I went up to the security guard and spoke quietly to her again. This time I made sure I was wearing my harassed-mother look.

'Where are you travelling to?' she asked.

'To Germany, and then England,' I replied.

'Lucky you. I wish I could join you,' she said, and taking a quick glance into my bag continued, 'OK, you can go on to the next room.'

I moved forward as calmly as I could. Then I heard an official behind me saying, 'Who was that woman you allowed through? We haven't searched her bag yet.' I kept walking.

In the room where the body searches were being conducted, there was a furious row going on between the woman official and a passenger. They seemed to be arguing over the passenger's jewellery.

'These are my personal belongings, my earrings, my rings,' she was saying.

'This is gold that you're trying to take out of the country,' retorted the official, and they started pushing and shoving each other.

'We had a revolution to be free, and now we are living under a police state!' screamed the passenger. 'This is my own jewellery! Leave it alone!'

Two or three of the security staff appeared, among them the
one I had just heard commenting that I had gone through
without a proper search. But I seemed to have been forgotten in
the fracas, and as they bundled the protesting passenger out of
the room, her adversary turned to me wearily and said, 'Do you
have anything to declare?'

'You're welcome to look,' I replied. I was relieved I didn't
have to lie. They gave me a thorough body search, asking me to
remove my chador and other items of clothing. They searched
me thoroughly – but not my bag, which contained all the films,
photos and documents.

'Fine. You can go.'

I almost dropped to my knees in relief.

All the time the plane stood on the tarmac I could still feel
my heart pounding nervously – what if someone came after me
and searched my bag even now? But the plane finally took off,
and as my fear dissipated I began to feel a growing sadness as we
travelled farther and farther away from my homeland.

Six hours later we were in Germany. At the airport I was
given permission to stay in Germany for a month, but although
I was looking forward to seeing Behnam and Faz, being so far
from Iran made me unhappy. I was afraid I might never be able
to return and began to regret ever having left.

The next day I went to the British Embassy in Frankfurt,
and after a short interview I was given a three-month visa for
England. I flew to London the next day and upon my arrival I
was welcomed by my children and some friends from Shíráz.

For several days I spent my time visiting old friends, but in
truth I was constantly thinking of Iran and the Bahá'ís there, as
if I could only fully experience life in the company of those self-
less souls. The more time I spent with friends who had left Iran
before the revolution, the more alienated I felt. This world with
all its comforts seemed meaningless, almost irrelevant to me,
and I longed to get back to Iran where I was needed so badly.

I flew back after sixteen days. I had both more vacation
days, and further time on my visa to stay longer, but I couldn't
bring myself to do so.

At the airport, just before the I went through passport
control, Behnam kept pressing the point that it would only be a

matter of time before I, like thousands of other Bahá'ís in Iran, would lose my job or worse. 'It is very dangerous in Iran right now,' he argued. 'Why are you so determined to go back?

The mother in me was sorely tempted to stay, but I knew I couldn't desert my friends at such a time. 'My dear, you know how much I love you,' I began, 'but my love for God is stronger.'

'If that is your reason,' Faz smiled, 'then you must go, and our prayers will be with you.'

The day I arrived home in Iran, my neighbour saw me and said, 'You're still here! I thought you were going to England.'

'I went to England and now I am back,' I replied with a smile.

The systematic offensive against the Bahá'ís continued unabated. In December, sixteen months after the abduction of the first National Spiritual Assembly of Iran, all but one of the members of the second were secretly executed.

One of those killed was Zhínús Mahmúdí, the chairperson. After her husband Húshang was kidnapped, along with the other members of the previous national assembly, Zhínús was fired from her position as President of the Department of Meteorology in Iran, and the Islamic Revolutionary Court confiscated all her belongings.

Undaunted by this injustice and full of optimism and energy, she filled a knapsack with all she had left and went on the road for over a year, staying in a different place every night and sleeping in a different bed, constantly visiting the local Bahá'í communities and sharing her experiences.

The last time she visited Shíráz she spoke to us in a calm, firm and detached manner, as if knowing this was to be her last visit. Shortly afterwards she was arrested by the Revolutionary Guards along with seven other national assembly members, and on 27 December 1981, after eighteen days of imprisonment and torture, she was executed.

It is hard to give a clear impression of this unique woman. However, perhaps this extract from a letter she wrote to the children of some close friends will help you to know her a little better:

Our world these days is very strange, yet fascinating!
Everything in our world is new. The relationship between
people is so astonishing, I don't think you would recognize them – I don't even think you would recognize us,
because in a way we have become strange too. We have
changed so much from what we were before.

The things that made us happy before do not make
us happy now; our values have changed. You might be
surprised if I tell you that life has never been so mean-
ingful. Our understanding of our surroundings and life
itself has never seemed so real. We spent so much time
running around day and night, for months, for years – it
was all meaningless. There is nothing to show for all
those years.

Now we have something priceless that brings us
true happiness. For example, we enjoy tribulation! We
enjoy our material losses! We envy the ones who give
their lives! We have become different people, yet we are
still proud of you. We know that even though we have
wasted so many years of our lives in the pursuit of empty
values, you won't. You will recognize the great responsibility you will have in the future – which is not so far
away. Get yourselves ready for it in these fruitful years
of your lives.

Not only are you our sole hope, you are the sole
hope of this world. You are the generation that has the
greatest responsibility in the history of the world, so get
yourselves ready for it. We will do our share here and
you do yours over there.

May my life be sacrificed for you.

The execution of Zhínús Mahmúdí and the seven other
members of the National Spiritual Assembly in the last days of
1981 brought the number of Bahá'ís killed in Iran since 1978 to
eighty-six. A week later the total reached ninety-three with the
execution of seven more Bahá'ís in Tehran, six of whom were
members of the Tehran assembly.

It was becoming increasingly obvious that the Islamic
regime of Iran had one clear objective in mind with regard to

the Bahá'ís: genocide. Starting at the top of the administrative structure and working their way down, the government was determined to wipe out the Bahá'í community. As arrests and executions continued within the borders of Iran, international sympathy mounted. I remember one reporter from a television network in the United States interviewing Áyatu'lláh Músaví-Ardabílí – the head of Public Prosecution in the Revolutionary Court of Iran. The interview was broadcast all over the country.

The reporter asked the Áyatu'lláh, 'Why do you persecute and kill the Bahá'ís in Iran?' The Áyatu'lláh nonchalantly replied, 'We have never killed anyone because of their religion. The Bahá'ís we have executed were either the leaders of this political sect or they were spies for Israel. We are going to continue our efforts to eliminate all their leaders, and so far we have been very successful. Then we will put pressure on the other Bahá'ís, and no doubt they will all come back to Islam in time.'

Each day it seemed to be someone else's turn to suffer. On 14 April 1982 it was Dr Zíyá Ahrárí's. On that day he received a summons from the Revolutionary Court to turn himself in six days later, six days in which he could have left Shíráz and gone into hiding. Instead, he remained on duty at the hospital until the last minute, without mentioning the summons to anyone. Then, confident in the knowledge that he had done nothing but help people and serve his country, he reported to the Revolutionary Court. The Religious Magistrate arrested him immediately and sent him to prison.

Dr Ahrárí was an outstanding doctor who was a pharmacologist at the Háfiz Hospital. Over the years, he had developed a number of drugs that eliminated the need for imports from other countries, and had received an award from the Ministry of Health in recognition of his work. For a few days after his arrest, the workers and doctors at Háfiz Hospital and other hospitals in Shíráz protested against his imprisonment – Dr Ahrárí was very popular among his colleagues and friends. But none of those protests made any impression on the authorities.

One day at the prison, armed guards gagged and blindfolded Dr Ahrárí and forced him to accompany them to the home of another Bahá'í so they could arrest him too. Luckily, the man's wife was at home alone, and the guards were cheated of their prey. But they decided that they would try and break the trust between the Bahá'ís, and so they shamelessly lied to the woman, saying, 'We didn't want to trouble you, but Dr Ahrárí insisted that we come to your house. He said there was going to be a large meeting here, and it was a good opportunity to make many arrests.' Dr Ahrárí could not say a word. Tears were streaming down his face, and it was those tears that told the true story: nothing could break the unity and trust among the Bahá'ís.

Mr Habíb Awjí was arrested at about the same time as Dr Ahrárí. He was born a Muslim and was originally very prejudiced against the Bahá'í Faith. At that time he was a baker in Shíráz, and not only did he refuse to sell bread to the Bahá'ís, he even swore at them as they passed his shop. In 1955, when the clergy rose up against the Bahá'ís and attacked the House of the Báb, Mr Awjí was one of the people who joined the mob.

The Bahá'ís at the time, however, not only showed no resentment for what he had done, they offered him genuine love and friendship. He began to investigate the Bahá'í Faith, and after many months he decided to become a Bahá'í. The men who had once refused to sell bread to Bahá'ís now found that his Muslim customers would no longer buy from him.

In December 1978, at the beginning of the revolution, a mob attacked his home, taking all his possessions and burning his house. They even tried to kill him, thinking that by doing so they would be praised by God in the next world. The shot injured his arm, and as a result he lost the use of it. His Muslim relatives were very upset and wanted to retaliate by killing his assailant, who was known to them, but Mr Awjí encouraged them to forgive.

They continued to insist on revenge. 'OK,' he told them, 'since you insist, I give my permission for you to kill him. But kill his ignorance and his prejudice, not his body. Go and tell him on my behalf that he should let go of his hatred and instead use the hands that God has given him to help the helpless and to serve humanity.'

Mr Awjí used to say, 'Oh God, you took from me the same arm that I used to attack the House of the Báb with. Now we are even.'

At about this time, a Society for the Promotion of Islam was formed, and committees with such titles as 'Islamic Committee' or 'Committee for Reconstruction' were set up everywhere. They dismissed the educated, experienced people so that – as they put it – 'the country's corporations and institutions would be under Islamic supervision.' In other words, they transformed offices and schools throughout the country into an extension of the mosques.

Several times a day, without warning, they would call the employees or students from their work to say group obligatory prayers or hear a lecture on Imám Husayn or another religious subject. Ordinary working people and intellectuals alike had reluctantly to comply.

The mullahs also set out to impose Muslim social practices such as the ban on alcoholic beverages and complete segregation of the sexes on all government departments, schools and universities, and even private businesses. The chador, of course, had been compulsory dress for women for some years.

To many Muslims, used to a fairly liberal, secular way of life under the Shah, these new rulings were anathema. Nevertheless, they were inhibited from standing up for themselves by the fear of losing their jobs.

I knew I wouldn't be able to keep my own job for much longer. Only a few months previously I had arrived for work one morning to find posters on the walls announcing the new laws passed by the Islamic Council. One of them, Article 28, stated that all Bahá'ís would be dismissed from government offices. I wasn't at all surprised to see the poster. By now, most Bahá'ís working for the government and in education had already been dismissed, and many in private businesses had also been fired.

A number of Bahá'ís with specialist skills who had lost their jobs attempted to open private businesses in their own area of knowledge and expertise, but the government quickly put a stop to this. Only in menial positions were Bahá'ís allowed to earn their livelihood – academics and doctors were now driving cabs or cleaning offices. But after a short time the mullahs began to take even that away from them, issuing orders to all cab companies to confiscate Bahá'í drivers' licenses. In fact, the only large company in Iran that still employed Bahá'ís in any capacity was the National Iranian Oil Company, and that's where I was working. It was quite clear from the posters that it would only be a matter of time before the management was forced to purge the office of Bahá'ís.

One day in May a group from Tehran came to our office, calling themselves the Committee for the Cleansing of Manpower. The head of the group called a meeting of about 200 of the employees, explaining that Bahá'ís had to be removed from the workplace. I noticed how embarrassed my boss was; he averted his eyes and tried to avoid looking at me. Some of my colleagues were also blushing, and glanced over at me to see how I was reacting, and to get my permission to speak in defence of the Bahá'ís. But I signalled to them to relax.

A few days later I was called into another meeting. There were six people there, not including the armed guard standing in the corner. As soon as I entered I heard the door being locked behind me. One of the members of the committee, Mr Najafí, said abruptly, 'We have heard certain things about you. Of course, we're hoping they're not true – that there's been some mistake.'

'Could you be a little more specific, please?' I asked. 'Has something been stolen or has someone, God forbid, committed murder?'

He glared at me. 'Just fill out this form and then we'll know who's guilty or innocent.'

I looked at the form in front of me: it asked for my name, place of birth, work history, religion, and a few other questions about my beliefs.

I answered all of them straightforwardly until I got to 'religion'. I quickly wrote, 'I am a Bahá'í'.

'I believe in all the living religions,' I wrote, 'in all the prophets from Adam to the present, including Muhammad and the religion of Islam. I believe in the next world and the existence of the soul. I also believe in the most recent messenger of God, Bahá'u'lláh, who . . .'

The second he saw the word Bahá'í on my form he ripped it out of my hands. 'OK. You're guilty and your crime is quite clear to us.'

I replied, 'My belief is not a crime.'

The session took about three hours. They didn't fire me that day, but I knew it wouldn't be long before they did. When I returned to my office I went through all my files and put them in order so the person who would be replacing me would be able to pick up my work where I left off.

About ten days later, I was summoned once again. When I entered I realized that none of the people from the last meeting were present except Mr Najafí himself. The new group included two people from my own office who had recently joined the Islamic Committee. One of them blushed when he saw me, and shuffled uncomfortably.

'None of the people from the last meeting agreed to come back here today to issue the order to fire you,' Najafí began. 'Your boss is very satisfied with your work and all of your colleagues like you. To be perfectly honest, I don't want to fire you either. You have already been given ten days to reconsider, and it would simply be enough for you to say that you are not a Bahá'í for you to keep your job.'

I replied, 'I would never renounce my faith,' and the questions and answers started again.

When Najafí realized that I wouldn't recant he started to threaten me. 'I know you rely on your husband's pension,' he said. 'I will order his pension to be cut off from today, and you will be required to repay at once the one-million tuman mortgage you got from the NIOC for your home. That will make you recant.'

'You're talking about material difficulties, not spiritual ones,' I answered.

'What would you do if we confiscated your house?'

'I would rent a room and live there quite happily.'

'What if I don't let you rent a room?'

'I'll go to the cemetery and camp there,' I said quietly.

Mr Najafí announced the meeting adjourned after about four hours of this, and I politely said goodbye. He was shaking with anger, but the other people in the meeting stood up respectfully and saw me out. Since I still hadn't been fired, I went back to my office.

When the supervisor of the accounting department saw me coming he called me over to his desk. 'I'm so glad I caught you,' he said. 'The accounting department has all the cheques for the month ready today. Go this minute and collect yours, before they fire you!' I very much appreciated his kindness.

The next morning at around ten o'clock, my boss called me into his office. When I entered the room I could see from his face that he had received the order for my dismissal. He looked pale, and in a very low voice, almost mumbling, he said, 'I am ashamed. I have worked here for thirty years and I have never liked firing anyone – not even those who have been dishonest, or who have made serious mistakes. And I have never had to fire anyone for their beliefs. Olya, how can I do this to you, one of my best employees?'

I understood of course that none of this was any of his doing, and so I asked him not to be upset. 'I received my cheque yesterday for this month,' I said, 'but I haven't worked a full month, so please calculate my salary so I can return what is owed to the company.'

He shook his head and said, 'This company owes you so much more. Every month they have deducted savings and retirement contributions from your cheque, and you still have vacation days owing. We are firing you without giving you your due, and now you want to pay back some of your salary!'

I received a letter stating that I was discharged because I belonged to 'the misleading sect of Bahá'ísm'. I went and said goodbye to each and every one of my colleagues, including Mr Najafí.

When I got back to the office to pick up my belongings, my friends were there. Some of the women were crying. The personnel manager came in and made a short speech.

'Friends, why are you crying?' he began. 'We are proud to have a colleague who is leaving her job because of her principles. She has not lost anything – she has gained something. Olya Roohizadegan is leaving this office with her head held high.' He finished his address and quickly left the room. It was 18 May 1982, my son Payam's third birthday.

Up until the last minute I continued to receive messages from the committee, suggesting that I still had time: 'Just say you are not a Bahá'í and you can have your job back.'

As they had threatened, they were not content with merely firing me; they stopped my husband's pension too. He had worked for the NIOC for thirty-two years. They also demanded that the one-million tuman loan be paid back immediately in one lump sum, otherwise they would repossess our house.

Neither of us now had any income, and we had no way of coming up with so much money. On top of it all, we had to keep sending money for our sons' education in England. We racked our brains to try and come up with a solution. We had only been given a few days, so there was no time to sell the house. We had some savings and we could come up with 450,000 tuman but that still left us 550,000 short. There didn't seem to be any way out.

A couple of days later, one of the Bahá'ís of <u>Sh</u>íráz, Mr Íraj Dihmu'bidí, dropped by to see how we were. When he heard about our financial crisis, he simply said, 'Don't worry; I'll lend you the money, and more if you want, and then when you sell the house you can pay me back.' It was a miracle. Morad and I were shocked for days. 'What if he changes his mind?' we thought. But he didn't. Mr Dihmu'bidí and his wife gave us a 530,000-tuman loan interest free, and other friends generously made up the difference so we were able to go to Tehran, repay the money, and be released from our mortgage with the oil company.

We were far from being alone in experiencing this type of persecution. A woman named Mrs Izadí, who had been fired from teaching at a government school because she was a Bahá'í, had managed to find a job as headmistress in the child-care centre where I was now taking Payam every morning. One day three men from the fundamentalist group Hezbullah suddenly turned up and called a meeting for the staff, children and parents.

'We have been informed that a Bahá'í woman is running this place and that there are some Bahá'í children here,' one of them announced. 'According to the Qur'án, these infidels must be removed. I'm now in charge of the Islamic Committee reorganizing this school.'

Mrs Izadí stood up and said, 'Yes, I am a Bahá'í and I am proud of my beliefs. I am not frightened of you and I will not, under any circumstances, deny my faith. If the parents and the Islamic Committee don't want me here, I will leave this minute.'

The Islamic Committee decided that since she had admitted she was a Bahá'í, she was not suitable to supervise Muslim children, but the parents objected to this decision and argued that this nursery was the best in Shíráz for its care, organization and cleanliness – and that this was due to Mrs Izadí's professionalism.

'This centre is being run very well,' said one mother, a relative of Áyatu'lláh Dastghayb. 'If they dismiss this woman I will remove my child from the school.'

But of course, the committee had the power to do whatever they wished, and Mrs Izadí was fired on the spot. Three-year-old Payam was barred from attending the centre, as were all other Bahá'í children.

In the early autumn of 1982, a young Bahá'í by the name of Suhayl Húshmand, a twenty-four-year-old house painter, was arrested by Revolutionary Guards and cruelly tortured. In yet another attempt to create distrust among the Bahá'ís, the guards then forced Suhayl to accompany them on their raids of Bahá'í homes, to make him appear responsible for identifying them. Under extreme physical and emotional pressure, it was rumoured, Suhayl had named other Bahá'ís who were still in hiding.

Whatever the truth of these claims, it was with careful timing and military precision that the guards descended on Bahá'í homes on 23 October and arrested about forty-five people, ranging from seventeen-year-old-girls to eighty-five-year-old men. This action was sanctioned by the order of one of the leading clerics in Shíráz, and the charges levelled against them were that they were Bahá'ís and therefore spies and heretics.

As soon as I heard what had happened I rushed to Nusrat Yaldá'í's house. She was now a member of the assembly and I feared the worst. As I approached her home I saw Kúrush, her twelve-year-old son, standing in front of the door. The moment he saw me he frantically signalled that it wasn't safe to come any closer, but the sight of the boy standing there alone made me go on.

I asked him if his mother was at home, or his brother Bahrám.

'Last night some armed guards came to the house and searched around,' he said, 'and then they took my mother, my brother and our neighbour Mrs Ávárigán with them. They wanted to take all the Bahá'í books, documents and tapes, but they couldn't fit everything into their car, so they said they would come back this morning for the rest. They told me not to leave the house or let anyone else go in!'

I asked Kúrush to come home with me but he insisted he must wait for the guards to come back.

I rushed to some other Bahá'í friends but none of them had any idea what had happened the night before, so I called Mr Yadu'lláh Mahmúdnizhád, the secretary of the assembly. There was no answer. I later found out that both he and his seventeen-year-old daughter Mona had been arrested.

For several days the local Bahá'í community was in a state of panic. Most of those arrested were assembly members or well-known Bahá'ís in the area. The reserve assembly members immediately stepped into their shoes, despite the danger their membership placed them in. A number of the remaining Bahá'ís who were on committees left Shíráz and went into hiding, and those of us who stayed behind were expecting the guards to barge into our houses and take away our loved ones at any moment.

For almost a month the guards did not let any family or friends of those arrested visit them in prison. I went to the prison a few times, and tried different approaches on the guards to try and persuade them to let me in, but it was no use. A guard named Mu'alimí, who officiated at the front gate of the prison, had the power to ignore the Religious Magistrate's or Public Prosecutor's order for visiting privileges if he felt like it; there were no proper regulations and no system of authority.

Mu'alimí held a list of the prisoners in his hand every day, and all the families of the prisoners – Bahá'ís and Muslims alike – gathered in front of the prison gate. First he would read out the names of the Muslim prisoners and let their families in for a visit, and then he would announce that Bahá'í prisoners had no visitors – after they had waited in the cold for seven, eight or more hours.

Even when visits were finally allowed it was difficult to find out about the conditions in which the Bahá'ís were being held, since asking prisoners about their treatment in prison was strictly forbidden. Occasionally, when a Muslim prisoner was released, he or she would describe the tremendous physical and mental pressure that was being put on the Bahá'ís to recant their faith and to reveal the names of other prominent Bahá'ís.

In November we suddenly heard that Mr Awjí had been executed. On the sixteenth, without any prior notice to his family, the morning paper had printed the news of his execution. His family immediately contacted the prison and asked, as was their right, for the body. However, Mr Awjí had been badly tortured in prison and the authorities did not want the family to see the state of the body. It is still not known how he was killed or where he was buried.

The following week we received the terrible news that Dr Zíyá Ahrárí had been executed. His wife, whose dignity in the face of her loss truly astonished me since I knew how much she had been dreading this moment, had to pay the court the 10,000 tuman they always demanded from Bahá'ís before they would allow her to bury her husband in the Bahá'í cemetery.

The impression that still stays with me most strongly from Dr Ahrárí's funeral is that of Hidáyat Síyávushí's mother supporting his widow and family, of her calm serenity even though she knew her own son had been sentenced to death at the same time and that she might hear of his execution at any minute.

On 25 November 1982, about five weeks after the mass arrests, the Public Prosecutor of Shíráz announced through all the media – television, radio and newspapers – that 'All orders of arrest have been cancelled, and no one under any circumstances has the right to enter your house, arrest or interrogate you. So beware! Do not let strangers onto your premises.'

Hearing this message, repeated over and over again, scared me even more. I had a feeling that this was only another one of their tricks and would probably lead to the arrest of even more Bahá'ís. I shared this thought immediately with the members of the Local Spiritual Assembly, but they were all very positive about the announcement and in any case, they said, they had surrendered to the will of God.

Four days later this same Public Prosecutor issued orders for the arrest of forty more Bahá'ís, and for the second time, the guards raided Bahá'í houses.

On the morning of the twenty-ninth I felt a strong conviction that something was about to happen. I took Payam out to the shops, and after looking in all the stores, I finally bought him a red tricycle that he liked. From there I went directly to my parents' house. After the demolition of the alley of the House of the Báb, they had rented a house near the airport. I mentioned to my mother that I had bought Payam a tricycle, so that if I was arrested he would have something new to play with that would help take his mind off my absence. I had also gone there to say goodbye; there was no telling when they would come to arrest me.

My mother became very upset. She didn't even want to contemplate what might lie ahead for me; from very early childhood she had herself endured persecution as a Bahá'í, and she had hoped her children wouldn't have to go through the same torment. I sadly left my parents and drove towards my house. It was already dark.

As I drove along I had a strange feeling that was totally unfamiliar to me, as if an indescribable force was keeping me from going home. The street leading to our house was very quiet and somehow I felt the presence of the guards close by, although I couldn't see anyone. I looked at the sky above; even the sky seemed oppressive. The closer to home I got, the stronger my sense of foreboding became.

At last I could see our house ahead. An unfamiliar jeep was parked in front of it. Immediately, I reversed my car and parked about seventy metres away, barely able to keep a grip on the steering wheel because I was shaking so much. I aimed my headlights at the jeep to get a better look at it. I could see three people inside. A voice in my head seemed to be telling me to get away from there. For a moment I was paralysed, but then I said to myself, 'It's only my imagination. I'd better just go home. Whatever is going to happen will happen. As my father always said, even a leaf wouldn't fall from a tree unless it was the will of God.'

I was deep in these thoughts when the jeep suddenly started up and roared off, down the street and away.

I went into my house and Morad was there. I could sense that he too was nervous. 'We just have to be calm, and take it one step at a time,' he said. 'There's nothing else we can do.'

I quickly set about hiding some of our valuables. First I put all our address books – containing names and addresses of many Bahá'ís – and diaries in a safe place. Then I began collecting up our bank books. Morad noticed.

'What are you doing?' he asked, surprised. 'You don't think they can simply come in here and steal from us, do you? We haven't committed any crimes.'

He promptly put the bank books back where they belonged. Soon afterwards he left to make his way over to my brother's and collect some of my relatives who were coming for dinner.

Around seven o'clock, as Payam was happily playing with his new tricycle, the doorbell rang. It was my husband, together with my two brothers and my brother-in-law. A moment later both doorbells on the front and back door rang at once. I knew straight away who it was.

One of my brothers went to the front door and called out, 'This man says he's one of your neighbours.'

'Don't worry,' I said. 'They are not the neighbours, they are the Revolutionary Guards. I'll go and open the door.' It had become well known among Bahá'ís that the guards often posed as neighbours when coming to make arrests, not realizing that we would have opened the door to them anyway. In the meantime Morad went to answer the back door, where there were four Bahá'í friends and a guard.

As soon as I opened the front door three armed guards barged past me and demanded to know if this was the Roohizadegan residence, if I was Mrs Roohizadegan and if I was a Bahá'í. I answered 'Yes' to all three questions.

I also explained that I thought the guns unnecessary, since I had done nothing wrong and was not intending to attempt an escape. This remark angered them. They said they were from the Revolutionary Court and had an order from the Public Prosecutor to search our house. I said to them politely: 'According to statements in the press and on TV and radio made by the Public Prosecutor himself, we are not to let anyone into our houses. All orders for searches and arrests have been cancelled.'

The guards looked at each other and then one of them said, 'We have a warrant to search your house from the Public Prosecutor himself.'

'Do you mind if I see it?' I asked.

He handed me the warrant for the arrest of local Bahá'ís, with a list of seventy-two names and addresses attached. I managed to memorize about twenty of the names before the guard realized what I was doing, and snatched the list back from me.

'I would like to telephone the Public Prosecutor and verify this warrant,' I said.

Their leader, who was a short, fat man, introduced himself as Guard Imámí. He dialled the number as we all waited in anticipation. 'Sir, can you confirm you gave us this order for the arrest of the Bahá'ís?' he said. He handed the receiver to my husband.

'Mr Prosecutor,' Morad began, 'didn't you announce yourself in all the media that all orders for the arrest of citizens were cancelled?'

'The announcement was not for you Bahá'ís,' the prosecutor laughed. 'I sent those guards to search your house and then arrest the ones whose names are on the list and bring them to the Revolutionary Court.' He hung up, and Imámí triumphantly instructed us not to move or touch anything. He was in charge now, and was keen to let everyone know it.

The phone rang and one of the other guards answered it. It was my husband's cousin, who immediately began to gabble on excitedly, assuming that it was my husband who had answered the phone.

We could clearly hear him saying: 'Morad, the guards have been attacking the houses of the Bahá'ís. Leave home immediately.' Imámí smiled and ripped the telephone out of the wall.

Two of the guards went into the other rooms and rifled through cupboards and drawers, while another remained standing in front of us to keep an eye on us. Suddenly I noticed that near me, on the top of the television, there was a document that identified all the members of the present National Spiritual Assembly. Carefully, without Imámí noticing, I managed to brush it with my elbow so that it fell down behind the television and out of sight.

However, a mentally retarded young girl who was visiting us with her family when the guards arrived had seen me. She began to point excitedly to the television. My heart was in my mouth. I looked at her sternly and frightened her into silence. Fortunately they did not realize why she had been so agitated, and the moment passed.

Imámí then took each of us in turn into the hall and interrogated us about our beliefs. I was worried about my guests, especially my brother-in-law, who had narrowly managed to avoid arrest on previous occasions; I'd never have forgiven myself if they had been arrested in my home. But miraculously, although the guards asked for everyone's name and for detailed information about them, they didn't seem interested in arresting anyone but me.

My husband offered several times to make tea for the guards, but they refused. They demanded our jewellery, gold and cash, our car keys and all our valuables including bank books, cheques, uncashed money orders, family albums and Bahá'í books. They were there, in fact, to rob us in the name of Islam. Imámí then said that one of us had to write down a list of the items they were taking away, as though that would somehow legitimize their actions.

All the time they were in the house, Payam, our innocent little child, was in a state of shock. They wouldn't even let me give him his dinner or put him to bed.

When they had gathered together all the things they wanted to take, Imámí told Morad to go out and put them in their car. Presumably, they didn't want the neighbours to see them stealing our possessions. They were finished at about midnight and told me I had to go with them to the Revolutionary Court. 'The rest of you are not required, but you must wait here until we are far away from the house before you leave,' Imámí ordered. As they bundled me into the hallway, I stopped to ask them what charges they were arresting me on. 'Participation in the Bahá'í administration,' Imámí answered.

'Can I at least say goodbye to my family?'

'We haven't got time for that sort of thing. Come on.'

'Please,' I said, looking him straight in the face.

Imámí quickly glanced at his fellow guards, and then turned back to me. 'Make it quick, then.'

I kissed my brothers goodbye and told them not to worry about me, but to assure my parents that I'd be fine. I was familiar with the court's policy by now, and so I asked Morad to try to bring Payam to visit me; as he was under four, there was a good chance they would let me see him.

I begged Morad to be strong. I saw how tense he was, his jaw tight as he struggled to keep control of himself. He simply had to stand there while several armed men took his wife away in the middle of the night.

As for me, in spite of everything my heart was filled with indescribable joy; the thought that I was being arrested for my Faith brought me a strange sense of fulfilment, unlike any other experience of my life. Only God was witness to the sense of wonder with which I embraced my husband and my child, not knowing when – or if – I would see them again.

As the guards pushed me into the car, I saw Payam running from the house towards us. He had struggled free from his father's arms, and was screaming and crying so loudly that all the neighbours were woken up and began to peer out of their windows. They didn't dare come out of their houses because they knew the guards were armed, and they had heard all about the previous arrests of Bahá'ís.

My little son clung to the car door handle and screamed frantically. One of the guards quickly got out and tried to release his hold on the handle. But Payam's grip was amazingly strong in his hysterical state, and in the end Imámí had to help his colleague get rid of the child. They threw him violently towards his father, and Morad caught him in mid-air.

By this time my husband had nearly lost control and yelled out, 'Where are you taking my wife at this hour? At least take me with you, or leave her here for now and I promise I'll bring her wherever you say in the morning.'

But they weren't listening. They sat me in the front seat with Guard Imámí at the wheel, while the others sat in the back pointing their guns at my head.

PART II

PRISON

In the Cell

The guards did not utter a word to me until we arrived at Sepah prison. I was relieved when I saw where they were taking me – it was where the other Bahá'ís were being held. As soon as we got inside the prison yard they asked me to close my eyes and bend down with my head on my knees.

Then the driver put his foot down on the accelerator and drove very fast round the prison complex, braking and accelerating and swerving sharply round the corners to frighten me. With my head down I couldn't brace myself properly, and they laughed as I was thrown about.

When the car stopped they blindfolded me tightly and gave me one end of a rolled-up newspaper to hold. They said since I was a Bahá'í I was unclean; therefore their hands would be contaminated if they touched mine. They led me into a room, shouting and swearing at me all the time. When we were inside someone exclaimed, 'We brought her.'

A voice replied, 'Which group does this prisoner belong to?' and the guard answered, 'Zionists. She is a spy for Israel.'

Just then I heard three gunshots outside, very close by. Immediately the thought rushed through my head that they had shot my husband and Payam, who had been trying to follow me to the prison.

I began to panic, but in a matter of seconds I managed to pull myself together and said to myself, 'I shouldn't let my feelings take over. Even if they kill my husband and son, I still have to stand firm and face whatever tests come my way.'

My concentration was broken by the sound of people yelling and swearing at me. A group seemed to be standing around me. Someone began to taunt me, 'Just look at her. She is a *Tághútí.*' This was the term they used to identify wealthy people during the Shah's regime.

'Look at the smart clothes she is wearing!' they continued, but they were just trying to intimidate me, because I was only wearing a basic black chador.

One of the guards started asking me questions in a hostile manner, asking for my name, family name, address, and so on, and finally my religion. I answered politely, 'My religion is the Bahá'í Faith and I am not a spy.' He mockingly imitated my voice and laughed at me.

For over an hour I stood in the middle of that room as the guards bullied and insulted me. But this was not a new experience for me. As a child, from the moment I became a Bahá'í at the age of eleven, I had encountered the same prejudiced attitudes in my school and in the streets, and eventually I got used to being persecuted for my religion. I remember fanatics coming to our house in the middle of the night to throw stones at the windows and shout abuse, several nights in a row, just to intimidate us.

All the time I was in that room they were bringing other Bahá'ís in, sometimes individually, sometimes in groups. When people entered the room I would know they were Bahá'ís because each time the guard announced, 'Keep away, keep away, this is another Bahá'í. Be careful not to touch these unclean people.'

At one point someone came into the room and said excitedly, 'We've got Farhád Bihmardí.' Another replied, 'Search his house thoroughly. He is the head of the Bahá'ís of S̲h̲íráz, you know!' They didn't understand Bahá'í administration, and thought that since Farhád was a member of the Local Spiritual Assembly, he must be the leader.

One of the guards eventually said, 'Take this woman [meaning me] to the cell so she won't find out how many Bahá'ís we arrest tonight.'

I was led into another room for a body search. The search was done by a girl named Sister Muhammadí; they called the male guards 'brother' and the female guards 'sister'. She searched me thoroughly and took the 100 tuman that I had in my pocket. Then, still blindfolded, I was given the newspaper to hold as they directed me to the cell.

First I heard the unbolting of heavy iron bars, then suddenly they pushed me against a cloth hanging from the ceiling and I was told to remove my blindfold. It was dark. The first thing that struck me was a shining pair of eyes staring at me, and then there was the harsh sound of loud, insane laughter.

For a moment I was shocked, but then I sensed other people around me, and heard myself cautiously saying 'hello'. A woman's voice responded warmly to my greeting and asked me if I was a Bahá'í. This lady, I soon discovered, was the political prisoner in charge of the cell. She held my hand and directed me to the corner where the rest of the Bahá'í women, who had been brought in an hour ago, were sitting. 'I've brought you another Bahá'í,' she announced. As my eyes focused I recognized the happy and familiar faces of 'Izzat Ishráqí and her beautiful daughter Roya, and Táhirih Síyávushí and Mínú Násirí. Mínú's father Dr Mihdí Anvarí had been executed more than a year and a half previously. All the women embraced me. We hugged and kissed one another.

About two hours later the iron bars opened again, and I immediately went to the door. They bundled in Shírín Dálvand, Mítrá Íraván and Rúhíyyih Jahánpúr. I hugged and welcomed them to the prison and they were greeted in the same manner by the other Bahá'í prisoners. Some hours later, Mahshíd Nírúmand was brought in. In that one night, about forty Bahá'ís were arrested in Shíráz and taken to Sepah, between 7.30 in the evening and three o'clock the next morning. The Bahá'í men were taken to a different cell.

There in the women's cell, we didn't sleep until the early hours of the morning, but spent the night happily sharing the stories of our arrests with each other. I found I had been lucky to escape the vulgarity and discourtesy of some of the female guards who conducted the body searches. They were illiterate young girls with repulsive manners, and one of them had even asked some of the elderly ladies to take off all their clothes, then clumsily conducted an internal search of their bodies.

The person in charge of the cell, Fakhrí Imámí, was a Muslim and a political prisoner who had repudiated her past

activities and 'returned to Islam'. Some of her relatives were
Bahá'ís and she was very sympathetic towards the Bahá'í prisoners. She had the complete trust of the guards, and therefore
considerable power over life in the cell. Fakhrí was very helpful
from the first night, both in Sepah and after we were all transferred to Adelabad Prison. She told us about the treatment we
could expect as Bahá'ís in the prison, how they pressured the
Bahá'ís physically and psychologically into revealing the names
and addresses of other Bahá'ís.

She told us stories about the other Bahá'ís who had been
arrested over a month ago, of how they had been put under
pressure to give our names to the guards, and how just half an
hour before we were brought in, they had been transferred to
Adelabad Prison so we wouldn't see each other to exchange
information. The ones they had transferred included Símín
Sábirí, Zarrín Muqímí and her mother; Akhtar Sabet; and seventeen-year-old Mona Mahmúdnizhád. At the same time they
transferred Ishrat Rawhání and Irán Ávárigán to solitary confinement. Nusrat Yaldá'í, a relative of mine by marriage, and
Ṭúbá Zá'irpúr were still being held in solitary confinement,
having been separated from the other Bahá'í women from the
beginning of their imprisonment, over a month ago.

Our accommodation in Sepah consisted of two adjacent
cells, each about four by six metres. There were as many as forty
to fifty people in each. All crammed together there were political prisoners, murderers, prostitutes, drug addicts and women
who were mentally or physically ill. They included people who
were sentenced to death, pregnant women and even nursing
mothers with their babies.

There were hallways on each side of the cells, two of them
very narrow and the other two about 1.5 metres wide. There
were two toilets and two showers in the wider hallways – completely inadequate for so many people.

Each cell had two windows secured by iron bars. The air
inside the cell was stifling since we could not open the windows
and so many people were all packed together. It smelt of vomit. I
soon discovered why. The general lack of hygiene and poor food
in the prison regularly led to sickness and diarrhoea. We all suffered from it, but the drug addicts suffered more than most. They

seemed to be sick all the time. In one corner of the hallway there was a television which was controlled by the guards. All they showed were scenes of the war against Iraq, official demonstrations, or religious programmes directed by the mullahs.

The floor was covered by an old, dirty carpet, and our sleeping facilities were limited to two very thin, dirty army blankets each, one to sleep on and one to cover ourselves with. When additional prisoners arrived, we had to share our blankets with the newcomers. The Bahá'í prisoners were supposed to keep to one side of the cell so that they wouldn't 'contaminate' the rest, so we were allowed to sleep on only one side in a row. This left us so little space that we had to sleep curled sideways because there wasn't enough room to turn onto our backs. There was a heater in the hallway which was turned off at night and sometimes even during the day, which meant that the prison was so cold at night it was hard to sleep. They woke us up every morning at 4 a.m. by turning all the lights on and announcing over the loudspeakers, 'Alláh'u'Akbar' – the Muslim call to prayer.

We Bahá'ís were not allowed to say our own prayers. Fakhrí told us that when the first group of Bahá'ís had chanted prayers together, the other prisoners and the guards were moved by it, and when the Religious Magistrate found out about this, he put a stop to it. We tried to say our prayers in the middle of the night when the others were asleep, but the guards soon realized what we were doing and prohibited that too.

Our blankets, plates and glasses were kept separate from the Muslims'. For every three or four Bahá'ís there was one plastic bowl to share, but there wasn't any cutlery at all so we had to eat with our fingers. On the first day they poured some soup into a bowl and said, 'This is between three of you.' We asked for spoons but they just laughed. 'Do you think you are in your own homes? Eat with your fingers!' The food was divided between everyone by the Muslim prisoners. They also gave us duties such as sweeping the floor and so on. The Religious Magistrate had told them, 'The Bahá'ís are unclean. Let them wash the dishes, but rinse them afterwards yourselves.'

At meal times the Muslims were made to sit separately from the Bahá'ís, but most of the educated ones preferred to sit with us. They were scornful of these orders and said, 'You Bahá'ís are much cleaner than us; you even seem healthier than we are.' Many were attracted by the fact that we were like one big family, and they envied the trust and affection between us. The other prisoners often fought with each other and caused disturbances, and the guards used to tell them, 'Learn unity and peace from the Bahá'ís.'

But no one could get a moment's peace in that cell. The drug addicts were not given any treatment and neither was there proper care for the sick, so these poor women would moan and groan in their pain and suffering, and the noise would keep us awake at night. Another thing that prevented us from sleeping peacefully was that the investigators were often in the habit of calling one or more of us for trial in the middle of the night. Every time we heard the harsh sound of the iron bars opening, all of us jumped and waited with bated breath to see what was going to happen and whose turn it would be. Were they going to take someone for torture, or even for execution?

As a mother myself, I really felt for the tiny children in that prison. However, I tried to avoid getting too close to the children during the day because of my emotional vulnerability as a mother. In the middle of the night, however, when I was saying my prayers, I often saw the very young children shivering in the freezing cold, and then I would go to them and cover them with my blanket.

Three days after our arrest, at ten in the morning, they called out a group of us including Shírín Dálvand, 'Izzat and Roya Ishráqí, Mínú Násirí, Mahshíd Nírúmand, Mítrá Íraván, Táhirih Síyávushí, Mahín Akhláqí and myself. They blindfolded us all and handed the first woman in the line the end of a rolled newspaper. The rest of us were told to hang onto the chador of the one in front and in rather a grim parody of a dance we moved slowly forward. They led us down the corridor, swearing at us the whole way, saying disrespectful things about the Faith and that we all deserved to die.

After a while they told us to stop and face the wall. A group of guards stood behind us and said, 'Do you still claim to be Bahá'ís?' We all said we did. Then suddenly they shouted, 'Fire! Kill the bastards!'

For a moment, I really thought they were going to shoot us, but instead of fear, I was filled with a sense of release – it was such a sweet feeling. I felt so relieved and even happy that soon I would be free from their clutches, but of course they were just trying to scare us.

After that little charade was over, they took us to another room and called us one by one by name. When it was my turn, I was told to remove my blindfold. There was a photographer in front of me, and three guards. One of them was very fat, and wore a mask that covered all of his face except his eyes and mouth. Before they took my picture they said, 'Introduce yourself.'

I gave my name. The man wearing the mask said, 'Are you from Jahrum?' and I hopefully replied, 'Yes, Brother,' thinking he too must be from Jahrum. But he yelled at me, '*Khejalat bekesh!* – Shame on you! You are a disgrace to the people of Jahrum. They are all such fine Muslims. They helped this revolution to be successful, but you, you dirty bastard, you became a Bahá'í. You should be shot!' He swore a lot but I didn't pay any attention to what he was saying.

One of them handed me a steel plaque that had a chain on both sides and a number on the front. He told me to lower my chador to my shoulders and hold the plaque out in front of me. I held the plaque out with my left hand, but he shouted angrily, 'Bring out your right hand so your Bahá'í ring, the evidence of your crime, will be in the picture too!' After they took my picture they sent me back to the cell.

At that time we had not really adjusted to being prisoners, and the swearing and abuse really affected us. When we got back to our cell, we each sat in a corner and tried to hold back our tears. Ṭáhirih Síyávushí started to cry softly. 'Each of us was somebody in this country. We had a profession and somehow served humanity,' she said – she was herself a nurse. 'Until three days ago, I was saving people's lives in the hospital, but now I have to waste my time in here listening to their insults.'

Within a few minutes, however, she had pulled herself together. 'No, we must not let these people upset us. We must be spiritually strong and firm in our faith.' Then gradually she started to cheer everyone up with her amusing caricatures.

Jokingly, she imitated the way the guards had talked to us. To
make us laugh she added, 'So, tell me, how did that kind Mr
Investigator yell at you?' Looking back it seems strange that, in
spite of all the pressure we endured and were still to suffer in
that prison, we managed to retain our sense of humour and to
laugh with the other prisoners.

Four days later they brought in Firishtih Anvarí and her
husband Dr Muhammad Anvarí, together with other members
of the Local Spiritual Assembly of Marvdasht. They brought
Firishtih to our cell.

Although she had been the last one to arrive in Sepah, she
was the first one in our group to be taken for trial. She was
gone for two hours. When she returned, she could barely walk.

I helped her in and sat her down. Quietly, because our moves
were closely watched by the guards, I asked her what had happened. Those who had come back from a trial were not allowed
to talk about what they had been asked, what they answered or
what they had endured. She told me her story in a whisper.

After they called me out of the cell, they took me to the
basement. We walked down a lot of stairs. There I heard
a lot of high-pitched screams, and when they removed
my blindfold I saw eight wooden tables with chains at
each corner. Someone was chained to each table and the
guards were whipping them with electric cables. I was
terrified. They threatened me with the same treatment if
I didn't recant my faith or refused to give them the
names of other Bahá'ís who were members of the committees. I just fainted, and when I opened my eyes I
found myself on the bed in the prison hospital. The
doctor had given me an injection. They insulted me
again and said, 'You can go now. But we won't leave you
alone.'

As she was talking I was picturing to myself the rough times
ahead, and the kind of people we were up against.

The next day they called Mahín Akhláqí, Mahshíd
Nírúmand and myself. They blindfolded us and gave me one

end of a piece of cloth. The guard held the other end and told Mah<u>sh</u>íd to hold onto the back of my chador and Mahín to hold on to hers. He said they were taking us for trial. 'We have to go down a lot of stairs, and you must do whatever I tell you.'

Obviously, I thought to myself, we were being taken to the same place Firi<u>sh</u>tih had been the day before. We had no choice but to do what we were told. That was the worst moment for me. I was filled with a dread of the unknown: Where were they taking us? What was going to happen to us? Would we be able to withstand the tests that lay ahead? That moment stands out sharply in my memory because I was so afraid of failing, of breaking under the pressure. As I stumbled blindly down the steps, I constantly prayed to God for courage and steadfastness.

When we finally got to the basement, they kept us standing there for a while and then separated us. I could hear terrible noises some distance away. Then the guard led me on further and the noise got louder and louder. It sounded more like animals squealing in pain than any human sound. It wasn't like any noise I had ever heard before. My heart was pounding in my chest. I wanted to scream from the depths of my being and somehow put a stop to the torture of these people I couldn't even see. At that moment I wished the whole world could witness for themselves the obscene behaviour of these inhuman, prejudiced creatures who seemed to know nothing of God, love or humanity, despite calling themselves followers of the holy religion of Islam.

In that basement I remembered the story that my father had told me of a time over fifty years ago, when a mob had attacked his father-in-law's house in Jahrum – then as now one of the most fanatical cities in Iran. It was 7 April 1926 and my father, who was then only nineteen and newly married, was the sole survivor. His father-in-law, hearing a crowd of Muslims break-ing into his house, immediately rushed to my father and urged him to hide in a secret niche in the wall, but my father refused to save himself.

Carrying shovels, axes and clubs, the angry mob burst into the room. Several local Bahá'ís were in the house at the time for a meeting. They were all herded together and the host and seven visiting Bahá'ís were clubbed and hacked to death. All the while these gentle people were saying prayers, making no effort to defend themselves.

My father was badly beaten but still alive. A rope was put around his neck and tied to the body of his father-in-law. Gleefully the mob dragged him round the town, stopping every now and then to torture him in front of the crowd. Unconscious and covered in blood he was eventually left for dead. He lay in a coma for forty days, but miraculously survived.

I often used to ask my father how he had been able to endure such extreme pressure and hardship, even seeing his father-in-law and Bahá'í friends killed in front of his eyes, and still stand firm. He replied, 'God always gives a person the power to remain true to the pathway of truth. During difficult times one draws closer to the Creator.' I could never understand this at the time. Although I trusted in my father's experience, it was still very difficult for me to grasp the reality of it. I heard it like a story, but I couldn't touch it. Until the moment I stood in front of those heartless people in that terrifying basement, I had always regarded it as a truth I would never be in a position to experience for myself. Now I wondered, as I listened to the dreadful sounds of torture, if I would also be able to find the strength.

'You have to answer all my questions.'

I was still blindfolded while I answered the guard, saying, 'My name is Olya Roohizadegan, I live in Shíráz, and I am a Bahá'í.'

He started to insult the Faith and said, 'I will make you become a Muslim.' Then he asked about my occupation, and I said, 'I used to work for the National Iranian Oil Company until I was fired because of my religion.'

He asked about my children, their names, their ages and their whereabouts, and then said, 'Do you love your children?' I said I did.

'According to the Qur'án,' he went on, 'you are an infidel and you have to recant your faith and become a Muslim. If you don't recant, your punishment is death. You will be hanged. But I will give you a chance to think it over and become a Muslim, because you have been misled.'

'Your honour,' I replied, 'I have not been misled. One can only become a Bahá'í through personal investigation of the truth, not by inheritance or imitation. Each Bahá'í, according to Bahá'u'lláh's teaching, should first acknowledge the truth by recognizing all the previous prophets and their holy books, and then become a Bahá'í. So you see, in order to be a Bahá'í, I have to believe in the truth of the holy religion of Islam, and then believe in Bahá'u'lláh who is the promised one of all ages and the Messenger from God whose advent all the prophets have proclaimed.'

He got really angry and said, 'It seems that talking to you is getting us nowhere. I'll make you recant by torture, and if that doesn't work I'll hang you myself.'

After some more abuse, that was the end of my first interrogation and I was sent back to the cell.

Four days later they called on Mahshíd and myself again. In the same pattern as before they took us down the stairs to the basement, and then separated us. Once again I heard the dreadful sounds of torture in progress. After keeping me waiting blindfolded for what seemed like hours, they took me to another room and sat me down on a broken stool. Someone said, 'I'm going to take the blindfold off so you can write, but you are not permitted to look around.'

When they uncovered my eyes I saw men wearing masks, and a blank wall. One of the masked men handed me a heavy file and said, 'Write the answers to my questions in this file.'

On the front of the file these words were printed: 'You are being prosecuted in the Islamic Revolutionary Court of Justice. If your answers are found to be untrue you will be dealt with under Islamic law and punished accordingly.' I was surprised at the size of the file they had put together on me, since it was only the beginning of my trial. Feeling curious as to what was inside, I hesitantly opened the file. There were several pages of accusations.

In addition to being a Bahá'í and a member of a Bahá'í committee, I was accused of being an enemy of God, and a spy for Zionism and Israel. An El Al ticket for a flight from Iran to Israel, carrying no name or other information, was there with a note saying it had been found in our home. The guards who searched our house had written pages of reports, which were also in the file.

It seemed they had dug a deep hole for me. But I was innocent and had put all my reliance in God, so nothing could worry me or weaken my strength.

The investigator began by saying that if I lied in my testimony he would get the order from the Religious Magistrate to give me one hundred lashes for each lie. I explained to him that I had no reason to lie about anything. I said, 'You are well aware of the fact that we Bahá'ís are innocent, and we are only here because of your prejudices.'

The first question was, 'Explain your belief'. I answered, 'I believe God is an unknowable essence. I believe in all the prophets of God from Adam to the holy religion of Islam. I believe in the next world and the permanency of the soul. I also believe in the most recent manifestation of God, Bahá'u'lláh, who is the promised one of all ages.'

The other questions were about my arrest, the Bahá'í administration and my responsibilities in it, my Bahá'í relatives, and the members of the Local Spiritual Assembly. The last question was: 'Who did you vote for in the 1982 election for the Local Spiritual Assembly?'

To this I answered, 'In Bahá'í elections, one's vote is highly confidential. Voting is general and open to all adult Bahá'ís, but even husbands and wives should not tell each other who they voted for, since Bahá'ís don't believe in electioneering, and we should elect the people we honestly think can serve the best interests of the community.'

In between questions, the interrogator kept asking me if I would recant and become a Muslim. Every time, I answered, 'Under no circumstances will I recant my faith,' and each time he got more angry, until finally he said, 'Have you ever thought what you will have to answer to God when you go to the next world?'

'The path I have chosen is nothing but the path of God,' I answered, but he swore at me and said, 'Your punishment is to be executed.'

I replied calmly, 'I am subject to the court's decision.'

He was very anxious for me to reveal the names of the members of the Local Spiritual Assembly and the committees, but I resisted and instead explained my own duties in the Bahá'í administration. My conscience would not let me reveal any names to enable them to bring other innocent souls to that dreadful place.

He was really rough with me that day. 'You have been brainwashed. You are a puppet of your leaders, and they are using you,' he said.

'In the Bahá'í Faith', I replied, 'we do not have leaders and we don't obey any individuals. We all believe in Bahá'u'lláh and we all abide by His teachings. You should read the books you have stolen from us.'

That day he threatened and pressured me so much that the other guards began to feel sorry for me and spoke up in defence of my honesty. That only made him more angry, but eventually he let me go and sent me back to the cell.

I thought my interrogation was over for that day, but at two o'clock they called me again, this time with Rúḥíyyih Jahánpúr and Mínú Násirí. They blindfolded us and took us for further questioning. On the way, the interrogator asked, 'Are you going to talk this time, or do I have to whip you?'

I recognized his voice, and said, 'Your honour, I have answered every one of your questions!'

'No, you three have not answered satisfactorily.' He didn't take us to the basement this time, but straight to another room where someone else was to do the investigation. As we were standing there, the new investigator came in and started yelling at me for no reason. 'Roohizadegan – member of the Protection Committee – why didn't you give complete answers in your previous session? Now you have to give me all the names and addresses of your fellow committee members.' Again I refused.

He then turned to Rúḥíyyih and Mínú. 'You two have not explained your involvement in the Bahá'í administration.' Mínú, however, had boldly explained her membership in the Bahá'í Education Committee, and she now repeated the information for him. The investigator, as he was yelling and swearing at us, called a guard and ordered him to go and bring Yadu'lláh Maḥmúdnizhád. Mr Maḥmúdnizhád, Mona's father, was an Auxiliary Board Member and secretary of the Shíráz assembly. I suspected the guards had been torturing him to make him name the members of different committees.

Ten minutes later we heard them bring someone into the room. It sounded as if he had trouble walking. The investigator said: 'Maḥmúdniẓhád, name the members of the Protection Committee.'

Honestly and innocently, but in a weak and strained voice, Mona's father named all the members, ending with my name. He obviously didn't know I was in the room, and I guessed he was blindfolded too. Then I began to ask myself, 'Is Mr Maḥmúdniẓhád really here or have they tried to trick us by making a tape? Maybe they've forced him to read out those names onto a tape.'

I was frightened and puzzled, and didn't know what to do. Should I also mention other names? I remembered the individuals who had been forced to recant their faith and then had come to the Protection Committee in tears. I was worried that if the guards found out their names and brought them to the prison they would be tortured until they recanted again. With that thought, I decided to persevere in refusing to mention any names.

The interrogator was yelling at me and threatening me with torture. I, however, wanted to speak to Mr Maḥmúdniẓhád to find out his reasons for giving out the committee members' names. I was only concerned about the Bahá'ís who had once recanted; they had trusted the committee. A week before his arrest I had given Mr Maḥmúdniẓhád a list of those Bahá'ís, and had emphasized to him then how important it was that we should protect their identities.

I got a grip on myself and said, 'May I ask a question?' I was told I could. Then I said quickly, 'Mr Maḥmúdniẓhád, when you came to my house we talked about my dismissal from the oil company, didn't we?' Before the interrogator could intervene, Mr Maḥmúdniẓhád replied, 'Whatever Mrs Roohizadegan is saying is absolutely true.'

I was reassured, because he knew I was referring not to our conversation about my dismissal, but to our discussion the same day about the Bahá'ís who had recanted. It was clear he was aware of the danger facing those believers and it seemed he had not had to name them. The investigator, of course, was furious,

and shouted, 'Stop it, stop it! You cannot speak to each other!'
He was incensed because he had failed to create mistrust
between us, and he immediately ordered Mr Maḥmúdniẕhád to
be sent back to his cell. Then he started yelling again and asked
me what I thought of Mr Maḥmúdniẕhád's 'betrayal' of me.

I answered, 'Mr Maḥmúdniẕhád was honest in his trial and
told you the truth. I respect him like my brother.'

I was sent back to my cell, but an hour later they again
called for Roya and 'Izzat Iẕhráqí, Mahẕhíd Nírúmand and
myself. As before, they covered our eyes and took us for interrogation. They also brought some of the men, including 'Ináyat
Iẕhráqí and Farhád Bihmardí. Our blindfolds were removed but
we were not allowed to look round.

The investigator said, 'See, all the members of the
Protection Committee and of the assembly are now here.' He
called out all our names, and from then on he called everyone
by their first names – except me. For some reason, he always
called me Roohizadegan. Perhaps he felt reluctant to use my
name Olya. It means 'Exalted'.

When I found out that most of the members of the committee were sitting in that room with me, and that most of the
members of the Bahá'í administration were already in prison, I
felt a great rush of relief, because up to that point I hadn't
named any of them in the interrogations and now I could stop
worrying about being forced to give their names. I thanked God
that I had not been put in a situation where I was compelled to
mention any names of Bahá'ís outside the prison, and that I was
only responsible now for my own destiny. With anxiety gone, I
felt much more relaxed and confident answering the investigator's questions.

He said to us all, 'If you don't give me the names of other
Bahá'ís we will torture you to death.' He pointed to Farhád
Bihmardí and said, 'Especially you! You have already received
200 lashes but you still refuse to give us your brother Faríd's
address in Tehran.' Then he told the other guard to go and
bring Mr Maḥmúdniẕhád before starting the trial, so that he
could advise us to reveal other Baha'ís' names.

When Mr Maḥmúdniẕhád appeared, the investigator said,
'Your friends and most of the members of the committees you

were a member of are here now, but they are not giving us any information. You had better advise them to co-operate.'

Mr Maḥmúdniẕhád bravely said, 'I am Yadu'lláh Maḥmúdniẕhád, the secretary of the Local Spiritual Assembly of Shíráz for 1982. I implore the friends . . .'

The investigator interrupted him at this point and said mockingly, 'Maḥmúdniẕhád, why didn't you say hello to your friends?'

Mr Maḥmúdniẕhád replied, with absolute humility, while the guard still crudely laughed at his own joke, 'I will say hello now!' And then he calmly continued, 'I implore the friends to tell the investigators if they were on any committee and to explain their responsibilities. At first, we failed to tell them our duties, but now we realize that it is essential they know exactly what our duties were as members of the Bahá'í administrative committees. They must understand that we are not a political group, and our work does not concern the government or any political issue.'

But the interrogators were not really interested in knowing about our activities. They just wanted to compile heavy files about us so as to somehow justify our execution; they were not interested in the truth. The fact that we were members of a Bahá'í committee already established our guilt, and that was enough for them.

The investigator said, 'Did you all understand that? Now, if you don't admit that you were a member of a committee and don't give us the names of the other members, we are going to torture you to death.'

Mr Maḥmúdniẕhád, who had obviously been badly tortured himself, said nervously, 'Your honour, please don't pressure them. Give them some time. I am sure they will all tell the truth, because we Bahá'ís don't tell anything but the truth and we have nothing to hide.' The investigator then told the guard to take Mr Maḥmúdniẕhád back to his cell.

After they took him away, they handed each of us our files and told us to start writing the answers to all the questions they were going to ask. The first questions in my file were:

1. How many meetings did the Protection Committee have in 1982?

2. Explain in detail the duties of the Protection Committee.
3. Name the Bahá'ís who had recanted.
4. When the names of the people who recanted were publicized and their pictures were printed in the newspaper, why did you remove and keep that part of the paper? What did you use it for?

To the last question I answered, 'Because you were printing pictures of dead Bahá'ís and non-Bahá'ís and calling them members of a misleading sect who had recanted and returned to Islam. We kept the pictures for our records and compared the names and faces to the list of registered Bahá'ís to see if they were really Bahá'ís or not, and if so whether they were still alive.' The other questions were:

5. In this year, how many Bahá'ís became Muslims and how many Muslims became Bahá'ís?
6. Where were the meetings held?
7. How many Bahá'ís who recanted their faith did you speak to?
8. Name the members of the Protection Committee.
9. How many of those who recanted were allowed to rejoin the Bahá'í community?
10. Explain in detail your direct and indirect activities within the goals of the Protection Committee.

I answered all the questions but couldn't bring myself to name any of those poor Bahá'ís who had been forced to recant. I concentrated on explaining the duties of the committee, and after I had written eight pages about it the investigator changed the questions and tried a different approach. He asked a lot of questions about the Universal House of Justice and the National Spiritual Assembly. They were very familiar with Bahá'í terminology.

The interrogations were now a daily occurrence. They started every day at 8 a.m., and sometimes went on until ten o'clock at night. Fifteen or sixteen people were questioned at the same time, in the same room, our questions depending on our duties in the Bahá'í administration. There were only five chairs in the interrogation room, which were given to the women prisoners, but if any of the men were particularly weakened by torture we insisted they sit on them instead of us. The rest sat on the floor in two lines, facing the wall, for hours on end. Throughout, we could hear the howling of those who were being tortured in that basement, and only the power of faith gave us the strength to endure it.

They were anxious and disturbing days. Sometimes we were called to the investigation room individually at odd times of the night to answer the same questions, repeated over and over. And always, both orally and in writing, the interrogator would keep asking us if we were willing to recant. Once he addressed us all together, saying, 'You will be hanged if you don't recant. You have only one way to regain your freedom and that is by recanting and becoming Muslims. Those of you who are willing to do so, raise your hands.'

There was total silence in the room and no hands went up. Then he said, 'The ones who want to remain Bahá'í and be executed in accordance with the law of the Qur'án, raise your hands.' Immediately all our hands shot up and he started swearing at us, because he felt threatened by our determination and courage.

One day I was suddenly presented with one of my own notebooks that had been confiscated in the search of my house. It contained the telephone numbers of many Bahá'ís and Muslim friends. The investigator told me to write down all the names and addresses corresponding to these phone numbers, but instead I quietly changed all the 1s to 4s and so on, disguising the numbers in any way I could; then I threw a tantrum and told them I couldn't remember the names and addresses, and they should just call the numbers and ask. I never saw the book again.

At the end of one of my sessions the investigator said, 'Since the Seat of the Universal House of Justice is in Israel, and you obey the Universal House of Justice, you are all spies for Israel.' I gave him a lengthy answer to this one as well, explaining that the Bahá'í headquarters are only in Israel because Bahá'u'lláh had been banished to the area, then Palestine, by the Persian authorities of the day. He was buried there and it is a place of pilgrimage for us now.

The interrogator then asked the guard to blindfold everyone and take all the others back to the cell. I was told to stand
up. When I did so he said, 'Now walk.'

'Where to?' I asked. 'I can't see what's in front of me!'

He said, 'Walk forward and I'll tell you.' As I stepped
forward I hit the wall and he started laughing. He ordered me
to walk round the room and every time I hit a wall he shrieked
with laughter.

That day, after sixteen hours of questioning, I had no
energy to walk; my feet were swollen and I was feeling faint. I
had become so weak by now that I used to pass out regularly,
and I could hardly walk the distance between the trial room
and the cell. But although physically we were losing our
strength, spiritually we were strong. This strength had even
impressed the Muslim prisoners, who often hugged and kissed
us when we returned to the cell, asking, 'What do they ask you
that takes so long? How do you manage to keep your spirits up?
Every time you come back you still have a smile on your face.'

Once we were asked to write down our life history in detail.
We had to describe everything we could remember from our
childhood to the day we were arrested. This part of the trial
took two whole days. In addition to the answers regarding my
past I wrote:

> Those days have passed away, and this period will also
> pass. But as for you who are in power and hold the
> balance of justice in your hands, you who claim to be
> the followers of Imám 'Alí and lovers of Islamic justice,
> I leave the decision to you. Is it not better to forget your
> prejudices and replace them with love and understand-
> ing? Is it not better for all the people of this country to
> be allowed to live in harmony? I am sure you are all well
> aware of the innocence of the Bahá'ís. I am sure you
> know that we are not politically active and that we
> obey the laws of this country. It is time to leave your
> prejudices behind and rely on your conscience.

They took me back to the cell. Even though there wasn't a
peaceful moment in that prison, there was such an incredible

feeling of love and unity among the prisoners. Most of us didn't know if we would be alive next day or next week. The atmosphere of that cell was of another world, another reality, completely severed from the everyday events of this one. It was there that we felt, in the highest degree, detached from every earthly concern.

The Pen

CHAPTER 6

The first few weeks in prison were extremely hard because we were not allowed to see our families even for a short visit, nor could we receive or send letters. Without any word from them, day after day, we were torn between our love for our Faith and our love for our husbands, children and parents.

Sometimes we felt overwhelmed by a sense of loneliness and despair. We all got very homesick and cried a lot, especially at the beginning, but we tried to hide our tears so we wouldn't depress each other. During interrogation days we were all under an enormous amount of strain, so afterwards we made light of the situation whenever we could to raise our spirits.

To amuse ourselves and help pass the time, 'Izzat Ishráqí and I used to imagine that when we were all released, her daughter Roya would marry my eldest son, Behnam. 'Izzat was constantly worried that she might break down if they ever took Roya away and tortured her. She was terrified that her love for her daughter would make her unable to bear it. Roya and I would try to cheer her up. I would say to her, 'One day we will all be released and Roya will marry Behnam, we will all be related and we'll live happily ever after!' We were just joking – Roya and Behnam had never met – but 'Izzat dearly wanted Roya to get married and have children one day, and this playful scenario kept our spirits up.

One of the problems we found in prison was coping with the boredom of prison life. In Sepah we were taken for interrogation most of the time, but on the days when we were left in the cell we had nothing to do. The other prisoners could attend to knitting and handicrafts to keep themselves occu-

pied, but we were not allowed to. There was no natural light in
the cells because the corridors bounded them on all sides, and
we were only taken outside for fresh air three or four times a
week, each time for about fifteen to twenty minutes. The area
allocated for exercise was about 100 metres square and surrounded by high walls. All we could see was a small patch of
blue sky overhead.

We all suffered from claustrophobia – physically and mentally – and longed to get back to a normal life, to be able to do
all the things we wanted to do. The emptiness of prison life was
very painful for me because I was used to a very busy lifestyle,
and I was constantly thinking of all the things I could do if I
were free. I was keen to get back to my job, and to be of use to
others, especially my parents who were old and needed
someone to look after them. My mother was ill most of the time
I was in prison.

Perhaps because the present was monotonous and the future
seemed so bleak and uncertain, we spent a lot of our time in
prison thinking back to the everyday bustle of life outside,
before our arrest. It was like a film playing constantly in our
heads. We would think what we might be doing at a particular
moment if we were free. We could be taking the children to
school, for instance, or be in the middle of a normal working
day, or be with our family at home in front of the fire.

Thinking back to happier times was our way of escaping the
present. At home we used to spend our free time walking in the
mountains near Shíráz or in its many parks. Shíráz is a beautiful
city, smaller than Tehran, and known everywhere in Iran as the
'City of Roses and Birds'. Like most Shírázís, we often went to
the parks or into the countryside for huge picnics – grandpar-
ents, aunts and uncles, and cousins galore. Thinking about
home always made me long to see the sky and wide open
spaces.

Shírín, on the other hand, always used to say, 'If I was free I
would go to a restaurant in Tehran and eat chelo kebab' – a
minced meat kebab with rice that is one of the tastiest and
most popular dishes in Iran. She always made our mouths water
talking about it. Food is such a basic part of daily life – and it
was certainly basic in prison – that at meal times we felt the

greatest longing to be at home with our families, eating our own food!

The food in Sepah was usually appalling – we shared a small piece of hard cheese for breakfast at 6.30, perhaps some warm, watery soup and bread for lunch, and if we were lucky a small portion of rice for supper. It was hardly nutritious, and no one had made any effort to make it appetizing either. In fact, the food in prison was so bad we used to make jokes about it, telling each other not to look too closely at it in case we discovered any special secret ingredients – like flies.

But one day, much to our surprise, the guards brought us chelo kebab, and we were all over the moon about such a treat, especially Shírín. However, before we had taken a bite, the door of our cell was thrown open and an old lady of about eighty was pushed inside. She was very weak and had been badly beaten and tortured. She was a Muslim and the sister of a famous tribal leader in Fars, called Khusru Khán Qashqá'í.

She had had over eighty lashes on her feet, and they were terribly swollen although not bleeding – the feet do not bleed unless beaten for many days, and then they bleed from the toe-nails. Táhirih, 'Izzat and I went over to comfort her, and asked her why she had been so badly tortured.

She replied:

Under torture I told the interrogator, 'Don't be too proud of your power and position. I am an old lady and I have seen many things. I can still remember the reign of Reza Shah. And where is he now? Reza Shah is dead and Muhammad Reza Shah, his son, has fled the country and no longer has any power. Now I want to give you some advice! Áyatu'lláh Khomeini's power will soon disappear, and so will your own.'

The interrogator was furious with me and ordered the torturer to beat me even harder – especially since I would not cry.

She was a truly courageous woman. After this we could not touch the chelo kebab. It was our first and last chelo kebab while I was in prison.

Although we were not supposed to wander around outside our
cell, except to go to the toilet, we were free to visit the adjoining cell as much as we liked. Consequently we spent a lot of our
spare time sitting together sharing our experiences in the prison
and before our arrest. We always had to be very careful what
was said and who was listening, because of the many informers
in the two cells, but we passed many hours in quiet conversation and got to know each other very well.

Each of us had our own concerns that preoccupied us in
prison, and we drew a lot of strength from each other in sharing
them. Nusrat Yaldá'í worried a lot about her twelve-year-old
son Kúru<u>sh</u> who had been left to fend for himself at home when
she and her husband and eldest son, Bahrám, were arrested. She
was also concerned about what would happen to her daughter,
who had been studying in Spain at the time of their arrest, supported by funds sent regularly by herself and her husband. How
could she possibly manage?

'Izzat, similarly, worried about Rosita, her youngest daughter
who was living on her own at home, and Náhíd, her eldest who
lived in Africa and was expecting a baby very soon. Was Náhíd
having a good pregnancy? Would her child be delivered safely?
Would she ever see the child? She was particularly concerned
that Náhíd might hear about her family's imprisonment and
become anxious about them.

We all worried about someone we had left behind – <u>Sh</u>írín
was concerned for her grandmother who was left alone at
home; Mínú Násirí, who had only just got married, worried
about her husband Farámarz, who had been out when the
Revolutionary Guards came to arrest her. She hadn't even been
able to say goodbye, and used to cry a great deal. It was obvious
she loved him very much. We used to comfort her and tell her
not to worry, but these seemed hollow words. Because her
father, Mihdí Anvarí, had been executed for his faith, the
interrogators deliberately put extra pressure on her during her
trials, knowing full well whose daughter she was.

As for myself, two days before I was arrested I had been making
a jacket for Behnam and I hadn't quite finished it. Only part of
one sleeve was left, and then I was going to send it to England in
time for his birthday in December. Although I had plenty of time

in prison, I knew I wouldn't be allowed to do the work, even if they let Morad visit and give it to me, and I was worried I might never have the chance to finish it. It seems odd now that such a small thing should have troubled me, but it constantly played on my mind in prison that if only they had arrested me a few days later, I would have been able to send the jacket to him.

I was also terribly concerned about Morad, of course, and how he was coping with Payam all on his own for the first time. Because of his job with the oil company, he had always travelled a lot, often staying away from home for more than a week at a time, so I'd always had to manage without much help from him. Now I noted, with a touch of feminist irony perhaps, that the situation was suddenly – and completely – reversed!

I longed for some news of my family but heard nothing. The total silence, the lack of even some second-hand news, weighed heavily on us. We all suffered from this separation, but we tried to keep up a cheerful appearance so as not to make it harder for the others.

One night two of the Bahá'í women who, like me, had small children and were missing them terribly, hid under a blanket so they wouldn't disturb the rest of us and prayed desperately for the strength to endure the pain of separation. Then they went to sleep. That night I dreamed that the part of the cell in which the Bahá'ís were sleeping was illuminated and the rest was pitch black. In my dream I thought, 'What kind of a light is this that has only lit up the Bahá'ís?' Then I heard a voice saying, 'Don't you know? Get up! Bahá'u'lláh is coming to visit the prisoners.' I awoke with a start and, God bless her, 'Izzat noticed and gave me a comforting hug.

The next morning the guards called me. I assumed I was being taken for questioning, but much to my surprise they didn't put on the usual blindfold as they led me out of the cell. As we reached the main door of our section I suddenly caught my breath. There, looking lost and forlorn behind the bars, was my little son Payam. Morad was nowhere in sight. I stood for a moment in a complete state of shock, suddenly disorientated. I couldn't take in the fact that Payam, whom I hadn't seen for three weeks – three long weeks during which my whole life had been turned upside down – was actually there in the prison.

At first I thought I was dreaming, but no, there he was standing only a few feet away, within reach. The guards heaved open the cell door and I slipped eagerly through. Payam didn't recognize me at first because I was so pale and weak and the head scarf and chador that were standard prison uniform covered so much of my face. Carefully I pushed the scarf back so he could recognize me and wouldn't be scared, and he walked hesitantly towards me. The last time he had seen me a gun was pointing at my head and I was being driven away by strange men in the dead of night. His confusion was understandable.

Poor little Payam clung to me and asked, 'Mama, where are we? Why aren't you holding me like before? I thought you would be coming from the other end of the hallway so I could run into your arms.' Whenever I picked him up from the child-care centre, he used to run towards me; I would crouch with open arms and he would jump happily into them.

Three guards and two masked investigators were standing nearby watching us closely and listening to our every word. Payam looked nervously at the masked men. 'Mama, who are these people?' he asked. 'What happened to their faces? Why are you here? When are you coming home? Don't you love me any more?'

I didn't know what to tell him, so I said quickly, 'This is a hospital, and these gentlemen are doctors.' But I could see that he wasn't really satisfied with this explanation. He kept looking around at the walls and at the masked faces of the guards.

After ten minutes, the guards came to take Payam away and I was ordered to go back to my cell. As I began to walk away he screamed and tried to wriggle free of their grasp. 'Mama, Mama, don't leave me!' he sobbed. 'I want Mama, I want Mama,' he screamed even louder, desperately trying to make me come back. I turned and tried to smile to reassure him, but my heart was breaking. I had no choice but to walk away, the sound of his screams ringing in my ears, gradually receding into the distance as he was taken further and further away from me.

When I got back to my cell, all the Bahá'ís were sitting in a circle praying. They thought I had been taken to be tortured, and they were saying prayers for my steadfastness.

Later the guards called the other two women who had been praying the night before, and took them to see their children. When they returned 'Izzat told them about the dream I'd had. They cried with joy, thanking God for this miracle. We had not seen our families for almost a month, but from that time onwards normal visiting rights were restored and women prisoners were allowed to see their families for ten minutes every Saturday.

On the day official visits were first allowed, we were all so excited we counted the minutes to the time we would see our families. An hour before visiting time we were all ready, our chadors neatly arranged, and waiting to go. We consulted about what we should and shouldn't tell our visitors, and decided not to say anything about how rude and insulting the guards and investigators had been towards us. At last, desperately trying to look cheerful and relaxed but with barely the strength to stand, we were led out to the visiting room escorted by a large group of male and female guards. We were shown to individual booths, each with a glass partition separating us from our visitors and a telephone through which we had to speak. We sat down to wait impatiently for our loved ones.

A few minutes later they opened the door to the room and in rushed our eager families. I was shocked to see how much weight Morad had lost in the twenty-seven days I had been in Sepah. He looked so distraught and exhausted.

He had obviously been neglecting himself and had let his beard grow, which made him look rather unkempt and miserable. I told him to shave, but he insisted he wouldn't shave off his beard until I was free. We didn't realize at this point that our conversations were being recorded, but later the investigator, during one of my interrogations, referred to this remark and demanded angrily, 'Why did you tell your husband not to grow his beard?' Muslims are not supposed to shave off their beards, only to trim them. After that we were even more careful what we said during visiting sessions.

After my release Morad told me that the night I was arrested he had sat with Payam in the living room all night and cried and cried. When I eventually got out of prison I was surprised to find that though Payam was only three, he knew many long prayers off by heart, having sat beside his father as he prayed aloud, night after night.

Poor Morad had spent all his time in those first weeks running around trying to find a way to get me out of prison. He had been to the S͟híráz Central Court four times to see the prosecutor to petition for my release. He had even appealed to my ex-boss at the NIOC for help, who had immediately responded by sending telegrams both from himself and on behalf of the women in my office. Morad had also traipsed backwards and forwards to Isfahán to try to contact Áyatu'lláh Muntazirí and through him Áyatu'lláh Khomeini, as well as sending letters and telegrams to various government heads and the National Consultative Assembly in Tehran to see if they could somehow help secure my freedom, all to no avail. To make life more difficult, he had to take Payam with him everywhere on these long, exhausting trips because after my arrest the poor boy had become very nervous and fractious. He wouldn't let Morad out of his sight for a minute in case his father left him too. He was so unsettled, he couldn't even bear to stay with my parents, whom he knew and loved.

Morad had come to Sepah every day with Payam to try to see the Public Prosecutor about me. Eventually late one afternoon he was called into the office.

'Sir,' said Morad, 'my wife has been arrested because of her Bahá'í beliefs, and is imprisoned. Her little son is missing her terribly, and I would be grateful if you could look into her case.'

The Public Prosecutor turned to the mullahs who were with him and laughed mockingly, saying, 'And the father of the child is missing her too!' They all grinned spitefully. 'But, as I have said before, we will deal with the Bahá'í cases quickly,' he continued. 'Now, would you kindly leave my office.'

The first Saturday after my arrest Morad and Payam had arrived at Sepah at 8 a.m. and queued for permission to visit. As usual, all the Muslim visitors were allowed in first and the Bahá'ís had to wait in the cold. It was a long day, especially for Payam. Eight hours later a guard Mu'alimí called them over.

'Why are you here?' he asked.

'To see my wife,' Morad answered politely. 'She has been here for a week and our little son misses her badly.'

'Payam wants to see Mama,' pleaded Payam, on cue, and the guard at last let them in. However, I was not allowed to go to the visitors' room that day.

Nevertheless, Morad was able to talk to Nusrat Yaldá'í, who had been in solitary confinement for over a month. He was the first Bahá'í she had been able to talk to.

'Where is Olya?' she asked, wondering why I was not visiting that day.

'She was arrested last week and they are keeping her in here, somewhere,' he replied.

'Oh no!' Nusrat exclaimed in horror. 'Poor little Payam.'

The second Saturday, Morad was at last able to meet some Bahá'í prisoners who had seen me, who reassured him of my well-being. All the talking was done through telephone headsets because of the partition, and with so many guards about they couldn't tell him much.

The following week, Morad again pleaded with Mu'alimí to be allowed in to see me. The guard flatly refused – my name was not on his list to receive visitors that day. By this time, Morad was very concerned about Payam. He seemed to be getting more and more fretful.

Morad appealed to the guard. 'This child needs his mother. He is only three! If you won't let me in, at least let the boy see his mother.'

Surprisingly, Mu'alimí relented and poor Payam reluctantly, suspiciously, went with him through the gate and into the prison. And that is how he came to be standing outside the door to our cell block that wonderful day.

I had thought, after my last, two-day trial, that my interrogation was over, which made me feel very happy. However, it was not long before they called me again. The investigator was terribly angry and screamed at me, 'Roohizadegan, you haven't given us enough information, but I'm prepared to give you another chance. Think hard, and if this time you don't comply I will take you to the basement and have you tortured.'

For about three hours they kept me blindfolded in a room, and every once in a while he came in, yelled at me and called me names, and went out again. I really didn't know what to say.

I thought perhaps he was upset because I hadn't expanded on the fact that I was the liaison between the local Bahá'ís and the assembly. But I couldn't figure out what he was talking about.

'Your honour, maybe you want me to tell you more about my travels to the areas around Shíráz,' I said tentatively.

But he yelled again, 'Listen to me!' Then he started to read from a notebook, 'The forty-fourth meeting of the Local Spiritual Assembly of Shíráz, at 7 p.m. Mrs Roohizadegan met with the assembly and gave the report of her trip to Jahrum and other areas. If the Sadíqí family moves from Jahrum the Local Spiritual Assembly of Jahrum will be under strength, and they will need three people to form it again.' (Nine members are needed to constitute an assembly.)

The investigator cried angrily, 'Do you want me to read more?' Then he continued, 'The forty-seventh meeting of the Local Spiritual Assembly, consisting of a majority of the members, was formed. Liaisons Mr Ahmad Muhadhib and Mrs Olya Roohizadegan were sent to Jahrum and surrounding areas to visit the Bahá'ís of those areas and also encourage the Sadíqí family to remain firm and stay in Jahrum.'

Then he uncovered my eyes and, shaking with anger, handed me the book and screamed, 'Open your blind eyes and see for yourself!'

When I looked at the notebook, I saw that it was the assembly's report book from 1978 – more than four years ago.

I said calmly, 'Your honour, in your opinion, do you think there is anything against the present government or the nation of Iran written in that book you are holding? Is there anything illegal there? Do you think this is evidence of a crime?'

He said, 'Yes, being a member of the Bahá'í sect is a crime in itself and you have to admit in your file that you were a liaison officer and an assistant.'

'Brother,' I said calmly, 'there is no need to upset yourself so much. Being a liaison officer or an assistant is not a crime.' Then I expanded on the responsibilities of such a person. 'Let's imagine,' I said, 'that you are a member of the Local Spiritual Assembly. That makes you responsible for the spiritual support of other Bahá'ís, and also the general welfare of the community. For instance, if someone has financial difficulties, you will make sure they get help. An assistant more or less does the same.'

My gentle approach pacified him a little. A few of the prisoners who witnessed this conversation, including 'Izzat and Roya Ishráqí, Shírín and Mítrá, were quite surprised by the way I handled the questioning. When we came back to the cell they said, 'Fancy you telling him, "Imagine you're a member of the Local Spiritual Assembly!"' And this became a great source of amusement back in the cell, my daring to ask the investigator to imagine himself as a member of the assembly.

After all that, however, he still didn't let go of this 'evidence' that he had found. He wanted more names from me. Again I explained my duties as a liaison and an assistant, including taking news to the Bahá'ís and visiting them. But again he asked me for names. He wanted complete names, addresses, occupations and the present whereabouts of all the members of assemblies in the area.

'If you would like to have their names,' I wrote, 'you can easily ask the local Islamic authorities and I am sure they will tell you all of them; or you can make an announcement in the media requesting that all Bahá'ís come forward, and I assure you that they will turn themselves in straight away. Only last year all the Bahá'ís wrote letters to the government and they all gave their names and addresses; the research shouldn't be that difficult.'

But the whole point of interrogating us in this manner was so that they didn't have to admit their persecution in public and let all the people of Iran know what they were doing to the Bahá'ís. One of the interrogators asked me once, early on in my trial, 'Do you know what is going on?' I told him that I hadn't heard any news from the outside world – at that time we hadn't had any visits. 'All the newspapers and radio stations are demanding, "What are you doing to the Bahá'ís?" Now why are they standing up for you?' he had demanded furiously. That is how we came to know that some people were beginning to protest publicly at the persecution of Bahá'ís, and the government was becoming more sensitive on this issue.

I remembered Áyatu'lláh Músaví-Ardabílí's media announcement endorsing the elimination of prominent Bahá'ís and how, at the time, despite the fact that they had just murdered eight of the nine members of the second National Spiritual Assembly, the persecutions seemed much more open. At that time, they would allow the families to receive the bodies of those who had been executed and give them a proper burial. They printed their pictures in the newspapers, admitting they had been killed because they were Bahá'ís, and companies wrote openly to Bahá'ís to inform them they were being sacked because of their religion. I received such a letter myself.

However, they had not anticipated that the rest of the world would react to this, and were taken by surprise by the international outrage their programme of persecution provoked. As a result, the government changed tactics. From then on, many Bahá'ís were executed in secret without their relatives even being informed of their deaths, and their bodies were buried in unmarked graves. Sometimes the families only heard the news several weeks or months later when a Muslim prisoner was released and contacted them.

This is why they didn't want to make any public announcements now. They preferred to bring a few Bahá'ís to prison and make them reveal the names of other Bahá'ís so that, first, they could break the trust between them and secondly, the mass of the people wouldn't find out.

For a long time I fought against this pressure. I couldn't bring myself to be responsible for more Bahá'ís being brought to that place and tortured. So, in desperation, I wrote the names of the members who were already dead or had left Iran.

That day I was under interrogation for sixteen hours, and I had begun to lose my strength. A few times I put pen to paper intending to write some names, but I couldn't. I prayed for assistance, but physical weakness seemed to be getting the better of me. Because of the continual tension, most of us women prisoners had very frequent periods, and since we were not getting enough nutrition this made us terribly weak and anaemic.

As I was thinking and praying, I blacked out. When I opened my eyes I found myself on a bed in the prison clinic, in a small single room. There was a drip-feed in my arm, and a doctor and a nurse were standing by my bed.

The doctor said, 'Go and tell her investigator that she has suffered shock, her blood pressure is very low and she is seriously ill. Ask him if he wants to continue with his investigation or whether I can go ahead and treat her.'

I felt a throbbing pain in my arm. When I looked, I saw dried blood around the area of the injection. My hand was swollen and bruised. The doctor noticed my concern.

'It's not my fault; you see, I am a prisoner here just like you are. I treat patients on their orders, and they also make me teach my skills to these sisters – the guards – who don't even have secondary school education. If you see bruising and feel pain, it's because they were trying to learn how to insert a drip-feed into your arm.'

They transferred me to the nurse's room, and she was very kind to me, putting me on her own bed and making me fresh orange juice. Then suddenly a guard came in and called her away. 'But this patient is almost in a coma,' the nurse protested. 'The doctor said I have to take care of her for three days!'

But the guard said indifferently, 'Leave her alone, it's not important.'

I looked at my watch; it was 1 a.m. Some time later, a guard came and dragged me back to the cell. When they opened the cell door everyone jumped, and came rushing to embrace me. 'Izzat and Ṭáhirih hadn't eaten. They had saved an entire plate of food, normally shared by three, for me.

The doctor was supposed to see me the next morning, but the guards wouldn't let him. For three days I was really ill, and then once again they started calling me for interrogation.

The investigator was now questioning me about the night I was arrested and the papers and documents they had found. He already had all the documents, including our employment files, salary slips, and education records in front of him, but he still asked me where I worked, what I did, and why I was fired. He asked about my husband's position, and what he was doing now. He said, 'I have investigated your background, and I see you have been a very good employee. Why are you making your life so difficult for yourself? It would be enough for you just to say one word, that you are not a Baháʾí, and I would send you back to your job and order your husband's pension payments to be reactivated. You can have a comfortable life, and you can continue as before.'

'I am a Bahá'í and I hope to remain one to the last minute of my life,' I replied. 'Your honour, please don't ask me to lie. I am a Bahá'í in my heart and I believe in Bahá'u'lláh. If I recant my faith because of my attachment to this mortal life, how could I be a truthful and loyal citizen of my country? We are not making our lives difficult – our lives have been made difficult by injustice and intolerance.'

I felt for the first time that he was affected by what I said to him. He asked, 'Where are your elder children now?' and I replied, 'They go to school in England.'

Later I found out that he had received a letter that my Muslim neighbours had sent to the authorities and Religious Magistrates. Its contents were roughly as follows:

> At midnight on 29 November 1982, a group of guards attacked our neighbour's house – Mrs Olya Roohizadegan – and arrested her. Isn't it true that Áyatu'lláh Khomeini said all Iranians can live freely under the protection of Islam? Why then have you arrested this innocent woman for her beliefs? We, the signatories of this letter, would like to ask the Public Prosecutor and the Religious Magistrate for her immediate release to put our minds at rest, and, more importantly, for the sake of her three-year-old son.

It was a moving letter and constituted a real challenge to the people in charge because about a dozen people, mostly 'hájís', that is Muslims who have made the pilgrimage to Mecca, and other prominent Muslims had signed it.

The investigator then removed my blindfold and said, 'You have been very honest during your trial so far.' He handed me a bag full of papers, pictures, notebooks, and other documents, all of which had been taken from my house. 'Go through these pictures one by one and give us the names of all the people and their addresses and phone numbers. First write the names on the back of the pictures and then in the file.'

It was a very difficult task, especially since I was still feeling so ill. However, among the photos was one of Rúhíyyih Khánum, the widow of Bahá'u'lláh's great-grandson, surrounded by Bahá'ís. I was very worried when I saw it because some of the people in the picture were Iranian and could be identified. Quickly, and without anyone noticing, I slipped the photo under my chador, intending to get rid of it somehow.

I asked the investigator if I could go to the toilet. He refused permission. An hour later I asked again, insisting that I couldn't possibly wait any longer, and at last he said I could leave the room. Roya and Shírín, who were under interrogation with me, also asked to be excused, saying that after ten hours of questioning they were in desperate need too.

Together we went to the prison toilet. Wasting no time. I tore the photo into tiny pieces and flushed it down the toilet. It took a long time to flush all the pieces away, and Shírín and Roya called out, 'Olya, what are you doing in there all this time? We must hurry back.'

I told them I would explain later. I had saved the picture of Rúhíyyih Khánum from the centre of the photo and I carefully hid it in my bra before we all went back into the trial room.

Later, I managed to smuggle the picture out of the prison stitched into the collar of a coat. All the other prisoners were very relieved when I did so because they were always worried it would be found and I would get into trouble.

How I survived that day's interrogation is beyond me. I was in the trial room from eight o'clock in the morning to 10.30 at night, and I fainted several times. But as my father had promised so long ago, 'God always gives a person the power to remain true to the pathway of truth'. Never before had I experienced such closeness to God as I did during that time. It gave me an incredible power and sustained me during those tests. I felt His presence in that room, and it seemed that even if they used their cruellest torture, my resolve and my love for God would only have become stronger.

Strangely, in the course of that long day the investigator's attitude completely changed towards me. For the first time, after all the swearing and shouting, he was polite. He actually called me 'dear lady' or 'Mrs Roohizadegan'. I don't know what had made him change his mind about me. Perhaps I had convinced him that I really believed in my faith, because during the interrogations I was always in control of my emotions, and did not react to his rudeness.

When the investigator wanted me sent back to my cell that night he asked me to get up first before he covered my eyes. He knew I was so weak that if he put the blindfold on me while I was seated I would fall over when I tried to get up. For the first time I was able to look around at the trial room.

I noticed a pen on the floor. Automatically I picked it up and put it on the investigator's desk, saying, 'Your honour, I hope your pen writes the truth and supports justice. And I hope your deeds also are just, because in the divine court of justice there will be no pen or desk, and the only measure will be of our deeds in this world. During these days of my trial I have caused you trouble. Since I can't return your favours, I will pray for you.'

'Sister, will you really pray for me?' he asked, surprised. 'Did you say that from the bottom of your heart?'

'I swear in the name of my three sons that I will pray for you sincerely.'

He shuffled through the documents on the table and pulled out some photographs of my sons for me to keep. I was touched. Then, amazingly, he took my hand from the folds of my chador and, without bothering to blindfold me, led me back to the cell himself. That was to be my last afternoon in Sepah Prison after thirty-two days.

Adelabad

CHAPTER 7

The now familiar clang of the heavy bolts on the main door made us start. One of the guards came up to our cell and began calling out our names from a list.

'Mrs 'Izzat Ishráqí, Miss Roya Ishráqí, Miss Shírín Dálvand, Miss Mítrá Íraván, Miss Mahshíd Nírúmand, Mrs Olya Roohizadegan. Collect your belongings and come with me,' he announced briskly, and he stood waiting by the cell door.

Quickly we began to gather up our things. We had very little with us in prison – a few spare clothes, some shampoo, a treasured bar of soap, toothbrush and toothpaste, a comb, a towel – little luxuries that our relatives had managed to persuade the guards to let us have. All was thrust hurriedly into a plastic shopping bag and we followed the guard out of the cell and into the corridor. There our interrogator, still masked, was waiting for us.

Everyone was very frightened. Were they taking us to Evin Prison in Tehran, where some of the other prisoners had been taken? It was over 600 miles away. How could our families visit us there?

The interrogator announced abruptly, 'Your interrogation is now finished and today I am sending you to Adelabad.'

We all breathed a sigh of relief. The first group of Bahá'ís had also been transferred there the day we were arrested, and some of the women in our group had gone there several days previously. We would all be together, at least, and we were thankful for that.

We were led out into the prison yard where some Bahá'í men were already waiting. I was feeling very weak and dizzy, so

I carefully sat down on the concrete and leant back against the stone wall.

'Why are you sitting down? *Boland-sho*! Get up! You lazy infidel!' An armed guard stood over me, screaming. I stood up gingerly, afraid of fainting there and then, but a few minutes later the bus came. We all clambered in, the men in the back, the women in the front, a cloth screen protecting our modesty. In present-day Iran men and women are not allowed to mix freely in public.

As the last guard climbed aboard, our interrogator came running out of the prison. 'When you get to Adelabad,' he shouted, 'bring back Símín Sábirí.' I tried to see from his face what might lie in store for poor Símín, but his expression was inscrutable. I shivered. Something about the way he stared at us so intently gave me the impression he was reluctant to let us go, as if he hadn't quite finished with us and might call us back at any moment for further questioning. He reminded me of the way a cat watches a mouse trying to creep out of the reach of its claws, still toying with the idea of putting out a lazy paw and continuing the game.

The bus slowly pulled out of the prison yard, and I sat back in my seat. Even though we were on our way to another prison, the fact that we were leaving Sepah, with all its painful memories, made us feel good.

It was just after 2 p.m. on 31 December 1982 when the bus turned into the gate of Adelabad Prison. It was much bigger than Sepah, a huge complex consisting of several multi-storey buildings, each with long rows of small cells arranged around a central well, rather like the prisons one often sees in films.

The guards bustled us off the bus and into the nearest building. Inside a group of prisoners was waiting to be taken back to Sepah. Símín was called down, and one of the guards who had accompanied us told her he had orders to take her back with him.

'But why?' Símín asked him, very disconcerted. We tried to signal to her reassuringly, but another guard moved us on. We were to be held in the fourth wing on the third floor, the women's section where prostitutes, drug addicts, murderers and political prisoners were housed. We climbed the long flight of iron stairs to the third floor.

All the Bahá'ís who had been transferred earlier rushed out to welcome us. The guard started shouting angrily, and began to call out the numbers of the cells we had been allocated. Mítrá and I were told to go to number thirty-one.

Just then Símín appeared. She had quickly given the guard downstairs the slip and rushed up to find out if we knew anything about her recall to Sepah. We told her not to worry – all we knew was that there was some confusion about the membership of one of the committees she was on. Perhaps they wanted to question her about it. As we were trying to reassure her, the guard who was supposed to be escorting her came panting up the stairs.

'How did you escape?' he demanded furiously, and ordered her back down the stairs. We all smiled. Símín was a very intelligent, courageous girl.

Mítrá and I set off to find our cell. They were all very small, originally designed for one prisoner, and each had a small steel bed with a thin foam mattress and a single regulation blanket. Because the prisons were now so overcrowded, two or three prisoners were housed in each cell. This made life especially difficult for us at night, because only one person had anywhere to lie down. We all shared as best we could, but it was hard to get enough sleep. The lack of heating didn't help – at that time of year it could get bitterly cold, and frequently did.

Prisoners were under strict control in Adelabad. We had to wear our uniforms – long coat, trousers, scarf and chador – at all times, whereas in Sepah we only wore the chador when we left our cell. At 10.30 p.m. all the lights were switched off and we were supposed to sleep. Our cell doors were shut and it wasn't officially permitted to venture out, even to use the toilet. At 4 a.m. we had to get up. Even during the day we were not supposed to visit each other's cells or to gather together too much, and the female guards were under orders to ensure that we didn't.

However, Sister Yaqtín, one of our guards, had been taught by Ṭúbá Zá'irpúr at the high school in S̲h̲íráz and because of the respect she had for her ex-teacher, she began to relent. She used to let us spend time together and never reported us to the

other guards, so generally we had more opportunities to talk
than in Sepah, largely thanks to the efforts of Sister Yaqtín.

Mítrá and I always ate our meals in 'Izzat and Roya's cell.
We had one plate and one plastic bowl to share between the
four of us – for which a fee was demanded – and a few plastic
forks and spoons that our families had sent in to us.

Prison food consisted of a tiny piece of bread and cheese for
breakfast; cooked white beans for lunch; and bread, yoghurt
and dates in the evening. All the fruit we received from our
families had to be handed over and then shared between all the
prisoners. Of course, Bahá'ís were left till last, so naturally the
best fruit had already been taken by the time our turn came.

A more annoying problem was how to wash our clothes.
The prison authorities considered our garments to be contaminated and so we had to manage our washing as best we could,
using soap and a small bucket in our cell, with water splashing
all over our feet. We didn't have anywhere to hang the clothes,
so we draped them over the cell bars with the bucket strategi-
cally placed to catch the drips. Because of the cold and damp, it
used to take four or five days for clothes to dry.

This caused another problem. It was so cold that winter,
especially at night sleeping on the floor with only a thin
blanket between you and the bare concrete, that most of the
time we had to wear all the clothes we possessed, on top of each
other, for the extra warmth. So the decision to wash an item
was not taken lightly.

However, one of the features of prison life that probably
irritated us the most at Adelabad was the issue of the toilets
and showers! There were only three of each for the whole of
the third floor, and they were always dirty. They had no doors –
whether for security reasons or from neglect it was hard to say –
so someone had to stand guard whenever we used them. This
was a daily indignity we women all felt keenly. Moreover, with
150 prisoners on our floor, we had to take it in turns to use the
showers, which often meant going for days without being able
to wash at all.

Nevertheless, despite all these difficulties and irritations, we
found Adelabad to be a kinder regime than Sepah on the
whole, and the atmosphere was much more relaxed.

Something that contributed a lot to this was the good relationship that was quickly established between the Bahá'ís and the other groups of prisoners. They all loved and respected us, and we, for our part, did what we could to comfort and support them. The drug addicts had a particularly hard time. As in Sepah, they were not prescribed any drugs or given any medical treatment, so they would sometimes shake uncontrollably and scream in agony as they suffered the effects of withdrawal. We would help them as best we could, but they needed proper medical attention, and we could only offer them friendship.

Many of our fellow prisoners were very sympathetic to our situation. They would say, 'We are here because we have committed a crime, or because of our political activities, but you haven't done anything. You are simply here because of your beliefs.'

In Adelabad, all the prisoners were in their second or third stage of the trial process. Every prisoner had to go through three stages in prison. First was what they called the examination or investigation stage, which was carried out in Sepah by masked investigators. During this phase all the prisoners were put under a tremendous amount of mental and physical pressure. The investigators had unlimited power, and no one could question their methods or insist that human rights were respected. After completing oral and written examinations, the investigators transferred the prisoners and their files to Adelabad, about three miles away.

The second stage of the interrogations continued in Adelabad and was conducted by the Public Prosecutor's assistants. Again, they were prejudiced and heartless people. Every day they called a group of prisoners at 5 a.m., put them in a car with armed guards and took them to the Revolutionary Court in Sepah for interrogation. These interrogations were very intense, and the Public Prosecutor's assistant repeated the same questions the investigators had already asked a hundred times over. But they did not usually take more than a day – only in a few cases, where the assistant wanted to put more pressure on a prisoner, were they brought back for further questioning.

At this stage there was no torture, but there was still overwhelming psychological pressure. If the Assistant Public

Prosecutor now wished to release a prisoner he could do so with a security bond, which in most cases involved property. If he wanted to pursue the case to the trial stage, he would send the file on to the court where the Religious Magistrate issued the final verdict. In this third stage, the magistrate only examined the prisoners for fifteen minutes or so – at the very most, one hour. At no time in this process were Bahá'í prisoners allowed any defence counsel to act on their behalf.

At the end of the three stages, the decision was either execution or a period of further imprisonment, during which they would try and force the prisoner to recant or would attempt to extract money from his or her family. This money served ostensibly as a security bond, though often prisoners would be executed in secret after the money had been handed over, or they might be re-arrested shortly after their release.

We always seemed to be waiting for some sort of miracle, anything, that might eventually lead to our release. Most of us still had some hope that one day we would be free. We all longed for our freedom – but not at any price. We had psychologically prepared ourselves for the worst because we were all very familiar with the long history of persecution Bahá'ís had suffered going back to the mid-nineteenth century when 20,000 were killed. After all, most of us had read about it in children's classes. So although we wanted more than almost anything to be released, we were resigned to accepting whatever awaited us.

A number of Bahá'ís were released while I was in prison. Where the authorities found that they were not prominent members of the Bahá'í community, they were released unconditionally, but most had to hand over the deeds of their house or a large sum of money as a bond. It could be anything from 150,000 tuman to 800,000, depending on how active they had been in the Bahá'í administration. Some were asked to find a Muslim willing to act as their guarantor, and all had to sign a written statement agreeing to turn themselves in whenever they were required to do so.

In reality, there didn't seem to be any particular reason why some were released and others killed, or why large bonds were demanded from some and not from others. The Public Prosecutor could demand whatever he wished. He could increase the amount if he felt like it, or even cancel the release order, as happened with several of my friends who were later killed.

Many Bahá'ís were released, it seems, in order to lead the authorities to other Bahá'ís. Theirs turned out to be a temporary release, and they were quickly re-arrested. Perhaps another factor that may have come into play was the occasional need to calm the situation for a while, especially when the spotlight of international attention was turned on Iran. Whatever the reason, Zarrín Muqímí's mother was released, much to Zarrín's delight, as were, among others, Mínú Násirí and Rúhíyyih Jahánpúr, who shared a cell with Mítrá and me for the few days she stayed in Adelabad.

For those of us who had to remain in prison, there remained the constant pressure to recant. Thank God, nearly all the Bahá'ís resisted the pressure to recant their faith. Many people have asked me since my release why the Bahá'ís did not recant to save their lives, and simply reaffirm their membership of the Bahá'í Faith later – when it was safe to do so. It may seem strange, but this was not an option we ever discussed. The issue simply never arose, and it is hard to explain to someone removed from that experience exactly why.

When you truly love someone, it is inconceivable to deny it, and similarly we all felt very strongly that we must stand by our beliefs – to stand up and be counted. This was partly to demonstrate the truth of a religion we were willing to die for, but it was more than a public expression of the integrity of our faith.

The persecution we suffered, the physical and mental torture, the deprivation of our freedom, cut off from our family and the comforts of everyday life, tested our personal faith to the limits. It was almost an article of that faith, therefore, to be resolute, come what may. It was also a test of our personal integrity.

When I got back from my final trial, I told Ṭáhirih that although I had been offered my freedom in return for a signed resignation from the Bahá'í Faith, I chose prison and a death sentence over life with my little son Payam.

'Well done!' she replied stoutly. 'Children are the greatest test for a mother!'

And so they turned out to be for one poor family. The total number of Bahá'í prisoners at that time was ninety-four, and ninety-two of them remained firm in their faith in Bahá'u'lláh. Only two became victims of the guards' shameless tricks and succumbed to the pressure to recant. This unfortunate couple was Firishtih Anvarí and her husband Dr Muḥammad Anvarí, who were members of the assembly of Marvdasht. Firishtih was the last woman to be brought in to our cell in Sepah, but she was the first to be tried. They put her under tremendous pressure, forcing her to watch the whipping of other prisoners in order to frighten her and weaken her resolve. They also confronted her with Mr Maḥmúdnizhád to confirm her membership of the Marvdasht assembly.

Every time she came back from a trial she was barely conscious. She was physically very weak and suffered from back pain; she also had a stomach ulcer, and since the prison food was not suitable for her, for days she ate just dried bread and some nuts that she had had in her pocket when arrested. To pressurize her even more, the interrogators put Firishtih in solitary confinement for a while. But she withstood the pressure throughout.

She had a very negative attitude towards the guards, which was understandable because the same people had killed her brother-in-law Dr Mihdí Anvarí, Mínú's father, in that same prison almost two years before. The Revolutionary Court had told his family on the day before his execution that they were releasing him in two days' time. That was why she could not trust the guards or the court.

In one of her trials they had asked her to define the Bahá'í Faith and explain the Bahá'í administrative structure. Firishtih refused to answer their questions and an hour later she returned to the cell and told us about it. That day we were all having lunch together. We asked her why she had been hesitant – any signs of weakness on her part would only encourage them to lean on her even harder. And that is just what they did. Minutes later her name was called again and she was taken for another interrogation session.

Four hours later she returned semi-conscious. She told us that she had been extremely humiliated. They kept kicking her chair from under her, sending her sprawling across the room, and constantly insulted her because she had not answered their questions. 'What kind of a Bahá'í are you,' they taunted, 'if you don't even know what Bahá'ísm is? You can't even describe the Bahá'í administration! How come you were elected to the assembly of Marvda<u>sh</u>t?'

Nevertheless, she managed to get through the investigation in Sepah and resisted all the pressure to make her recant during the second stage at Adelabad. The final stage was the trial in the Revolutionary Court with the Religious Magistrate, Áyatu'lláh Qazá'í.

The magistrate straight away ordered the guard to bring in her two small children, who were waiting outside the court-room. The guards put the children on her lap as she was being questioned, creating an extremely emotional situation in which to play on her vulnerability as a mother. The children, who had not seen their mother for nearly two months, clung to her, and looked imploringly into her eyes. The Religious Magistrate took advantage of this and said, 'You are condemned to death. The decision is yours. Do you prefer to be hanged, or to go back to your children and take care of them? Your husband is also condemned to death, and your children will soon be orphans.'

She began to shake, and the sight of her children imploring her to stay with them eventually broke down her last defenses.

The Religious Magistrate had won, and with a heavy heart she proclaimed, 'I am not a Bahá'í.'

Her husband, Muḥammad Anvarí, was also on trial that day. As Firi<u>sh</u>tih explained to me later in the cell:

> When the magistrate sent for my husband and told him that I had recanted, he was very upset. He got on his hands and knees and begged me to change my mind. 'Firi<u>sh</u>tih, I know they forced you to recant. I will kiss your hands and feet if you will only change your mind.'
>
> But I told him, 'I can't tolerate this any more. I can't take such pressure. I just want to get out of here and leave <u>Sh</u>íráz and go somewhere far away to live in peace with my children. I can't bear to be apart from them any longer.'

'Don't think the guards will leave you alone,' he warned. 'No matter where you go, they will come and find you.'

It was clear as Firishtih told me the story that she was extremely distressed. 'I don't know why I did it,' she sobbed. 'I had no control. I couldn't deal with the pain I saw in my children's eyes.'

Firishtih spent that night in tears, huge shuddering sobs wracking her body leaving her exhausted and drained. 'Bahá'u'lláh,' she cried out in her despair, 'You know my heart. You know I still believe in you, but how could I choose between you and my poor children?'

In the morning, Táhirih and I went to comfort her. We told her that it wasn't too late; she could still go back to the magistrate and say that she was a Bahá'í. But she had already chosen another path. She was released the day after my trial, and when they brought me back to the cell the other prisoners told me that the video of Firishtih's trial had been shown on the prison's closed circuit television.

Two weeks after her release, some Revolutionary Guards went to her house asking her to become their wife. They told her, 'Now that you are a Muslim, according to the laws of the Qur'án you are no longer married to your husband, and you can marry one of us.' This upset Firishtih so much that she went straight to Adelabad to tell her husband what had happened.

When she explained to him that the guards wouldn't leave her alone and kept harassing her, he was badly shaken. This process of manipulation by the Religious Magistrate and the guards resulted in Dr Anvarí recanting his faith as well, so that he could protect his wife from their attentions.

Following his release, a story was printed in the newspaper with their picture under the headline, 'Bahá'í couple returned to Islam'.

Ṭúbá & Nusrat

CHAPTER 8

We all suffered in prison, but Ṭúbá Zá'irpúr and Nusrat Yaldá'í
probably suffered the most. They were both subjected to severe
torture, which most of us Bahá'í women were spared; those two
as well as Mihrí Ḥaqíqatjú and Maḥbúbih Mumtází were made
to endure terrible floggings.

Ṭúbá, at fifty-one, was one of the oldest of the Bahá'í prisoners and both she and Nusrat were arrested with the first
group of over forty Bahá'ís towards the end of October 1982.

Ṭúbá had been a teacher at the S̲h̲íráz high school, but had
retired some time ago. After the revolution her pension had
been cut off because she was a Bahá'í. She is an excellent illus-
tration of 'Abdu'l-Bahá's statement, 'The end is unknown'.
When she was a young girl she had married a Muslim without a
Bahá'í wedding ceremony and had stopped participating in
Bahá'í community activities. Later on, however, she and her
husband had a Bahá'í marriage ceremony and she soon began
making up for lost time, and in fact became a highly valued
member of the community. Her Arabic and adult study classes
were very popular, especially among the youth, and she kept
the classes going right up until the night of her arrest.

They kept Ṭúbá and Nusrat in solitary confinement for
fifty-five days. Before I was arrested, I had tried to visit them in
prison but the guards wouldn't let them see any visitors at all. It
was very hard for them. When the first group of Bahá'ís were
moved to Adelabad, just before my arrest, they kept Ṭúbá and
Nusrat back, and they were still in solitary confinement in
Sepah when I arrived, over five weeks after their arrest.

No one had had any news of them at all, and we were all
very concerned, as it was common knowledge that the prisoners

in solitary confinement were put under the greatest pressure. However, one day a Muslim woman named 'Itrat was brought to the cell; she had shared Ṭúbá's tiny cell for a short while when there had been no space elsewhere, and she told me:

> She was always so calm and patient. Whenever the guards brought her back to the cell after flogging her, she used to cover up her injuries from the whip lashes so they wouldn't upset me. The damage to her feet and legs was so severe that her toenails started falling out and the prison doctor had to remove blood clots from under her skin. On one occasion they broke one of her fingers. She couldn't sleep for several nights because of the pain, yet I never heard her complain, nor say a bad word against the guards; instead she spent her time praying for perseverance.

This woman was so impressed with Ṭúbá's courage that she herself became a Bahá'í while in prison.

A few weeks after my arrest, I was sitting in my cell reflecting on the fact that I was an eye-witness to the experiences of most of the Bahá'í prisoners in Sepah at the time – I was on trial with them in the same room and often listened to their answers, and we talked about our experiences afterwards. Mínú Násirí said later, when we met up in the USA, that I was like an interrogator myself, always asking questions. She still remembered how, every time one of the Bahá'í women came back to the cell, I would ask very detailed questions about the interrogation and try to memorize their answers. She knew I was propelled by a desire to try and record information for the outside world.

It was this desire that shaped my sense of mission. Although I was repeatedly told I would be hanged if I did not recant my faith, whenever I remembered the dream I'd had as a girl, where 'Abdu'l-Bahá had appeared to me and told me that doors would always be open to me, I felt sure that one day I would be free. And when that day came, I was determined to tell the world the full story of what had happened to us all.

As I sat pondering this in my cell that day, I realized that I had never been on trial with Ṭúbá or Nusrat, and because they were still in solitary confinement I hadn't had a chance to talk to them at all.

Suddenly I heard the clang of heavy bolts sliding open on the cell-block door. I quickly got up to peer through the cell door to try and find out who was being brought in. Nusrat Yaldá'í was shoved violently through the doorway and into my arms – had I not been standing there she would have fallen. As soon as she recognized me she threw her arms around me and we both began to cry. I was still standing by the door supporting Nusrat when, a moment later, Ṭúbá was thrown into the cell.

My first reaction on seeing my two friends after such a long time was a sense of great relief and joy. This was immediately followed by shock as I took in the changes in their appearance since we had last met. Two very different women looked back at me that day. Both were terribly weak, and poor Ṭúbá had to lean heavily on me for support. They had lost a lot of weight and their grubby clothes hung limply from their shrunken bodies. Nusrat, always petite, now looked shockingly thin and fragile.

Both suffered from poor health, plagued by stomach ulcers and in Ṭúbá's case severe migraine headaches. Because of the ulcers, prison food was like poison for them, but they were not allowed a special diet and had to manage as best they could, often existing on just a piece of bread a day. Kúru<u>sh</u>, Ṭúbá's son, came to the prison several times with the medication his mother needed for her migraines and ulcer, as well as some fruit, begging the guard to take them to her. He always refused.

Perhaps not surprisingly, prison seemed to have aged them. Lines of pain now deeply etched their faces, their skin was grey and dull, their eyes tired and listless. But what contributed most to the illusion of the passage of *years* rather than *weeks* was the sight of Ṭúbá's once glossy brown hair, now returned to its natural grey.

Solitary confinement meant more than just living on one's own in a tiny cell. Their hair was filthy and matted after nearly two months without a comb or shower. After Nusrat's arrest, I had taken some shampoo with me on one of my prison visits and asked the guard to give it to her, but he had refused.

Prisoners in solitary confinement were not allowed out of their cells to shower or wash themselves. Even permission to go to the toilet hung on the whim of the guard on duty. Nor could their relatives send in a change of clothes and Nusrat, who hadn't had time to pick up any spare clothing when arrested, still stood in the same clothes that she had put on so long ago.

Ṭúbá and Nusrat had been put under virtually non-stop physical and mental pressure for almost two months. Despite the suffering and indignities they had endured, I never heard them complain, either then or later. While we sat in the corner of that cell, they told me something of their experiences in Sepah. This is Ṭúbá's account:

Four days after my arrest they took me for my first interrogation. The interrogator asked me my first and last name, and I said, 'My name is Ṭúbá Zá'irpúr.' He didn't believe me and said, 'You are lying, your name is Qudsíyyih, not Ṭúbá.' Try as I might, I couldn't convince him that I was telling the truth. He took me to the basement and gave me fifty lashes. Then he insisted I write down that my name was Qudsíyyih. I said, 'Why should I lie about my name?'

'Suhayl Húshmand told us your name was Qudsíyyih Zá'irpúr,' he said.

'I taught in the high schools of Shíráz, and you brought all of my identification papers including my birth certificate here with you on the night I was arrested. If you just read them you will soon see that I'm not lying to you.' After they looked at my birth certificate they realized I was right. Then they put me in a small cell on my own. They brought me back for interrogation the next day, saying, 'You were a member of the assembly of Shíráz and you didn't confess this in your file.'

I replied, 'I have never been a member of the assembly of Shíráz.' They didn't believe me, so I was given 100 more lashes. After every ten strokes they would wait for a while to let the shock recede so I would feel the pain more. I swore to them that I was telling the truth, and asked why they insisted so strongly that I had been a member of the assembly. The interrogator said that Bahrám Afnán, who had himself been a member of the assembly, had written in his file that I had been elected as a substitute member for the third reserve group. I told him that I might have been elected as a reserve member but I had never been told. He wasn't convinced.

They brought my file and, while they were torturing me, they demanded I write down that I had been a member of the Local Spiritual Assembly. I said, 'I won't lie in my file, so I will write, "By force of the guards, who claimed Dr Afnán had told them that I was elected a reserve member of the Local Spiritual Assembly . . ."' But they refused to accept such a declaration and continued whipping me. I fainted a few times from the pain.

They took me back to my cell, and the next day tortured me again by giving me another seventy-four lashes with a wire cable on the soles of my feet and on my back. The whipping was so severe that for three days blood poured out from under my toenails, and they forced me to walk on my tortured feet so that I would suffer even greater pain.

The interrogators often came to my cell in the middle of the night to deprive me of sleep. They wanted the names of all the people who attended my classes, even the children's classes, and the names of the National Spiritual Assembly members and the local committees. I had made a firm decision not to identify anyone so that they wouldn't be put through the suffering I was going through. But the guards never left me alone; they kept coming to my cell bringing my file with them and trying to force me to write down names of Bahá'ís. They wanted me to announce through the media that I was a spy for Israel, and had now recanted and become a Muslim.

'Bahá'ís do not interfere with politics, and I am a Bahá'í. I will never recant, and I shall never tell those lies on television or anywhere else,' I told them. But I was suffering so much that every day I begged God to

let me be killed. I even looked around the cell a few
times trying to find something with which I could free
myself from the clutches of these inhuman and wicked
people. But later I was ashamed of myself for having
even thought about it; it wasn't becoming for a Bahá'í
to think that way. Anyhow, I never named anyone, and
never brought imprisonment upon other people; I have
brought with me the blank piece of paper from my file.

When I looked into Túbá's suffering eyes, I seemed to see the
eyes of 'Abdu'l-Bahá. I began shivering uncontrollably. I put my
head on her shoulder and begged her to stop because I couldn't
bear to hear about her painful experiences any more.

Even though Túbá's health was poor and she had been kept in
solitary confinement for such a long time under intense, continu-
ous pressure, the heartless interrogators continued to take her out
of our cell for long trials. One day, when they came to take her for
yet another session of interrogation, one of the guards swore at
her and spoke to her rudely. She calmly responded, 'Your honour,
it's a great shame that you use your tongue the way you do. I am
old enough to be your mother. Your tongue should be used for
praising God, not for rude and insulting words.'

The man replied angrily, 'I would be ashamed to have a
Bahá'í mother like you.' And Túbá, who was highly educated
and always courteous, had to tolerate the insults of a group of
ignorant and illiterate guards.

She was a very patient and tolerant woman who always
tried to keep everybody else's spirits up. To me she said, 'Endure
whatever happens to you, but if you are released one day, you
must tell everyone about what happened here.' And she told
me that during her trial one day the interrogator had arrogantly
insisted that despite all the torture and hardship she was suffering, she was putting herself through it for nothing, because no
one was ever going to hear about it. At that moment I knew I
had to get out and take her story, and the stories of all the
others, with me. I promised myself and Túbá that I would.

One day when they took us outside for fresh air, I noticed
there were marks on the ground here and there, like bloodstains.
I asked her if she knew why they were there. She told me, 'The

guards bring the prisoners here after whipping their feet and
force them to run on the concrete so they will feel more pain.'

I asked her, 'Which lashes are more painful, the ones on the
soles of the feet or on the back?'

'The ones on the feet, of course. Every time I was tortured
on the soles of my feet I felt the pain shoot up through my
whole body, right into my head. It even seemed to affect my
brain and I couldn't think properly.'

Even though she was physically very weak, she was spiritually as strong as a rock. She always used to walk up and down in
the cell, and encouraged us to do the same, saying, 'The cells
are not large enough, but still you mustn't stay sitting down; try
to move.' In prison there wasn't much for us Bahá'ís to do. We
were not allowed to do any handicrafts, and the only thing we
had to read was the censored version of the daily newspaper
and a poetry book of Háfiz, whose poetry is associated with
fortune telling. One day we were all feeling a little down and I
asked Túbá to read a poem for me for fun. She laughed and
asked me to make a wish and open the book, which I did. Then
she read me the beautiful poem on the page where I had
opened the book. This is part of it:

> O lapwing of the East wind! To Sheba I send thee,
> Behold from where to where I send thee!
> Alas! a glorious bird like thee in the dust-heap of grief,
> Hence to the nest of faithfulness I send thee!

Everyone cheered up when they heard this poem, because they
felt, we all felt, that this verse, along with my dream of 'Abdu'l-
Bahá, suggested I might be released.

'Now, tell me what you wished for,' Túbá demanded.

'I implored God to help me to stay firm during these tests,' I
replied. 'And then I asked Him if I could see my children once
again.'

'To be honest with you,' she said quietly, 'what I wish for is
to be free from these people and go to the United States to visit
my daughter.'

Túbá was kept at Sepah Prison for more than two months,
most of which was in solitary confinement. On 26 December

1982 she was transferred to Adelabad along with seven other Bahá'í women. I was transferred almost a week later.

Only a few days after I arrived in Adelabad, Ṭúbá was taken for the second stage of her trial. After eight hours of questioning, the prosecutor told her that her crime was evident: being elected as a reserve member of a Local Spiritual Assembly, and conducting classes – they said she had misled the youth. She had also been a member of a committee that had encouraged those who had recanted to come back to the Faith. For these activities, the Islamic Revolutionary Court found her guilty and condemned her to death by hanging.

Poor Ṭúbá had only been appointed to the Protection Committee a few days before she was arrested. 'They didn't even give me a chance to attend one meeting!' she joked. It seemed that a few members of the Shíráz assembly had told the investigators, under torture, about her activities. Ṭúbá said, 'I wrote in my file that I was sure my friends had told them the truth; that maybe I had forgotten some details. I didn't want the guards to take advantage of the situation.' Her sacrificing soul and her forgiveness were so admirable that even if I wrote volumes I wouldn't be able to do her justice.

Four days later, she was called for her final trial with the Religious Magistrate. 'For the last time,' he said, 'I ask you to recant and come back to Islam. If you do, I will let you go, otherwise you are condemned to death by hanging.'

'I would much prefer to be executed,' she replied.

On 12 March 1983, along with two brave men, Yadu'lláh Mahmúdniẓhád and Rahmat Vafá'í, she was hanged. Ṭúbá Zá'irpúr was the first Bahá'í woman to be killed for her religion in Shíráz. The Revolutionary Court refused to return their bodies to their families for burial.

Nusrat was born into a distinguished Bahá'í family in 1937 in Nayríz. She and her husband Ahmad had three sons and a daughter. Bahrám, the eldest, was born in Shíráz in 1955.

Because of our family connections (we were related by marriage) and also through Bahá'í gatherings, I had known the family for twenty-three years. From the beginning of their married life until years later, Nusrat and her husband lived in two small rooms with their children and his mother, where they were very happy and contented. One of the two rooms was always used for Bahá'í meetings. Their hospitality was legendary; the door of that small but lovely home was open at all times to Bahá'ís and non-Bahá'ís alike.

After some years they were able to buy the whole house, and they took in a few families who needed shelter at the time. After the confiscation of the Shíráz Bahá'í Centre and the office of the Local Spiritual Assembly, their house became an important place for Bahá'ís to gather.

For years Nusrat was a member of several Bahá'í committees, travelling widely for the Faith, and she also taught children's classes. She had been appointed an assistant shortly before her arrest. She often spoke at large meetings and had a talent for speaking well. It was unbelievable that she did all this despite not even having a high school education. The guards in prison often swore at her and accused her of lying about her lack of education.

The day Ṭúbá and Nusrat were brought into our cell in Sepah for the first time, Nusrat was able to tell me about her arrest and interrogations.

Bahrám was hosting a committee meeting that night. About ten minutes after everyone had left, four armed guards came into the house. One of the guards asked my name. I answered, 'Nusrat Ghufrání,' my maiden name.

He said, 'Known as Mrs Yaldá'í, a member of the Local Spiritual Assembly of Shíráz.' I was surprised at how much he knew about me. They then started to search the house; they collected our Bahá'í books and some documents and brought me, along with Aḥmad, Bahrám and Mrs Ávárigán, our neighbour, to the prison.

Two days later I was called for trial. The investigator asked me the names of members of the Local Spiritual Assembly plus the reserve members and other committee members. I had already made a commitment to myself and refused to reveal any names. The investigator then blindfolded me and took me to the basement.

There a female guard removed some of my clothes and then, wearing a thin blouse and a pair of trousers, I was told to lie down on my stomach on a wooden table. She chained my hands and feet to the table and yelled, ' 'Abdu'lláh, the prisoner is ready.' 'Abdu'lláh was the guard whose job it was to flog the prisoners.

Under those painful lashes I screamed out the name of God. 'Abdu'lláh taunted me, saying, 'If Bahá'u'lláh is the truth, why doesn't he rescue you from my hands?' Every few strokes he would pause for a few seconds and then continue, so that I would feel the pain more keenly. The female guard kept swearing at me and making crude remarks about my activities in the Faith, and the interrogator stood beside the table, holding my file and encouraging 'Abdu'lláh to hit me harder so I would give up and 'talk', as he put it.

That day I was given fifty lashes on my back and fifty on the soles of my feet. I almost fainted from the pain and my body was covered in blood. From the beating on my feet, my legs were horribly swollen up to the knees. But the guards just threw me into the prison corridor and opened the bars of the cell so that I could crawl in. At that time I was still in the communal cell in Sepah. They told all the other prisoners to keep away from me. They warned them that if anyone was seen talking to me or helping me they would be tortured too.

No one dared to come near me at first. At last, a lady named Mahvash, who was imprisoned with her two-year-old son, came over and helped me. Mahvash was a very well-educated young woman who used to work in the electronics industry in Shíráz. She was a Muslim and a political prisoner. 'If the worst comes to the worst they'll kill me for helping you. I have no fear of that,' she said. She removed the clothes that were stuck to my flesh, and helped me put on clean ones. She cleaned away the blood and then rubbed Vaseline on my back. I fainted. The next thing I knew I was back in the trial room; they had dragged me there unconscious.

For two days they tortured me constantly. They wanted me to go out with them at night to point out the Bahá'í houses, and to confirm the activities of the ones who were already in prison. They said that, because I was a member of the Local Spiritual Assembly, I had to denounce the Faith in the media and publicly urge the Bahá'ís to return to Islam. But I told them that I was only a small drop in a whole ocean, and my denial of the Faith would not put out the flame of God.

I later met Mahvash in Sepah myself. She was very young, only twenty-six years old. She told me what she knew about Nusrat's experiences.

When the heartless guards threw her so savagely into the passageway and I saw her dreadful injuries and looked at her sweet face, I couldn't stop myself from helping her. She was shivering, her body was covered with her own blood, and her blouse was embedded in her flesh. I announced loudly, in the public cell with eighty prisoners – some of them prison spies – 'I am not afraid of anyone. As a human being it is my duty to help her. It doesn't make any difference whether she is a Bahá'í or a Muslim; she is still a human being.'

They had tortured poor Nusrat very badly. After I changed her clothes she fainted from the pain. At the same time the investigator yelled to Sister Imání who was in charge of the inside wing, 'Get Nusrat Yaldá'í ready for trial.' She yelled back, 'Brother, she is unconscious, she can't walk.' The investigator didn't care. He came in angrily and dragged her down the corridor and into the trial room himself.

That first day in the cell Nusrat said to me, 'Olya, I can't see my back. Come with me to the shower and look at it, and tell me what it is that hurts so much.'

We went to the shower (it was her first for nearly two months) and when I looked at her back, I saw deep cuts under her right shoulder blade that were still not healing. I couldn't bear to look and had to turn away. 'Nusrat, what did they do to you?'

'They flogged me two days in a row, and the pain was so severe that I fainted, but they must have continued while I was unconscious.'

On the last day of my trial in Sepah, the investigator had admitted to having subjected Nusrat to terrible torture. I had just offered to pray for him. 'Will you really pray for me?' he had asked. I assured him that I would. 'Sister, do you think Mrs Yaldá'í, who we tortured so badly, will also pray for us? Didn't she tell you what we did to her, how hard we tortured her?'

'All the Bahá'ís will pray for you, even Mrs Yaldá'í,' I replied.

When we got to the cell he called Nusrat. I went inside and she rushed out anxiously, not knowing why he was calling her or what he was going to do to her next. The investigator spoke to her kindly.

'Mrs Yaldá'í, I have decided to finish your trial as soon as possible so I can send you to Adelabad to be with your friends.'

He obviously knew how intense and pressured the trials were in Sepah and that it was the most difficult stage for any prisoner. In prison the Religious Magistrate had absolute power. He issued the orders for torture, and decided on the number of the strokes. Sometimes he left the decision up to the investigators, who would use every possible trick to try to get the prisoners to give them information.

Torture was very common in the prison, and we all carried this fear within us at all times. At any minute the guards could come in and take someone out of the cell. The prisoner would ask herself, 'Are they taking me for trial? Are they going to torture me? Are they going to hang me?'

The investigators, it was clear, were determined to extract 'incriminating' information on other Bahá'ís and to force the prisoners to recant. Consequently, though they leaned hard on us all, they leaned hardest on those who were the most prominent members of the Bahá'í community – the assembly and committee members and Auxiliary Board Members. Nusrat had been both an assistant and a member of the assembly, while Túbá, a class teacher as well as reserve assembly member, was accused of misleading the youth. Perhaps their anger was also aroused by her knowledge and her tremendous perseverance under pressure.

Nusrat told me that the time she spent in solitary confinement was the hardest. She used to lie awake at night and pray that she would not have to face severe tests. 'During the day I was on trial and at night they wouldn't let me sleep. Sometimes, because of the pressure on space, they sent three or four other prisoners to my tiny cell and since it was only furnished for one, the rest of us had to stay up all night. However, the others were very sympathetic and offered me the chance to rest. "Mrs Yaldá'í," they said, "you have been tortured and you're very weak; you had better sleep and we'll stay up." '

Nusrat was always confident that I would eventually be released. We often discussed the possibility, and I promised her that if I ever got out I would tell the world what had happened in that prison. Perhaps if enough international pressure was placed on the Iranian government, we might all be freed.

However, towards the end of my stay in Sepah, I was called away for a trial that lasted all day. That was the day they brought out a copy of the 1978 minutes of the Shíráz assembly in which I was mentioned by name. When I got back to the cell, Nusrat asked me what had taken so long. I told her about the minutes.

She asked sadly, 'Olya, do you think they'll let you go after this? And will you ever be free to tell our story?' I reassured her that if God willed it, nothing would stand in the way of my release.

Nusrat Yaldá'í was the last Bahá'í to be transferred to Adelabad out of our two groups. They kept her longer to put even more pressure on her. During her time in Sepah, they confronted her twice with Mr Maḥmúdniẕhád, and once with her son Bahrám. They asked her to encourage Bahrám to talk, and since she knew they would torture him if he didn't, she said to him, 'My dearest Bahrám, tell them about your activities in the committees. We don't have anything to hide from them.'

Four days before my release she was finally transferred to Adelabad after her long, painful imprisonment in Sepah. Her safe arrival was a cause of great joy and relief to all the other prisoners.

The Maḥmúdnizhád Family

I first met the Maḥmúdnizhád family in 1960, at a time when they were living in Yemen and had come back to Iran to visit relatives. They later had two little girls by the names of Taránih and Mona, who were both born in Yemen. In 1969, when the government of Yemen expelled all foreigners, the family returned to Iran and they finally settled in Shíráz.

Yadu'lláh Maḥmúdnizhád was brought up as a Muslim, and he had investigated the Bahá'í Faith and become a Bahá'í independently. As soon as they arrived in Shíráz he immediately set about making himself useful in the Bahá'í community. I worked with him for seven years in different Bahá'í activities.

From 1977 Mr Maḥmúdnizhád served as an assistant to Yadu'lláh Vaḥdat. He later became secretary of the Shíráz assembly, and also gave Arabic lessons and classes for the youth.

In 1982, when opposition to the Bahá'ís was at its fiercest and gatherings were closely controlled by the government, Mr Maḥmúdnizhád went from house to house to visit and encourage the local Bahá'ís. To create less suspicion among the mullahs and guards, he took his wife and his younger daughter Mona with him. He always said, 'Young Mona must understand the responsibilities of being a Bahá'í.'

A week before he was arrested we had a meeting in our house. A minute after he and his wife had arrived, the doorbell rang. I looked out of the window and saw three bearded men, obviously representatives of one of the Islamic groups. Before I opened the door, I asked the Maḥmúdnizháds to go out through the back door and wait. The men were from the local mosque, and said that they had come to find out how many people were living in our house so that they could give us the proper number of food coupons.

The next day Mr Maḥmúdniẓhád came to our house again. He told me, 'After we left your house yesterday and got out of earshot, my wife and I could not stop laughing at the thought of Bahá'í houses being surrounded by armed guards before they dare ring the doorbell!'

He had a lively sense of humour, and he was extremely humble, particularly when it came to his work for the Bahá'í Faith. He was not a wealthy man. He and his wife and two daughters lived in a small two-bedroom apartment on the fifth floor of an apartment complex in the south of Shíráz.

The first time I went to their home Mona was only eleven. I don't recall why, but for some reason we went to Mona's room. It was a very simple, tidy room, and she had a poster on the wall decorated with the Bahá'í symbol, which she had designed herself. Mona loved handicrafts and used to make flowers out of paper or clay. She also liked painting and sewing.

Most of our talk that day was about Mona's talents, her maturity and her deep faith despite the fact that she was so young. The burning and looting of Bahá'í houses in Shíráz and the surrounding areas and the destruction of the House of the Báb had a tremendous impact upon her. Her faith was strengthened greatly by the persecution she witnessed and the Bahá'ís' courageous response to it.

The day the House of the Báb was finally destroyed, Mona made a pilgrimage to the ruins. When she returned home she said to her mother, 'Mama, can I come into the house with my shoes on today? They have walked on the ruins of the House of the Báb.' Then she sat down at her desk and wrote an article about the sacred house.

Mona was extremely intelligent and studied the Bahá'í Faith conscientiously. When she was fifteen, her father started an advanced class teaching Bahá'í writings. Although they were intended to be for mature Bahá'ís with a deep knowledge of the Faith, she showed more aptitude for the classes than anyone else. She immediately memorized whatever writings her father was teaching us about, and pleaded with him and all of us to let her join the class every week.

Soon, she was conducting children's classes herself. She made a special effort, following the advice of the National Spiritual Assembly, to memorize the writings and prayers so she could be spiritually self-sufficient in case one day she couldn't have access to Bahá'í books; she even compiled a little booklet of prayers for the students in her children's class to memorize.

Whenever and wherever I saw Mona, I found in her the humility and dignity of a mature Bahá'í, along with the innocence and purity of a sweet child. She was very pretty and graceful, with long brown hair and beautiful green eyes. She was tall and slim, and her voice was very soft. She always wore a beautiful smile. In school she was very popular, and even though most Bahá'í students in Iran had been suspended from school by then, Mona was still attending.

Two days before her arrest Mona and her father came to our house. We spoke about the persecution the Bahá'ís were suffering. I asked him, 'Mr Mahmúdnizhád, how long do you think this will go on? How long will the Bahá'ís have to suffer such prejudice and oppression under Khomeini's regime?'

'My dear,' he replied, 'study the Bahá'í writings. They have already described the calamities in Iran and in the world at large. We Bahá'ís have a difficult test before us, but we have to recognize it and remain firm. Khomeini has come to assist the progress of the Faith,' he continued, with an optimistic smile. 'This is only the beginning of the revolution on this planet. Calamities will continue to occur until humanity has reached a higher consciousness, and until we all practise the unity of mankind and live together in peace and harmony.'

When the guards attacked the Mahmúdnizháds' house two days later, they arrested both him and seventeen-year-old Mona. Mr Mahmúdnizhád was kept in solitary confinement and badly tortured. I met him twice during interrogations in Sepah. Later I was with Mona in Adelabad. She was always worried about her mother and sister, and often came to my cell to talk about them. Since I was arrested a month after her, I was able to reassure her that they were being very strong and courageous, and were doing all they could to get her released. Sometimes, if there were no guards nearby, she would stay and chant prayers in her beautiful, soft voice. One day I told her,

'Mona, I heard about how you and your father were arrested from your mother, but I would really like to hear it from you.' She happily sat down and told me her story:

It was around 7.30 in the evening of Saturday, 23 October 1982, and I was studying for an English test when our doorbell rang. My father answered the door. Four armed guards pushed their way into the house. My father asked them to identify themselves. They said, 'We are the guards of the Revolutionary Court of Shíráz. We have a warrant to enter your house from the Public Prosecutor of Shíráz.'

My father calmly asked to see the warrant, and one of the guards handed him a piece of paper. My father looked at it and said, 'Please come in, the house is yours to search.' For three hours they looked around, opening every drawer and closet. They took our family album and found some pictures of Bahá'ís who had already been executed, including one of Mr Bakhtávar. They questioned my father about it and he answered truthfully, 'This is a picture of Mr Bakhtávar.'

Then the guards asked me, 'What is your religion?'

I replied, 'The Bahá'í Faith.'

The guards collected some of my father's Bahá'í documents, books and photographs and told him that he and I should go to the Revolutionary Court with them.

My mother protested, 'If you want to take my husband, OK, but where are you taking this little seventeen-year-old girl at this hour of the night?'

One of the guards replied angrily, 'Don't say "the little seventeen-year-old", you should say "the little Bahá'í teacher". With what we have read of her writings today, we are sure she will be a Bahá'í teacher in the future.'

I tried to calm my mother down. My father said, 'Farkhundih, don't worry. I love these brothers like my own sons and I am sure it is the will of God for them to be here now and to take Mona and myself away with them. Just leave everything in God's hands and don't worry about Mona. These brothers look upon Mona as their own sister.'

I said goodbye to my mother and left with my father and the guards for Sepah. In the prison yard they blind-folded us. I was taken to a room where they insulted and belittled my beliefs and yelled at me. They separated me from my father and I was body searched by a female guard in another room. Then they blindfolded me again and took me to the public cell where they took my blindfold off and left.

I was standing in a large, dark room and for a while I couldn't see anything. My eyes had not yet adjusted to the darkness of the cell. A prisoner came up to me and directed me to a space on the floor in the corner where I was obviously supposed to sleep. She asked me why I had been arrested. I answered, 'Because I am a Bahá'í; I haven't done anything wrong.' I guessed the time to be just before midnight. She gave me two thin, dirty blan-kets.

It took a while, but eventually I got used to the darkness and could see. The cell was like a hall, and many young girls and women were sleeping on the floor. I didn't know anyone, as I was the first Bahá'í in that cell. I had no idea where my father was. I lay down in the corner and silently said prayers thanking God. I felt as if I was standing on a balcony and getting closer to the moon. But the worried look on my mother's face was still before my eyes. I prayed for her perseverance and for my father's too. I decided to go to sleep like the others and wait until tomorrow to see what destiny had in store for me.

I was lying there, deep in thought, when the cell door opened and a woman came in. I didn't recognize her. I found out later that she was Mrs Irán Ávárigán, but I didn't know she was a Bahá'í at the time. I got up and went to the washroom, then I returned and went to sleep.

Later the cell door opened again and another woman entered. This woman kept repeating, 'You must give me my pills, I suffer from very bad migraine.' But no one paid any attention to her. It was Mrs Zá'irpúr. I couldn't see her face properly in the dark, but her voice sounded very familiar. They brought her to our corner. As soon as she looked at Mrs Ávárigán she exclaimed, 'Irán, is that you?' Mrs Ávárigán then recognized her. I went closer because the voice was very familiar.

Mrs Zá'irpúr said, 'Mona, is that you? What are you doing here? They've even arrested you? Oh my God!'

I felt a warm glow in my heart when I recognized Mrs Zá'irpúr. Even though they had taken me away from my home and my loving family, I was brought to a new family in prison where all the women were like a mother to me and all the young girls were like my sisters.

That night they arrested over forty Bahá'ís and they brought all the Bahá'í women to that cell. As soon as Mona realized that a lot of Bahá'ís were being arrested and were expected to arrive in Sepah, she became determined to welcome and comfort them. Mona was of course the youngest, and her youth and sweetness endeared her to the Muslim prisoners, including the murderers and drug addicts, who were imprisoned with her. They used to call her 'the little prisoner'.

She loved her father very much, and in prison most of her thoughts revolved around him. Whenever we talked of him she said, 'I know they will execute my father because he freely admitted that he was the secretary of the Local Spiritual Assembly. But I am completely resigned.'

Once, in Sepah, they had confronted her with her father and ordered him to tell her to talk. 'We are not a political group, and we have nothing to hide,' he said, then continued, 'Mona, whatever they ask you, answer them bravely and honestly.' She had told them she taught Bahá'í children's classes.

She often rested her chin in her hands and became lost in her own spiritual world. After so many years, I still vividly recall her sweetness and hear her lovely voice in my head, chanting prayers with a heart full of love.

I had the good fortune of being with Mona in Adelabad, where she underwent the last two stages of her trial. She described her final trial to me.

The prosecutor insulted and humiliated me, saying, 'Your parents have deceived and misled you. They have forced you to imitate them in following the Bahá'í Faith.'

'Your honour,' I replied, 'it is true that I was born into a Bahá'í family and initially learned the Faith from them, but I want to assure you that I have exercised my own reason and accepted the Faith after my own investigation. One doesn't become a Bahá'í by imitation, only by individual investigation of the truth. You have access to several of our books, you can read them for yourself to confirm this. My parents never insisted on my becoming a Bahá'í.'

The prosecutor looked at me astounded and said, 'Young girl, what do you know about religion?'

'Is there a better proof of my faith than the fact that I was taken out of school to be brought here and undergo long hours of trials? Can't you see that it is my belief that has given me the confidence to stand in your presence and answer your questions?'

Then he asked me to say a prayer. I put away the file and quietly and respectfully recited 'Abdu'l-Bahá's prayer:

O God! Refresh and gladden my spirit. Purify my heart. Illumine my mind. I lay all my affairs in Thy hand. Thou art my Guide and my Refuge. I will no longer be sorrowful and grieved; I will be a happy and joyful being. O God! I will no longer be full of anxiety, nor will I let trouble harass me. I will not dwell on the unpleasant things of life. . . .

The prosecutor stopped me in the middle of the prayer with a wave of his hand, and remained silent for a little while.

I felt that he was affected by the prayer, but his prejudice had blinded him. 'Why didn't you chant the prayer?' he asked. 'On the night you were arrested, the guards found many tapes of your chanting. Your crime is quite obvious: you were misleading young people by making recordings of prayers in your beautiful voice.'

'Your honour, in your opinion is the chanting of prayers a crime?'

'Yes. What harm did you find in Islam that made you turn to the Bahá'í Faith?'

'But I do believe in Islam, your honour – because the basis of all religion is the same. However, I also believe that, according to the needs of human beings in different ages, God sends us different messengers and laws to guide us.'

The prosecutor said, 'We must obey the Qur'án. You must either accept Islam or face execution.'

'I kiss the order of execution,' I answered without a moment's hesitation.

An order for Mona's release was issued twice while I was in prison. In the second stage of the trial the Assistant Public Prosecutor offered to release her on a security bond but would not accept the family's apartment, which was subject to a mortgage, as security. So Mona remained in Adelabad. Then the Religious Magistrate issued an order for Mona's release on a security bond of 500,000 tuman. Mona's mother took the bond to the Revolutionary Court, but the Public Prosecutor said, 'You must leave this security bond here for yourself. I will give you twenty-four hours to turn yourself in to the court, because we have discovered that nine years ago you were a member of the Social Committee and we have the documents to prove it.'

Mona's mother turned herself in the next day. She was in prison for five months, and later wrote to me, sharing her experiences of the difficult time following her husband and daughter's arrest.

Nearly four weeks had passed since Mona and Yadu'lláh were arrested, and I had heard nothing from them. I had gone to Sepah many times in the hope of getting a chance to see them, but every time I was turned away disappointed. It was Friday, 19 November 1982 and as I sat by the window looking out at the people moving around on the streets below, going about their normal lives, oblivious to what was going on around them, I lost control. I couldn't stop crying. It was as if a dam, at last, had burst. I was calling to God out loud, 'Oh God, I want my child; I want Mona from you. I haven't even heard from her; I want my baby.' I looked up at the sky and cried, 'The little birds are free but my little bird is trapped in a cage.'

That was a very difficult day. The next day, Saturday, I went to Sepah with tearful eyes and a broken heart. And when I got there, after days of not knowing what had happened to all the prisoners and being left completely in the dark, we were at last told we would be allowed visits – although no conversation was possible. We waited from one o'clock in the after-noon until 7 p.m. that night. Finally they brought the Bahá'í women in and asked them to form a line on the other side of the glass partition.

We stood on opposite sides of the glass, just looking at each other. Seeing Mona again after so long reduced me to tears. She gestured to me, asking me to stop crying. I immediately wiped away my tears. I wanted to tell her that my tears were not tears of grief but of joy at seeing her again, which I am sure she knew, but she didn't want to see me crying at all. We stood and looked at each other until I was told to leave.

Later Mona told me they had been on trial from one o'clock in the afternoon to 3 a.m. the following morning, and our visit had been just a short break in a long, difficult day for them.

The first Saturday in December, we had gone to Sepah to see Mona as usual, only to be informed by the guard on the gate that she was no longer there. They had transferred her to Adelabad. Anxiously we rushed to Adelabad. As soon as I saw Mona in the visiting room I snatched up the receiver and asked her how she was. She had caught a cold, and had piled on all the clothes she had, one on top of the other, to keep warm. They had moved the prisoners from Sepah to Adelabad almost a week previously, and hadn't bothered to inform us. During this time she had caught a chill because of the cold wintry weather and having only one blanket to sleep on.

I looked at her slight figure muffled up against the cold and lost my self-control. 'Please forgive me for crying,' I apologized, 'but I can't help it. I miss you so much, my darling.'

Strong as a rock, Mona held back her tears; I could see them welling up in her eyes but she managed to control herself. She tried to cheer me up: 'Mama, we are very comfortable here. Compared to the last prison [Sepah], this is like a mansion. They give us breakfast, lunch and dinner! It's almost luxury!'

Mona always tried to comfort us. She was always concerned about others, showering us all with her love and happiness. Before the visit was over she told me, 'The minute you find out they have brought Father here, bring him extra blankets so he won't catch cold.' When the time came for me to leave, Mona kissed her fingertips and put them up against the glass partition. I did the same, and after that whenever we said goodbye we did the same thing.

Taránih, Mona's sister, also wrote to me later about the family's experiences.

My mother turned herself in on Saturday, 22 January 1983. I couldn't believe they would arrest my mother too. I was hoping they would ask her a few questions and let her go, but they had different plans for her. On the Saturday, which was our visiting day for Mona, my mother was detained at the Revolutionary Court. I didn't know what to do, but I decided to go and see Mona on my own.

The first thing she said after saying hello was, 'Where is Mother, is she all right?'

At this point I didn't know where Mother was; I didn't know whether she was OK or not. I replied, 'She is in Sepah. She had to take care of some things for Father.' She didn't ask any more and I didn't add anything. Of course, in our visiting times we could not talk about the things we really wanted to, but by looking at each other we could say a lot. In Mona's eyes I saw detachment and a deep, indescribable happiness. When the visiting period was over we said goodbye. My mother was taken to Adelabad that same night.

On Saturdays I went to see Mother and Mona, and on Wednesdays, which was the men's visiting day, I visited Dad. The night Mother was arrested was horrible. I couldn't believe how suddenly everyone around me was gone, and that night I cried my heart out. I didn't know whether or not they had sent my mother to Adelabad, where Mona was, until the following Saturday when I saw them both standing side by side on the other side of the glass partition. It was a beautiful moment.

Mona's mother later told me about her own experiences in prison beginning with the day she arrived in Adelabad.

As I was going up the iron stairs to the third floor, some of the prisoners who were with me ran ahead quickly and told Mona that I was coming. Astounded, Mona came out to welcome me. When she hugged and kissed me we made no attempt to control our emotions – we both started to cry. She held me tight and welcomed me to my new home. Then she brought me some leftovers from lunch and dinner and set us a small dinner table.

A few other Bahá'ís came to the cell, and as I ate dinner I told them about the situation outside the prison and what each family had been doing on behalf of their loved ones inside. It was a busy night. They all had questions to ask and things to inquire about, until the lights were turned off and it was time to sleep. I was to move into Mona's cell, which she shared with Ṭáhirih Síyávushí. Since there was only one bed in each cell they let me sleep on it. Mona slept on the floor beside the bed and Ṭáhirih slept by the door.

Mona explained to me how different prison life was from life outside. She told me one must spend more time praying alone, and one should suffer within oneself but never cry.

'When you are among others,' she said, 'you must laugh and give them positive energy.' Another thing she made a special point of telling me was that I must take care not to show extra love and affection to her. She said that all of us were alone in that prison, and begged me to be even more of a mother to the others than to her. As she wished, I did not even kiss her again until the last day, and I tried to spend more time with other friends. Mona had also told me, 'Mother, be yourself here. At decision-making times don't copy anyone. Follow your own heart. The only thing that hasn't been taken away from us is our individuality.' On my first night she was wonderful. She truly comforted me and gave me confidence.

Mona liked to be alone a lot of the time. She wanted to have intimate communion with God, and whenever a cell was vacant she was there saying her prayers. She was a very creative girl and as well as painting she loved to write; it was very difficult for her in prison, not being able to do any of the things she loved. The fact that she had managed to send out two letters to us was amazing, since prisoners were not allowed to write anything. Although she spent a lot of her time in prayer, whenever she found a free moment she spent it with the non-Baháʼís. She spent hours talking to them and teaching them songs, and they were always eager to grab her and whisk her away to their cells. She was very popular with everyone.

One day a Muslim prisoner who had been for trial in Sepah brought some sour plums back. She gave each of her friends one and brought one for Nusrat Yaldáʼí. She said, 'I know you like sour plums. I'm sorry I don't have enough to give everybody one, but I have one left for you. Eat it and don't tell anyone else.'

I was sitting with Nusrat at the time. She accepted the fruit and thanked the woman warmly. When she went out, Mrs Yaldáʼí turned to me and said, 'I can't bring myself to eat this. Here, you have it.'

I thanked her and said, 'No, I can't accept it; it's yours.'

Just then Mona was passing by the cell. Nusrat called her in, placed the plum in her hand and said, 'My dearest Mona, this is the only one, go and eat it.' Mona took the plum and disappeared. A few minutes later she came back with a small tray. She had removed the stone and divided the plum into seventeen tiny pieces, and had decorated the tray with plastic forks and knives. She had such a sincere and creative mind. She called all the Bahá'í prisoners into the cell and gave each one a piece. We were all touched by what she had done and laughed, because they were such small pieces. I, for example, got only a tiny piece of the skin!

A few weeks after Farkhundih Mahmúdnizhád's arrest, the Bahá'í prisoners were given the chance to visit immediate family members who were also imprisoned for the first time. She later described the scene to me.

The Ishráqí family were sitting quietly in one corner on their knees, holding hands. On the other side, Mrs Yaldá'í and her son Bahrám sat with their arms around each other. All the friends who had been deprived of seeing each other for such a long time got a chance to be close to one another. Mona, my husband and I were holding hands. Mona and I both knew they would execute him.

'These hours of separation will pass in no time,' he said. 'Before you realize it we will all be together again. Do you remember, my dear, that when we decided to go to Yemen, I went on ahead to find a home and prepare it for you? It is the same now. I'll go first to the next world and make a home for you to come later.' Then he looked at Mona and said, 'Are you heavenly or earthly?'

Mona replied, 'Heavenly,' and no further words were exchanged between them. Mona just kissed her father. Those two didn't need to speak to one another, they could just look at each other and know what each one was thinking.

After a few minutes, my husband began calmly asking about the whereabouts and well-being of our relatives and friends. That was the last time I saw him.

The day I announced the tragic news of my husband's execution in the prison, all the prisoners, Bahá'í and Muslim, came to comfort Mona and me. They were all broken-hearted and many were in tears.

Mona comforted them. 'Please don't cry for me – I don't feel alone. I know you are all sharing my grief. You are all like my aunts.' Then she looked at the younger girls and said, 'And all of you are like sisters to me. But we must stay strong – we haven't passed our own test yet. Now we have to pray that those who have been martyred will intercede for us with Him to enable us to pass our tests.' Then she began to chant in her lovely sweet voice. That day and the next few days were passed in grief and joy combined.

Taránih also described to me her last visit to her father.

Neither of us knew that it was to be our last meeting, but he said to me, 'Tell your mother that although we have always shared our happiness and our grief, we have to suffer separately now and go through our tests alone. This is our chance to prove our true love for one another and for Bahá'u'lláh. This is our destiny.'

His face was lit up. Tears of great happiness filled my eyes, keeping me from seeing him properly. I asked him, 'Father, how come from a family of four, three of you were Bahá'u'lláh's chosen servants and I was deprived of this great bounty? What have I done that I wasn't worthy of being imprisoned for my Faith?'

He replied, 'Do you think you are free? You on the outside are in the harsher prison. With all this oppression, you are prisoners too.'

I knew I would never have the chance to embrace him in this world again, to rest my head on his chest.

But, as he advised, I concentrated on what would result from their imprisonment and execution, and I resigned myself to God's will.

Four days later, on 13 March, I received the news of my father's death. He had been martyred the previous day along with two other wonderful human beings, Ṭúbá Zá'irpúr and Raḥmat Vafá'í.

My husband brought the tragic news to me at ten o'clock in the morning. He was crying hysterically. Even though I knew my father's spirit of sacrifice, and after his arrest I always knew he would be killed, when I heard the news my whole body trembled with the shock and I screamed. I couldn't control myself. My one-year-old daughter Nora woke up because of the noise we were making, and she too began to cry.

At length I got a grip on myself. I said, 'Father, you told me yourself that the spirit of the martyrs will make this tolerable for the ones left behind, and that they will send us strength. So where is it?' I swear to God, at that moment my whole being became calm. I felt peace within me as never before in my life.

I decided to go and see the body, and finally succeeded in getting permission to do so. I saw the bodies of all three martyrs. We weren't allowed to collect the bodies, of course, or even to get close to them.

The next Saturday was visiting day with my mother and sister. They knew that there were two men martyred with Mrs Zá'irpúr, but they didn't know who. Most of the prisoners had guessed, however, that one of those two men must have been my father. Now the terrible duty of confirming this tragic news rested on my shoulders.

I had already recognized the wonderful spiritual state they were both in, but I was not expecting the gift of strength that came to me when I needed it. When it came to delivering the news to them, I was filled with an indescribable joy and happiness. I congratulated both of them, and they did the same in return. I said to Mona, 'Dad is gone to the next world.'

'I know,' she said. 'Good for him. Lucky him.'

Táhirih & Zarrín

CHAPTER 10

The first time I met Ṭáhirih Síyávushí was at the Vaḥdats' house in Shíráz in 1977. The next time I saw her was five years later, when I was lovingly embraced by her in that dark, cold cell in Sepah Prison. She had been arrested an hour before me.

Her husband Jamshíd was a cousin of Hidáyat Síyávushí, who had worked in the optician's shop before he was taken to Sepah. Ṭáhirih briefly told me all that she and Jamshíd had had to endure in the past few years.

In 1977, Jamshíd and I decided to move to Yásúj. At the beginning of the revolution, in 1978, we were attacked, and they took our home, our belongings and Jamshíd's new shop. I was also fired from the hospital where I was nursing.

After that we returned to Shíráz penniless. We started out again with nothing, and for a while we had a very difficult life, but we were content with the little we had. I approached several hospitals for a job, but they all said that, even though they desperately needed my services, they couldn't hire me because I was a Bahá'í.

Recently, after months of looking, I found a job in a private hospital. Jamshíd also started up a small clothing shop three months ago. After four years of being without our own home, constantly moving from one place to another, we could at last stand on our own feet again. Only last week we managed to buy a refrigerator, a bed and a few small pieces of furniture. But it seems they couldn't leave us alone even with so little, and now we are both here in prison.

Jamshíd was arrested at the end of October, in the street after dark, and taken directly to Sepah. Two days later, at ten o'clock at night, four armed guards brought Jamshíd home. I was shocked when I saw him. He was shaking like a leaf and could hardly keep his balance. I rushed over to him to ask him what they had done to him, but they were keeping a close eye on us so I kept quiet and didn't ask him too many questions.

I guessed they had come for the Bahá'í registration book and for the community's funds. Jamshíd was in charge of looking after both the registration book and the money, and he didn't want to give them up. They had clearly tortured him to try and get the names of other Bahá'ís.

To frighten both of us they separated us and locked me in another room. I could hear them telling Jamshíd, 'Either you give us the book and the money or we will kill you right now.' I was terrified; I knew they were armed. I started screaming and pounding on the door. Since they didn't want me to attract the neighbours' attention, they opened the door and let me out.

I could see from Jamshíd's face how desperately he wanted to resist their pressure. 'Táhirih,' he said, 'I gave the registration book to Ahmad. I don't know where he put it.'

Jamshíd had in fact hidden the registration book and told his brother Ahmad that, if he was arrested, Ahmad was to remove the book and give it to someone he trusted, so that the names of the Bahá'ís would be kept safe.

I kept quiet. Jamshíd moved reluctantly towards the place where the book was hidden. He sighed painfully, and the tears were running down his face as he fought with himself. On the one hand he had to endure torture in prison to protect the names of the local Bahá'ís, and on the other hand he valued honesty and didn't want to lie. I took a chance in front of the guards and went towards Jamshíd. I held him by the arm and helped him walk, and just by a look I reassured him that the book had been removed and that Ahmad had also left the city.

Since they were unable to find the registration book, the guards took Jamshíd back to prison. A month later, they came back and arrested me. My charge was membership of the Bahá'í Publishing Committee.

Ṭáhirih and her husband had been married for twelve years now, and were very much in love. She was thirty and he was thirty-four, and they didn't have any children. In prison she constantly repeated his name and cried for him. She used to spend hours telling me stories about their relationship and describing his personality and habits. 'Olya,' she said, 'I am terrified they will kill him and I won't be able to live without him.'

She always said she wished to sacrifice her life for Jamshíd. Ṭáhirih's spirit of sacrifice and love was astonishing. Even in those dreadful conditions, she took care of everyone and helped them in any way she could.

In prison many people used to get sick and since the facilities were so limited we had no choice but to continue eating with our fingers from the same plate. Ṭáhirih knew that I was squeamish about eating from the same plate as a sick person, so every time she noticed me in that situation she would say, 'Olya, why don't we change places?'

She always offered to wash our clothes for us while we were taking a shower – for the first few weeks most of us had only one set of clothing, and it wasn't until later that they allowed our families to bring us a change of clothes. Ṭáhirih, however, had cleverly brought a second set of clothing with her when she was arrested. When the guards came to her house that night, she'd had the foresight to pack spare clothes and some toiletries.

In my own case, I had asked the guards if I should pack and they had refused to allow me to bring anything with me to the prison. It was around two weeks later, after much pleading, that the prison guard eventually let Morad bring me some of the things I needed. In the meantime, I used Táhirih's clothes to change into while I washed my own. We had to wear thick stockings, trousers and a long tunic, a head cover and chador when we went for interrogation, but since most of us had come in our everyday clothes we were wearing sheer stockings and didn't have any thick ones. Táhirih had two pairs, so for the first week or so most of us used hers. Once, when they suddenly called me to trial, she took off the ones she was wearing and gave them to me. I said, 'They might call you as well, and then if you don't have any to wear you will be in trouble.'

'It doesn't matter,' she replied, 'you wear these, and go now.'

When I returned I immediately gave her back the stockings, and then we sat and talked about our trials and the pressure we were under. She suddenly turned to me and said, 'Olya, I want to give you these stockings.'

'Táhirih, if I get out of here one day and leave Iran, I will keep these as a memento of our troubled days together, and they will remind me of all your sacrifices.' At that time there wasn't the slightest chance I would be set free. But now I treasure the stockings she gave me in prison.

Táhirih's trials were held separately from ours, and one day she was called to trial and not brought back to the cell. We were all worried about what had happened to her. A few days later, a political prisoner was brought in and told us that Táhirih was being held in solitary confinement. To intimidate us, the investigators sometimes transferred prisoners from the main cell to a single one. Ten or twelve days later they transferred Táhirih back to our cell. She told me that she had been questioned very intensively in that time, but had managed to avoid talking about any Bahá'ís other than Jamshíd and herself.

Whenever we could, we gathered together in the cell and spent time joking and laughing to ease the pressure. Everyone had something to say, especially about their own prospects of being killed. Táhirih was very humorous. 'Ya Bahá'u'lláh,' Táhirih would say, 'could you *not* choose me, please. I don't want to be a martyr. I want to remain a Bahá'í *and* live.' Then she would laugh lightly and continue, 'Ya 'Abdu'l-Bahá, I don't want to be a martyr. It's not compulsory, is it? I wish you would put Jamshíd's hand in mine and let us live as Bahá'ís together. I don't mind if we have to camp on the streets – so long as we are together and we are Bahá'ís.'

Some of the other prisoners would improvise a performance on the reaction of their friends and relatives to the news of their execution, and make us all laugh. But Ṭáhirih always said seriously, 'These fanatical people, with all their prejudice towards us, will kill us all.' I think she knew in her heart from the very beginning that she would be killed, but she would laugh and say, 'Listen, we must be careful not to leave our mouths open when they are hanging us, because if we do, our tongues will hang out after we are dead and we'll look ugly. So remember to keep your mouth shut and smile.'

She often made me count my blessings by reminding me, 'We don't have to worry any more. Remember how frightened we used to be, about being attacked by the guards at night and getting arrested? At least now that we are here we don't have *that* fear any more.'

Visiting days were the hardest for Ṭáhirih. She used to sit in one corner deep in thought. Aḥmad, Jamshíd's brother, had had to leave his pregnant wife and his children to escape from Shíráz. But every Wednesday and Saturday, his wife travelled on the bus with two small children and bags of fruit, clothes and money, to visit Jamshíd and Ṭáhirih. She then had to wait by the gate for seven or eight hours each time and listen to the guards' insults and swearing in order to see Jamshíd or Ṭáhirih for ten minutes or less through the glass partition. This broke Ṭáhirih's heart every time. 'All her sacrifice and selflessness make me feel ashamed of myself,' she would say.

When the guards learned that Jamshíd was a member of the Samaritan Committee, and that he was born in Jordan, they started to torture him more than the others. For seventy days they kept him in solitary confinement in Sepah. They knew how much Ṭáhirih and Jamshíd loved one another and took advantage of this fact, trying to use it against them by telling each that the other had recanted, but it did not work. Every time they told Ṭáhirih this story she bravely replied, 'I am a Bahá'í.'

'Aren't you his wife?' they would ask.

'When it comes to belief, everyone is responsible for his or her own.'

The investigator became infuriated by Ṭáhirih's strength, and took her into the interrogation room to tell her, 'If you don't recant, I will give the order for Jamshíd to be tortured to death.'

'I am a Bahá'í and I will remain a Bahá'í,' she answered bravely. 'I will never recant my faith under any circumstances.'

'If you only knew what we have done to Jamshíd. If you saw him, you wouldn't recognize him. We have tortured him so much that there is no Jamshíd left for you.'

Ṭáhirih, who loved Jamshíd so much, begged them to tell her how Jamshíd was. They brought him into the room, and for fifteen minutes let them see each other. She came back to the cell shaking like a leaf and crying.

They brought Jamshíd into the room, supporting him on both sides. As soon as I laid eyes on him I screamed. He was only skin and bones; he was like a ghost. He could hardly keep his balance, and blood and pus were oozing out from under his toenails. But spiritually he was very strong. He kept comforting me, saying, 'Ṭáhirih, don't worry about me. I will live.'

I told him, 'Jamshíd, if they kill you, I will see you in the next world. We will be there together.' At that point I felt that Jamshíd wanted to tell me what they had done to him so that if I ever got out of prison I could tell the National Spiritual Assembly.

He pulled up his shirt and showed me his back. The lashes had caused his spine to become infected. He said to me in front of the interrogator, 'Ṭáhirih, I have endured seventy days of torture and seventy sleepless nights. I don't know what more these brothers want from me. They torture me during the day and then they won't let me sleep at night. They keep asking for the registration book with the names and addresses of all the Bahá'ís of Shíráz. They say I have to go with them and show them the houses of Bahá'ís. They also ask for the names of all the committee members and their addresses, especially the names of the members of the Local Spiritual Assemblies in the area. I keep telling them I don't know anyone other than myself who has been a member of an assembly, but they don't believe me. They charge me with helping Bahá'ís in need and say that if I hadn't helped them they would have become Muslims.

'I gave them the receipts of the four truckloads of goods, including furniture, clothing and food, and the money the Bahá'ís donated to our Muslim brothers and sisters who suffered in the earthquake and the war. This act should have shown them that we wanted to help anyone who needed it. We believe in helping all the human race, regardless of their religious background or their skin colour. An ounce of justice would have been enough for them to know that we are innocent.'

At this point one of the investigators seemed to be moved by Jamshíd's protest and told him, 'We know you are not lying. Now we want to take you out for some fresh air.'

Although prisoners in solitary confinement were kept in dark, stuffy conditions and longed for fresh air, Jamshíd asked, 'Your honours, if it wouldn't be too much trouble, would you take me to the main cell instead so that I might visit my friends? That would make me much happier.'

I suddenly noticed deep cuts on Jamshíd's neck and wrists. I asked him what they were. One of the investigators said, 'Jamshíd has been a naughty boy. He has attempted suicide twice.'

'Ṭáhirih,' he said quietly, 'forgive me, but after so long in solitary confinement, suffering constant physical and mental torture, I couldn't take it any more and I decided to kill myself. Sometimes they taunted me with crude insults because we don't have any children. They kept asking me, "Is it you or your wife that is to blame?" Or they would wake me in the middle of the night and tell me I had to go with them and show them the homes of Bahá'ís.'

The next day they took Ṭáhirih to see Jamshíd again, and this time she came back smiling. 'What do we have here that I can

take for Jamshíd?' she said cheerfully. 'I think one of the investigators was moved by what Jamshíd said yesterday. They have
transferred him from solitary confinement back to the main cell,
and they told me I could bring some fruit for him, since he hasn't
had any for the whole time he was in solitary confinement.'

Luckily, that day Morad had visited and had brought some
sweet lemons, apples, oranges, pistachio nuts and dried fruit.
Ṭáhirih joyfully took some sweet lemons, apples and nuts and
went back to see Jamshíd. But a few minutes later she returned,
still carrying them, and said, 'The guards are just toying with us.
We are completely at their mercy and they can do whatever
they please to torment us.'

I vividly recall the day, about two weeks after her transfer
to Adelabad, that Ṭáhirih went for her final trial. When she
returned that afternoon, she walked into my cell calmly and
with dignity. She was smiling joyfully, and her face shone.
'Ṭáhirih, what has happened? Why are you so happy?' I asked.

'Until now,' she told me calmly, 'I thought they were going
to kill Jamshíd alone, but today the Religious Magistrate gave
the order for my execution. I will now accompany my husband
on this journey.'

From that day on I never saw her cry or look sad.

Zarrín Muqímí was born in 1954, in a village near Iṣfahán called
Abíyánih. She was the third child in a Bahá'í family. She
obtained a degree in English Literature from the University of
Tehran, and was an excellent student all through her academic
years.

After she finished her studies she moved to Shíráz with her
parents, who were involved in the maintenance of the House of
the Báb and its surrounding buildings. They lived in one of the
houses in that alley. She worked as a translator and accountant
in a petrochemical company near Marvdasht, but at the end of
1981 she was fired for being a Bahá'í. She was always proud of
the fact that she had lost her job because of her Faith.

Zarrín was tall and slim, and always dressed simply. Unlike
other girls of her age, she was never a follower of fashion. She
loved studying, had a wide knowledge of the Bahá'í writings
and the Qur'án, and knew the book of Aqdas by heart.

Adelabad Prison

Entrance to Adelabad Prison

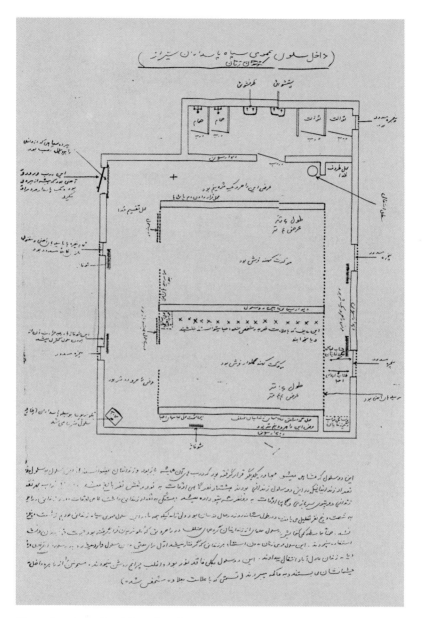

Two drawings by Olya showing the layouts of the prisons where she and the other Bahá'ís were kept. Above: Diagram of interior of Sepah Prison. Olya surreptitiously measured the building with her hands and feet. Facing page: Diagram showing interior of Adelabad Prison and Olya's notes.

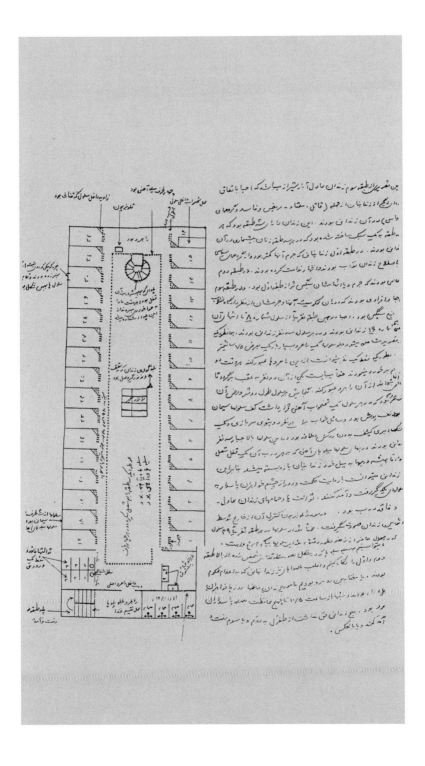

Right: Olya in Iran after the revolution wearing the compulsory head covering for her passport photograph.

Payam's second birthday party in <u>Sh</u>íráz.

Jam<u>sh</u>íd and Ṭáhirih Síyávu<u>sh</u>í – husband and wife were both executed for being Bahá'ís.

'Ináyat and 'Izzat I<u>sh</u>ráqí with their daughter Roya – all of whom were executed.

Top left and right: Mona and her father Yadu'lláh Maḥmúdniẓhád.
Bottom left and right: Zarrín Muqímí and Símín Sábirí.

Top left and right: Nusrat Yaldá'í and <u>Sh</u>írín Dálvand. Bottom left and right: Mah<u>sh</u>íd Nírúmand and A<u>kh</u>tar Sabet.

Bahá'ís gathered around mass grave where the bodies of the ten Bahá'í women were buried.

Olya, after here escape from Iran, presented as a key witness at the European Commission for Human Rights in Brussals.

She taught Bahá'í children's classes, was a member of the Youth Committee and just before her arrest was appointed as a member of the Publishing Committee and an assistant, as I was. While the Bahá'ís were being subjected to fierce opposition and their every move was closely watched, she fearlessly put her books under her arm and travelled from house to house, encouraging the Bahá'í youth.

Zarrín had had a remarkable gift for reciting poetry even as a child, and as she grew older she wrote beautiful, poetic articles and essays. On the occasion of Dr Mihdí Anvarí's and Hidáyat Dihqání's execution, she wrote movingly about the mystery of sacrifice and about the bravery of Dr Anvarí's son and daughter, her personal friends; and after visiting prisoners in Adelabad, she described the spirituality and courage of the prisoners in terms that were prophetic of her own experience as a prisoner a year later. This is an extract from that poem:

I have come from Adelabad tonight.
What can I write, how can I pen a description of that
    place?
In what tongue can I portray the sort of world it is?
Which words can express what I beheld with humble,
    earthly eyes?
Sweet vision or bitter reality?
I blink my eyes to see . . .

I have come from Adelabad tonight,
The abode of detached lovers,
Of moths burnt in the flame of the love of God.
Within those heavy, towering walls,
Souls mightier than the walls lie chained.
If only I could ask those walls: What hast thou beheld?
Recount it to me! Tell me of the whisperings of love,
And of the murmurings of prayers that waft
Through the iron bars at the hour of dawn,
Of tear drops that slowly fall upon the cheeks! . . .

I have come from Adelabad tonight.
I have returned from the land of the enamoured,

From the land of the afflicted lovers, guests at the feast of
     tribulation.
Inquire of me as to what I have seen!
Ask me, so that I may recount to you that I beheld
The blazing flame of faith in the eyes of that intoxicated
     lover,
I saw his head held high, heard him exultantly proclaim:
See, I finally attained my heart's desire! . . .

I have come from Adelabad tonight,
The abode of harvest-burnt Majnuns
And lovers gazing at the face of the Beloved.
I have come from the boundary between life and eternity,
Between the universe of dust and the world of the
     Kingdom!
And you, O wayfarer, should you some day pass by that
     spot,
Tarry a while, fix your gaze on those high stone walls,
Look at those iron gates;
Then close your eyes and hearken with the ears of the
     spirit,
That perchance you too might hear
This murmur rising from every single stone:

This is the Vale of Love, hold thy steps!

Zarrín was under tremendous pressure for five years prior to
her arrest, particularly because of her involvement with efforts
to protect the House of the Báb. I remember seeing Zarrín and
her father speaking kindly to fanatical Muslims and explaining
Bahá'í teachings to them while they were in the act of destroying the holy house. Zarrín and her parents were among the
first group of Bahá'ís arrested in October 1982. I never saw
Zarrín in Sepah, but I heard from some of the prisoners about
her direct and brave response to the questions of the guards
and the interrogators, and how impressive her strength had
seemed to them. Later, when I was transferred to Adelabad, I
got a chance to speak to her, and she described her experiences
to me.

When I was in Sepah the investigators put me on trial every day for long hours, asking me questions about my beliefs. I was on trial with Bahrám Yaldá'í, because we were both members of the Education Committee.

One day, they put me in a room on my own and kept me blindfolded for seven hours while they asked questions. I answered the questions from my knowledge of the Qur'án and Bahá'í writings. Then the investigator suddenly said, 'Now, Brothers, what do you have to say to this girl? I myself have nothing more to say. She claims she is a Bahá'í, and that the promised one whom we are all waiting for has come. If you have any questions, you can ask her yourself.'

There was a moment of silence and then I heard the sound of several people leaving the room one after another. I said to the investigator, 'I don't know what is going on here. How many people were here during my trial?'

'I have asked you questions many times, and I told them all about your bravery, your perseverance and your knowledge but they didn't believe me, so I asked them to come here today and see for themselves.'

He asked me what I thought my sentence would be.

'Ultimately, execution, but I would prefer to die and have told you the truth rather than be guilty in the divine court of justice.'

Another day the investigator was insisting that I recant. I said, 'I am a Bahá'í, and under no circumstances will I recant my faith.'

He said, 'Up to what point will you adhere to your beliefs? To the moment of execution?' I replied that I would, but he wouldn't give up and kept repeating that I must recant.

'Your honour,' I said, 'for days you have been asking me the same questions. I have written and signed numerous statements that I would prefer to die rather than recant. I don't think it is necessary to keep repeating the same question! I gave you a definite answer the first day. If you propose the same thing for years to

come, I will still give you the same answer. Why don't
you leave me alone?' I began to sob. 'In what language
must I tell you, my being is Bahá'u'lláh, my love is
Bahá'u'lláh, my whole heart is Bahá'u'lláh.'

'I will tear your heart from your chest!' he shouted
angrily.

'Then my heart will call out and cry, "Bahá'u'lláh,
Bahá'u'lláh".'

He rushed out of the room, moved by my display of
emotion, and when he came back he found me still
sobbing.

'You are still crying, Miss? We are human beings
too, you know – we have feelings too.'

They used every trick to torment us and to try and
break the trust between us. One day after a long trial in
Adelabad, the investigator called on me and my parents
to go to Sepah, and there they confronted us with
Suhayl Húshmand. I could tell he had been tortured,
although we were blindfolded during the entire trial; it
was obvious they had forced him to confirm false
charges against us. They said, 'Suhayl here has admitted
that Mr and Mrs Muqímí went to Israel a few years ago
on a spying mission; the three of you must admit to the
fact that you are spies for Israel and the Universal
House of Justice.'

I was very naive about their devious methods at
that time and I believed them. I said, 'Suhayl, I hope
God forgives your lies. We are not spies and we don't
have anything to hide. Every individual Bahá'í is forbidden to take part in politics. Anyone who breaks this
rule and becomes involved in political activities is not a
Bahá'í. We have been ordered to abide by the laws of
the government of the country we live in. My parents
went to Israel years ago, purely on a pilgrimage.'

'Your honour,' my mother said, 'I am an old and
uneducated woman. I don't know anything about spying
and politics. Once I went to Israel to visit the Bahá'í
holy places, just as you go to Iraq to visit the grave of
Imám Husayn. Does that make you a spy for Iraq?'

Zarrín's mother was released shortly afterwards, without any security bond being demanded, but Zarrín and her father remained in prison.

Because of Zarrín's extensive knowledge of religion, she was especially at risk. The more learning we revealed, the harder they leant on us and the more guilty we became in their eyes. I specifically mentioned to Zarrín, the night before her final trial, that she should be careful. 'The prosecutor is a very prejudiced man, and if he finds out how knowledgeable you are, it will antagonize him and he will order your execution.'

She looked at me and smiled. The last thing on her mind was her freedom. 'Now that we have this opportunity, we must teach them the truth and help them to understand it. We can't afford to be scared of what they might do. We have to be honest, answer every question they ask us in detail and not leave anything unexplained. We have to put the Faith before ourselves and our own lives, and sacrifice absolutely everything for the truth.'

A few minutes later she returned to my cell holding a piece of elastic, a needle, some thread and her black chador which we had to wear every day. 'I must sew this piece of elastic to my chador so I can easily put it around my neck and not worry about it slipping from my head. Then I can concentrate on what they have to say to me tomorrow and not be distracted.' This was how she prepared herself, calmly and decisively, for the next day.

She woke up at 4 a.m. to pray, and then kissed us goodbye. At five o'clock they called her to the lobby, and it was 8 p.m. when she returned. She had been charged with participation in the Bahá'í administration, being a spy for Israel, a Bahá'í class teacher, a member of various local committees, not being married, and refusing to recant her faith. She had been sentenced to be hanged unless she recanted, and she had courageously told the prosecutor: 'I have found the truth, and I will not give it away at any price.' She was twenty-eight.

Símín, A<u>kh</u>tar & Ma<u>h</u>shíd

CHAPTER 11

In prison, Zarrín's closest friend was Símín Sábirí, who was very like her in many ways. Símín was among the first large group of Bahá'ís arrested in October 1982. She was twenty-four, the youngest of a large family, and the youngest assistant in <u>Sh</u>íráz. She was a member of the Bahá'í Education Committee, a liaison for the Local Spiritual Assembly and she taught Bahá'í children's classes. In December 1978 when angry mobs looted and set fire to the homes of many Bahá'ís in <u>Sh</u>íráz, the Sábirís' house was attacked and later confiscated.

Símín was a brave, cheerful and lovable girl who had studied at secretarial college and worked for an agricultural firm in <u>Sh</u>íráz. During her trials she was fearless and outspoken about her involvement in Bahá'í activities, and very direct in her lectures to the interrogators about the validity of the teachings of Bahá'u'lláh. After prolonged and intense interrogation in Sepah she was transferred to Adelabad before my arrest and we were like ships that pass in the night – she was taken back to Sepah for an interrogation session in the very bus that brought us from Adelabad. We were all very impressed by the way she managed to give the guards the slip that day so she could try to find out from us why she was being recalled.

Two days later she came back. She said they had put tremendous pressure on her to give them a list of committee members but in the end they let her go. Despite the trauma of going back to Sepah, she had been glad to have the chance to spend some time with Rúhíyyih Jahánpúr and Nusrat Yaldá'í. 'I at least had the opportunity to make poor Mrs Yaldá'í laugh,' she said.

Símín always found something to laugh about. Whenever someone in the prison was upset, she would joke and joke until they laughed. She was absolutely sure about what was going to happen to her, however, because before her arrest she had had a dream in which Bahá'u'lláh had told her He was going to take her away with Him. She always used to say, 'Zarrín, Mrs Zá'irpúr, Mrs Yaldá'í and I are going for certain.'

She was filled with love for Bahá'u'lláh, and very proud of the fact that all the Bahá'ís in prison expounded fully on the principles of the Faith during their trials. 'Because there is such a large group of us together in prison, we will be recognized by the world,' she said. 'The Islamic regime will be forced to announce the banning of Bahá'í administrative activities, and make it illegal to practise the Bahá'í Faith. Then the world will know about us.'

A favourite joke of hers that always made us laugh concerned dying and going to 'heaven'. She used to say that when she died she was going to turn everything upside down in heaven, just to make things more difficult for the angels, so that they would go through something of what we all had to endure down here on earth. Of course, Bahá'ís don't believe in heaven as a place up in the sky, but her imagination was so active she used to have us doubled up with laughter.

I never saw her depressed or unhappy except one early morning when she came to my cell with tears in her eyes, saying, 'Last night I had a dream that Zíyá Ahrárí came to Adelabad and asked all of us to explain what we had done for the Faith. I answered, "We have made the principles of the Faith known to the guards, and have tried to clear up any misunderstandings so that they would look positively on the Faith." But Dr Ahrárí replied, "You haven't done anything yet. The cause of God needs the blood of the Bahá'ís. That's why we have given our lives to His cause." '

With tears running down her face, Símín said: 'It is just as Dr Ahrárí said, we haven't done a thing yet.' From that day on she couldn't sit still. She went from cell to cell repeating, 'We haven't done anything yet.'

I vividly remember the last stages of her trial. One afternoon she returned to the cells and told us cheerfully: 'The

Religious Magistrate has sentenced me to death by hanging. He
wrote sixteen charges against me, and said that if I would say
only one word to indicate that I was not a Bahá'í, I would be
released. I told him I would prefer the sentence of death.'

Akhtar Sabet was born into a poor Bahá'í family in Sarvistán in
1958, the daughter of a small shopkeeper. She was brought up
in an environment where Bahá'ís were frequently attacked and
persecuted. In school she had always been hard-working and
popular, and her teacher had told her mother that she was
exceptionally intelligent and talented. Akhtar always assisted
her classmates in their studies and homework, and even though
the parents of the other children knew she was a Bahá'í and
were often prejudiced against the Faith, they trusted her more
than anyone else to be with their children.

Akhtar was twenty at the beginning of the revolution when
mobs attacked the Bahá'ís of Sarvistán, plundering and burning
their homes and businesses. Her family were among the 300
Bahá'ís who were made homeless that night. They managed to
escape from Sarvistán, crossing the mountains and valleys on foot
to reach the relative safety of Shíráz, where they eventually settled.

Akhtar resumed her education and got a degree in paedi-
atric nursing, then began work in one of the hospitals in Shíráz.
She carried out her duties as a nurse with love, care and dedication, often staying late and working overtime for no extra pay
when there were patients needing special attention. She was a
down-to-earth girl who preferred to make her own clothes and
dressed very simply, but elegantly.

From childhood Akhtar had always loved participating
actively in the local Bahá'í community. Her mother told me:

The night before her arrest I knew in my heart that
something was going to happen. I pleaded with her to
leave Shíráz for a few days. I said, 'You know they are
looking for people who are well-known in the Bahá'í
administration. You are a member of a committee and a
Bahá'í children's teacher. They will come for you.'

But she answered, 'My dear Mother, we have to rely
on God. What He has ordained for us will happen. We

haven't done anything wrong, so why should we be scared?'

A<u>kh</u>tar's parents were not at home when, on 23 October 1982, a group of guards attacked their house and the houses of other Bahá'ís in <u>Sh</u>íráz, arresting over forty people and taking them to prison. A<u>kh</u>tar's sister was the only witness to her arrest.

Her trial was shorter than most people's, and we all thought she would be released quite quickly.

Her imprisonment caused great concern to her colleagues at the hospital where she had worked, and the president of the hospital, a Muslim, called the Public Prosecutor and said, 'Why are you keeping a poor innocent soul like A<u>kh</u>tar in prison? Why don't you let her go? We need her help in the hospital. She was our best children's nurse.'

The Public Prosecutor replied, 'Her crime is that she is a Bahá'í and active in the Bahá'í administration. Therefore, she must be punished; but if she says she is a Muslim we will release her.'

A<u>kh</u>tar always used her medical knowledge to care for the other prisoners' health, despite the lack of even the most basic facilities. We shared the same cell for a while in Adelabad, and I remember one day I had a pain in my chest, probably due to the lack of fresh air and all the tension I was suffering. A<u>kh</u>tar pleaded with the guards to get me a doctor, but they wouldn't, so she took over my care, using her experience as a nurse, and treated me with some salt and sugar until I gradually felt better.

When Ṭúbá Zá'irpúr was transferred at last to Adelabad in a weakened state, A<u>kh</u>tar devoted herself to looking after her. She washed her clothes, helped her shower and did everything she could to make her life more comfortable. In fact she was kind and considerate to everyone; it didn't matter if they were murderers, prostitutes, or drug addicts. The other prisoners always invited A<u>kh</u>tar to their cells and appreciated her warm-hearted and gentle nature. Every day she used to get up early and walk in front of the cells, carefully and quietly chanting prayers in her lovely voice. She never complained about all the difficulties in prison and on visiting days she always faced her family joyfully and confidently. She always asked her parents and her sister and brother to pray that she could do what Bahá'u'lláh wanted her to do.

I distinctly remember her final trial. They called her at five o'clock in the morning and took her, under armed guard, to the Religious Magistrate for the final verdict. They brought her back after a short time.

'Akhtar, what did they say?' I asked her.

She smiled and said, 'Like the others, he told me "Either you come back to Islam or you die." '

We were all gathered around her. 'Akhtar, why didn't you try to talk to them?' we asked. 'You weren't as involved in the administration as the others. The guards are more interested in the ones who were more active, like members of the assemblies, or the liaisons and assistants.'

Akhtar said, 'I simply told the Religious Magistrate that I was a Bahá'í and I would not recant. That is all I said. I didn't plead or anything.' Then she continued, 'I am completely unconcerned, because I am sure it will not be the will of the magistrate nor mine that determines my destiny. Whatever God has ordained will happen.'

The charges against her were that she was a Bahá'í; that she taught Bahá'í children's classes; and that she was not married. She was twenty-four years old, and she was sentenced to death.

Another of the young prisoners was Mahshíd Nírúmand. Mahshíd was born into a Bahá'í family in Shíráz in 1955. Her father was a technical worker, and though they were not a wealthy family, they had a comfortable life. Mahshíd was a quiet person who normally kept to herself, but at times she could be very funny. She had a naive, childlike quality about her, but was also very mature and intelligent.

Mahshíd was a good student and passed her exams every year with good marks. Túbá Zá'irpúr was one of her teachers for a while. She went on to Pahlaví University to study physics, but because of her special interest in geophysics, she took extra courses in geology as well. Had university policy permitted it, she would have liked to have stayed on after her graduation, and in another six months she would have achieved a double major and received her second Bachelor of Science degree.

As well as English, which was the working language at university, Mahshíd learned French and German by attending optional courses. After finishing all her studies so successfully, and even though she had paid back her student loan in full, the authorities refused to give her a degree certificate because she was a Bahá'í.

Mahshíd was a very conscientious person, both in her work and her private life. She believed that the opportunity to serve was God's favour to the individual, so one had to take full advantage of this favour and always give of one's best. Her mother later told me that she used to wake herself up in the middle of the night to pray and meditate. She found it easier to concentrate when everyone else was asleep and all was quiet.

Before she was arrested she, always said, 'I wish I could trade places with someone in prison.' Just before her arrest, as if she could foresee what would happen, she prepared herself by reviewing the prayers she had memorized, and studied some new writings so she would be able to answer the investigators with actual quotations. She kept a set of clean clothes ready so she would be prepared to go to prison at any time. She even started to sleep on the floor without a pillow, telling her mother, 'I must build up my tolerance to hardship. If one day I am arrested and have to go to prison, I must be able to sleep on the floor.'

It was not long before her premonitions were realized, and she was arrested and taken to Sepah. We were arrested on the same night, and then transferred to Adelabad together just over a month later, so I came to know her very well, although by nature she was shy and retiring.

Mahshíd was as hard-working in prison as she had been at home. The younger Bahá'ís took responsibility for the tasks we had been given. 'You are like our mothers,' they argued. 'How can we sit and watch you work? Let us do it.' Mahshíd took on the job of washing all the dishes.

Although we were very close and united in prison, and shared the same beliefs, it didn't mean we were all alike. Quite the contrary. Mahshíd, for example, was a very serious young woman, always neat and tidy. Roya Ishráqí, on the other hand, had a very bubbly, easy going personality, and couldn't resist playing practical jokes on her in Adelabad to cheer her up. One of her favourite pranks was to slip into Mahshíd's cell just after she had finished tidying it, and mess it all up again. When Mahshíd got back from her interrogation or visiting one of the other prisoners, everyone would laugh as she tried to find where Roya was hiding.

Roya was always the first to wake up, and another of her antics was to sneak into Mahshíd's cell in the morning and strip her blanket off crying, 'Wake up, lazy bones!' Mahshíd feigned a long-suffering attitude, taking it all in good spirit.

Mahshíd had great inner strength, and she always comforted her parents during family visits, and urged them to be patient and firm. I remember that during her first visit with her parents she brought out her hand from under her chador and showed them her clenched fist as a symbol of strength and steadfastness.

She was incredibly brave and honest during her interrogations in Sepah, which were usually conducted at the same time as mine; she always avoided mentioning any names, but explained in detail her own activities and services. Mahshíd's replies to the interrogators were always calm and measured, in contrast with my own impulsive desire to shout back at them. She was always worried I would get myself into trouble with my quick tongue, and used to say, 'Olya, be careful! Don't talk back to them.'

Once they took Mahshíd alone to the basement where they tortured prisoners. Hours later they brought her back to join us in the interrogation room, and then sent us all back to the cell. Mahshíd told us what had happened.

When they separated me from you I was blindfolded and taken to the basement, and they made me sit on a wooden table they use when they whip people. I could hear people screaming and crying all around me. The guards swore at me and insulted me. Later they uncovered my eyes. There were chains hanging from the four corners of the table, and two investigators wearing masks were standing in front of me.

There was also a man who called himself 'Abdu'lláh – he was the one who tortured the prisoners. He had a wire cable in his hand and was threatening to whip me. Sometimes they yelled at me and sometimes they begged me to recant and to give them the names of the other committee members. I simply told them, 'I will not recant or give you any names even if you tear me apart.'

'Abdu'lláh began to get angry and kept playing with the wire cable in his hands and threatening me. I said, 'I have told you everything you wanted to know.' They were so inhuman that I was sure I would be flogged. I asked as calmly as I could, 'On which side would you like me to lie down? Do you want to whip my back first or the soles of my feet?' My composure just made them laugh.

One day I came across Mahshíd lying on the floor of her cell staring at the ceiling, deep in thought. I went to her and asked, 'What's wrong, Mahshíd, has something happened?'

She simply smiled, replying, 'No, nothing important,' but I persisted and she said, 'For two nights running now I've had the same dream. I know they will execute me. Even if they let everyone else go, I know they will execute me. But I am not afraid. I have surrendered to His will.'

'Mahshíd, why are you saying this? We all hope that these misunderstandings will soon be put right and our innocence will be proved to the Revolutionary Court.'

'You will know, when I am executed,' replied Mahshíd with a smile, 'that my dream was a true dream.'

Mahshíd was transferred with us to Adelabad after over a month of non-stop interrogation, and on 16 January she was taken to the Revolutionary Court for prosecution. Four days later she faced her final trial before the Religious Magistrate. She was charged with being a Bahá'í, attending Bahá'í classes as a child, being a Bahá'í class teacher, being a member of the Youth Committee, giving money to the Bahá'í fund, being unmarried, and being a supporter of Zionism. She, too, was condemned to death.

'Sweetness'

Shírín Dálvand was born into a Bahá'í family in Shíráz in 1956. Her real name was Shahín, but because she was such a lovely child she was always called Shírín, which means 'sweetness'.

Shírín was very calm, caring and affectionate. Not only was she extremely loving towards people, she had a very soft heart for animals and even plants. Her mother told me there was a plant that Shírín was allergic to growing in the family's back yard. Her father wanted to uproot it, but she wouldn't let him do that. She preferred to cover her face every time she passed the plant rather than have it destroyed.

Throughout her school years Shírín always earned the highest grades. She was accepted into the Pahlaví University in Shíráz at nineteen, majoring in sociology. While there she researched and wrote a thesis about drug addiction and what it was that made certain people more prone to it than others. Her report was so thorough and contained such useful insights from her interviews with addicts that it was later used by her professors when teaching their own classes. As well as working hard at her studies, Shírín was an enthusiastic member of the Youth Committee and later the Bahá'í Education Committee. Just before her arrest, she had been appointed to serve as a liaison for the Local Spiritual Assembly of Shíráz.

She was arrested just a few hours after me. 'Izzat, Roya, Mínú, Ṭáhirih and myself were already in the cell, quietly sharing stories of our arrest when once again we heard the clang of the iron bolts on the main door sliding open. Every time the cell doors opened the mentally ill prisoners would laugh loudly, a strange, ugly sound to the ears of a new arrival.

Consequently we would leap up to greet the newcomers quickly and reassure them.

It was about 3 a.m. when S͟hírín was brought in together with Mítrá Íraván and Rúḥíyyih Jahánpúr. I went to hug S͟hírín, who was the first one to come into the cell, and for a while we all greeted each other and asked about news. S͟hírín told me the story of her arrest.

> I was at Mrs Jahánpúr's house for dinner. At eleven o'clock, the guards burst in and asked everyone to identify themselves. When I told them my name they looked on their list and said, 'Your name is on here, you must come with us.' They wanted Rúḥíyyih to come too.
>
> My family and friends had suggested that I leave S͟híráz for a while and go to Tehran because there was a danger I might be arrested, but I couldn't bring myself to leave them all at this critical time. This was an opportunity to sacrifice and be firm. The Bahá'ís desperately needed each other's support. How could I leave S͟híráz?
>
> Last night we had a meeting of the committee, and Mahs͟híd Nírúmand, Roya Is͟hráqí and Mítrá Íraván were all there. We talked about ways in which we could support the youth under the present circumstances, and although everyone thought there was a good chance of getting arrested even as we sat in that meeting, we decided to go ahead with our projects without any fear or delay. I was completely ready for my arrest. I had already explained to my grandmother what she needed to do when I was imprisoned.

At the beginning of the revolution S͟hírín's family, herself included, had left Iran for England, but S͟hírín had returned because of her studies and was living with her grandmother. Her family, living in Newcastle-upon-Tyne, kept up with the news in Iran, and they could see that the opposition to the Faith was becoming more intense. They constantly asked her to leave Iran and rejoin them in England, but her response was always, 'My blood is no thicker than that of other Bahá'ís in Iran. How can I leave when so many of my friends' lives are in danger?'

A few days after our arrest they started putting us on trial, and we were each called at least once – except Mítrá and Shírín, who hadn't been called at all. Shírín was very patient, and never talked about her worries or fears, but at night in her sleep she would sometimes call out. Before we had been forbidden to chant prayers in prison, we used to ask Shírín to chant for us because she had such a lovely, soothing voice.

On 24 December, after nearly a month of imprisonment, I was sitting in the corner of our cell feeling very depressed. It was my eldest son Behnam's birthday, and he didn't even know I was in prison because I wouldn't let Morad tell the boys. Every time they rang from England and asked to speak to me, poor Morad told them I was at my brother's house, or had just popped out. We thought it would save them unnecessary worry.

Shírín saw my tears and swiftly came over to sit beside me to ask why I was so sad. I explained to her, and she replied quietly, 'Never mind, tomorrow is my birthday as well.' We hugged each other and she said happily, 'Now I feel you are my mother too.'

The next day, as we were dividing out the food the guards had left outside our cell for lunch, Shírín announced to everyone, 'Well, today is my birthday. Last year my mother sent me a beautiful night-gown from England, which I had been saving for my wedding night. This year, I am in prison for my beloved Bahá'u'lláh.'

I can't explain our feelings at that moment. We had nothing to give her as a birthday present, so we each took some food from our plates and gave it to her. That was how we celebrated Shírín's birthday.

That day was, coincidentally, the day we were finally permitted our first visitors. There was an indescribable excitement among the Bahá'í prisoners, and we were reminding each other to smile so our families wouldn't guess what we were going through. Since neither Shírín nor Mítrá had yet been on trial, they were worried because the policy at that time was that prisoners could not have visitors until they had been on trial at least once. Shírín sat in a corner crying quietly.

'I feel so sorry for my grandmother,' she said. 'Today, like every day, she will come hoping to see me. If they don't let me see her today on my birthday she will be heartbroken. And when my parents telephone and find out that all the other prisoners except me have been allowed visits with their families, they will be worried to death.'

But when the time came for us to see our families, much to our surprise the first person they called was Shírín. We were all so happy for her, even the non-Bahá'ís. She was able to see her grandmother that day and to talk to her through the glass partition for a few minutes.

Later, I told her, 'Shírín, you have a wonderful protector. God is always looking after you. Even though your parents are not here, He does not let you feel alone.'

There were a few occasions in prison when the situation looked bad for Shírín, but the minute she became unhappy enough to cry, something would happen and the impossible would be achieved. She was a special being.

That day her grandmother sent her some new clothing as a birthday gift. She took the items out of the plastic bag one by one and admired each in turn. Then she noticed a small mirror wrapped in some tissue among the clothes. We were all surprised, because prison regulations did not permit prisoners to have mirrors, and we all admired her grandmother's cleverness for having wrapped it in such a way that the guards had not detected it.

Shírín passed the mirror around, and we were all able to see our tired, yellow faces for the first time in a month. When Shírín first saw her face in that mirror, she said with a heart full of hope, 'With God's help, I will look normal again when I am released.'

She had also been given two pairs of slippers, and since I didn't have any, she gave one pair to me. The night I was arrested I was wearing high heels, but we were not allowed to wear them in prison, because according to the Religious Magistrate a woman's footsteps should not be heard by men. He said the sound aroused men's sexual desire. Since many prisoners had their feet whipped, they couldn't wear high heels anyway. We all wore slippers or soft, flat shoes. Sometimes our families, in their love and concern for us, sent us things that got us into trouble in prison. For example, my family once sent me a brand new, glamorous night-gown. I was very lucky the guards didn't see it and I had a chance to send it back. It made us all laugh to think of my wearing a flimsy night-gown to sleep in that cold, filthy prison cell.

Our families really had no idea about the conditions we were living in, because on visiting days we tried to look happy and healthy so they wouldn't lose heart. We never talked about the conditions in the cell or about the way we were treated. This made visiting days something of a test, because on the one hand we were extremely pleased to see our families, but on the other we hardly had the energy to stand on our feet, let alone to try and look strong and cheerful.

The following day, Shírín was called to trial for the first time, and luckily I was with her. She was brave and straightforward, courageously admitting her membership in the Youth Committee and explaining its responsibilities, but never mentioning any names during her trial. She had promised herself that she would not be the cause of anyone else's suffering.

Each day, Shírín's trials were twelve to fourteen hours long, and I was with her for most of them. The only thing that worried her was the fact that the investigators might question her parents' absence from Iran. Luckily, Shírín's grandmother pretended to be her mother in order to be allowed to visit her; that was why the guards did not suspect her family had left the country. She also had a brother-in-law who had been named to the investigators as an Auxiliary Board Member but who had left Iran. Shírín was afraid that if they found out he was related to her, they would torture her to try and get his address outside Iran, and his and his family's lives might be put in danger even though they lived abroad.

Her concern was valid because the investigators always asked for the complete addresses and phone numbers of those people who had left Iran. She was constantly worried about the safety of her family. I recall the time her grandmother managed to let her know her parents were extremely anxious about her and they were considering returning to Iran. It upset Shírín to think that her parents might come back under the present conditions, just for her sake. They could easily have been arrested and imprisoned as well.

'Besides,' she said, 'I don't want my mother to leave my brother and sisters in England and come here and see me, looking such a mess and so pale, through prison bars. If I am to be killed, I want my mother to remember me as the Shírín she pictures in her mind now, healthy and full of energy.'

One day Shírín woke up crying. She had had a dream about her mother, where she heard her mother calling and she kept answering, but her mother couldn't hear her. Though she was awake now, she said, she could still hear her mother calling her name. 'Izzat and I embraced her and tried to comfort her in her loneliness. 'Don't worry,' I reassured her, 'God willing, we will be released soon and I will take you to England and put your hand in your mother's.'

But Shírín replied, smiling through her tears, 'Even if I am released, I will stay in Iran as long as I am needed here.'

I repeated my offer in private, saying, 'Shírín, if they release us, would you come with me to England so that you can be with your parents and I can be with my children?'

She didn't answer my question at first but her eyes seemed to say, 'How could we leave our friends in the present situation? This is the time to sacrifice our own preferences.' I persisted, and this time she said quickly, '*Nah. Man Nah* – No, not me.'

Shírín's grandmother was extremely kind to her. She always brought her the best fruit, although Shírín never got any of it because it went into the communal fruit basket. But she had made friends with all of the prisoners, Bahá'ís and Muslims, and she never begrudged sharing everything she had. I could never tell who among the prisoners was her closest friend because she talked to everyone in the same loving, sincere manner.

One day the investigator asked Shírín, Mítrá, Roya and Mahshíd why they were not married. They each answered. One of them said, 'It hasn't been a part of my destiny yet.' Another said, 'I haven't thought about it yet.' Shírín replied, 'Inflation has made it very difficult to get married these days!'

'Don't give me that,' snapped the investigator. 'Just admit that you haven't married so that you can be free to attend meetings and become members of committees for corrupting young people. One of the charges we have against you all is that you are not married.'

In fact, Shírín was deeply in love with Hidáyat Síyávushí, Jamshíd's cousin. He had been in prison for over a year when Shírín was arrested, and was under sentence of death. They had already made a private agreement to get married, but were not formally engaged. Apart from their families, only a few of the Bahá'í prisoners knew about it. Shírín endured their long separation with her usual patience, but she told me privately how much she worried about him. She had tried to visit him in prison, but as she wasn't a relative the guards wouldn't let her in. Now, even though they were both being held in Sepah, they never had a chance to meet.

The Saturday after Shírín's birthday, we were waiting for our visitors to arrive when in rushed my mother at the head of the queue, looking very worried. When she sat down she put her head in her hands. I asked her what had happened, but she replied, 'Nothing.'

I begged her to tell me her news, no matter how bad it was. Could it be little Payam? Had Morad been arrested? Some of the other visitors said, 'Tell her, it's better that she knows.'

'Hidáyat was hanged yesterday,' said my mother.

'Thank God!' I replied. 'At last it's over for him, and he stayed strong to the end.'

When I got back to the cell, I laid out all the oranges Mother had brought for me and invited all the Bahá'ís to come and say prayers. Everyone was anxious to know what had happened, and as gently as I could I told them about Hidáyat. Shírín gasped and burst into tears. She cried and cried.

Later, when all was calm, we had a short memorial service for him in my cell, and Shírín recited this prayer from memory:

O God, my God! Thou hast lighted the lamp of Thy Cause with the oil of wisdom; protect it from contrary winds. The lamp is Thine, and the glass is Thine, and all things in the heavens and on earth are in the grasp of Thy power. Bestow justice upon the rulers, and fairness upon the divines. Thou art the All-Powerful, Who, through the motion of Thy Pen,

hast aided Thine irresistible Cause, and guided aright Thy
loved ones. Thou art the Possessor of power, and the King of
might. No God is there but Thee, the Strong, the
Unconstrained.

In both Adelabad and Sepah, due to the dreadful conditions, Shírín came down with a bad cold and a kidney infection. All of us suffered sickness of one sort or another, but the guards were not in the least concerned about our illnesses. Finally, after practically begging for help from a female guard, three of us were allowed to visit the prison clinic in Adelabad.

The clinic's doctor was, as I have mentioned, a Bahá'í who had not been involved with the community for many years. He had also, coincidentally, once been my family doctor. I was so weak and pale that he didn't recognize me at first, and he kept asking my name and studying my face.

The doctor said that all three of us were seriously ill and in need of treatment, and that Shírín and I needed an injection. Since the Revolutionary Court had prohibited male doctors from touching female patients, the injections had to be given to us once again by untrained young girls, and they bruised our hands so badly they were quite sore for a few days afterwards.

After the second stage of Shírín's trial in Adelabad, she returned looking happy, and gave us the good news that she was to be released from prison. 'The prosecutor ordered my release, along with Rúhíyyih, Mínú and Mítrá, on a security bond of 40,000 tuman each. Mínú's husband was standing by the court entrance during the trial, and he immediately gave them a cheque for 40,000 tuman and took her straight home.'

The prosecutor later increased the security bond required for Rúhíyyih and Shírín to 80,000 tuman each, but for Mítrá Íraván it was left at 40,000. The three of them only had to wait for their families to bring in the house deeds or other documents equivalent to the sum that had been set for their release and they would be free. We were all so happy that night.

The next day at noon Rúhíyyih's family brought a document to the court and she was released. But Mítrá Íraván's family refused to give the court the 40,000 tuman required, and her release order was cancelled.

Shírín meanwhile was eagerly expecting her grandmother
to bring the security bond and rescue her. Three days passed,
and I was taken in for the second stage of my trial before the
same prosecutor as the other women. As I was being questioned, I saw a number of Bahá'ís coming into the prison to
enquire about their loved ones. They all entered very politely
and asked calmly about their children, parents, spouses and so
on. But it made the Public Prosecutor very uncomfortable, to
the point where he refused to answer any more of their questions. Then Shírín's grandmother came in to see him.

She was holding the security bond for the release of her
beloved granddaughter. She came forward and presented the
document to him, saying, 'Your honour, this is the document
you requested for Shírín's freedom.'

He looked at her coldly and said, 'It is three days since I
ordered her release. You were supposed to bring it earlier.'

'I needed some time to prepare it, your honour,' she pleaded.

'You are too late,' he said dismissively. 'Only today I sent
her file over to the Religious Magistrate for her final trial.'

The poor old woman began begging him to find the file and
release her granddaughter. But nothing she could say touched
his heart. The helpless woman at last left the room in despair,
but she returned three times, each time pleading desperately for
Shírín's freedom. 'Your honour, you ordered her release along
with Rúhíyyih Jahánpúr. She was set free, yet Shírín is still
here.'

'Rúhíyyih has only been released temporarily,' he replied.
'We had her sign a form saying she would turn herself in for a
final trial. In four days' time we will send for her again to
appear before the Religious Magistrate.'

That evening, as soon as Shírín saw me returning to my
cell, she ran towards me happily saying, 'Did my grandmother
bring the document? Am I going to be free soon?'

I didn't know how to tell her. I held her hand and drew her
into my cell. I knew how strong she was and I had witnessed
her bravery so often during our trials, so I told her frankly what
had happened in the prosecutor's office.

'I don't think I will ever be released,' she said. She sighed
and tears rolled down her cheeks. 'I feel so sorry for my grand-

mother. God knows what she has gone through in these past few months.'

Then she looked at me calmly and said with absolute resignation, 'If you ever leave Iran and see my family, send my love to each and every one of them, and please, Olya, tell the world the whole story.'

The Ishráqí Family

CHAPTER 13

'Izzat and Roya Ishráqí were the first familiar faces I saw when I walked into that dark cell the night I was arrested. The Revolutionary Guards had come for them at 8.30 p.m., a few hours before they came for me. What a warm reception 'Izzat and Roya gave me on my arrival. It was like coming home!

I first got to know the Ishráqí family when the guards confiscated the homes of those Bahá'ís living in the alley of the House of the Báb and two elderly sisters, members of the Afnán family, had been evicted. I remembered that the Ishráqís had offered to shelter homeless Bahá'ís, so I took the two women over and they were lovingly offered a room, even though the house was barely big enough for a family of four as it was.

'Ináyat Ishráqí was born in 1921 in Isfahán, but had moved to Shíráz to work for the National Iranian Oil Company. He had already retired before I started working there, but his colleagues often referred to his kindness and honesty and he was very popular with everyone. His pension was cut off in 1982 because he was a Bahá'í, and this made life difficult for the family, but somehow they managed.

'Ináyat was a member of the Marriage and Counselling Committee, which offered advice to Bahá'ís with personal problems. He was also an assistant, and a member of the third reserve assembly for Shíráz. By the end of November 1982, following the October arrests, the third reserve assembly had already stepped into the shoes of its two predecessors.

'Izzat, his wife, was a member of the same committee, and Roya, who had been studying veterinary science at Shíráz University until all the Bahá'ís were suspended, was a member

of the Youth Committee and taught Bahá'í children's classes.
All three were arrested that night, leaving the youngest
member of the family, seventeen-year-old Rosita, alone.

This was not the first time the Ishráqís had been arrested.
A year earlier the guards had arrested all four of them, as well as
an American house guest, and kept them in Sepah for three
days. I had then had the responsibility of sending the account
of their arrest and imprisonment out of Iran.

That first night in the women's cell in Sepah, we stayed
awake until the early hours of the morning talking about our
experiences at the hands of the authorities. 'Izzat told me about
their arrest.

A few hours before, we were at my brother's house
having dinner. It was as if I knew something was
going to happen; I was worried and uncomfortable. I
suggested to my husband and daughters that they
should go to Isfahán for a few days, but my husband
said, 'How could we leave Shíráz under the present circumstances, when all the Bahá'ís are in danger, and in
need of each other's support?' He added, 'Also, since I
have been elected as a member of the Local Spiritual
Assembly, I would not be able to forgive myself if I left
Shíráz now.'

Roya and Rosita laughed at me and said they were
not afraid. Whatever was destined to happen would
happen, and we would just have to accept it, they said.

We returned home, and as soon as we turned on
the lights three guards burst into the house. After
searching the whole house for several hours, they put
all the Bahá'í documents and books into a sack. They
insulted me and my husband and ridiculed our religion,
and then ordered us to get ready to leave.

As we were preparing to go they checked a list they
had in their hands and saw Roya's name was also on it;
they told her she had to come too. I looked at her and
saw an expression of joy and delight on her face. 'I am
coming with you, Mama,' she said. The guards, who
were not ashamed to use bad language in front of the

seventeen-year-old Rosita, took the three of us with them and left her behind, alone and in shock.

In prison 'Izzat often spoke about her other three children who were out of Iran – one daughter and two sons. Náhíd, her eldest daughter, was expecting a baby and lived with her husband in Nigeria. Vahíd, her second son, was in Australia and her eldest, Sa'íd, lived in Texas. She was very happy that she had had a chance to speak to Sa'íd and his wife in the United States a few days before her arrest. She told us about the Persian words that her American daughter-in-law had learned and repeated over the phone. She always remembered them all with love and affection, but she was extremely worried about Rosita, at home alone. She was afraid that the guards would harass her. Roya always calmed her down.

'Izzat was deeply concerned about the young girls with us in prison. She asked me to talk to them and advise them that, because they were young and had a future ahead of them, it would be wiser if they didn't admit their part in the Bahá'í administration. She argued that since the guards were not interested in the truth anyway, it would be better if they didn't admit to anything and tried to save their lives.

When Roya heard this she just gave me a look filled with so much meaning that I immediately understood what she was thinking. She smiled and said firmly, 'If I hide the fact that I participated in the Bahá'í administration, then what is left for me to say? We haven't done anything wrong, or anything against the government or people! It is essential that we explain our activities and the nature of the Bahá'í teachings thoroughly so they realize that Bahá'ís are only interested in unity and world peace.'

Roya, Shírín Dálvand, Mítrá Íraván and Mahshíd Nírúmand all decided that they would clearly explain their responsibilities in the Youth Committee, but without mentioning anyone else's name. On the first day of the interrogations, Roya bravely admitted her activities in the Youth Committee, and also the fact that she was a teacher of Bahá'í children's classes. She proudly explained that she had been active in the Bahá'í administration since she was a child and that the goal of the Bahá'í community was to bring unity and peace on earth. Then she expanded on Bahá'í teachings and principles and also the duties of the Youth Committee.

Roya had just turned twenty-two and was a vivacious, happy girl. She sacrificed every bit of comfort she had in prison to help others. Her character and the strength of her faith made her very popular among all the prisoners, but especially with Fak͟hrí Imámí, the political prisoner who was in charge of the cell at Sepah. Roya willingly helped her keep the records of who was supposed to go for questioning and who had to clean the floors or toilets on our cell rota. With so many prisoners in the cell block at that time, Fak͟hrí had found it very difficult to cope, and she really appreciated Roya's help. In return, whenever she heard of a new order or any other news she immediately shared it with Roya, and out of respect and affection for her she was kind to all of us.

'Izzat went through a rough time. Most nights she sat up by the young girls, worrying about them and praying for their freedom. She daredn't sleep in case the guards came to take one of the girls in the middle of the night – she wanted to be there to comfort them. She and I became very close, and we used to talk for hours, sharing all our inner feelings.

I remember once 'Izzat was telling us how popular Roya was among the Bahá'í families, and how many young men had asked her to marry them. But Roya had always said it was not the time to get married, but the time to support the Bahá'ís in their difficulties. She turned to Roya: 'Now see, if you had got married and moved away, this wouldn't have happened, and you wouldn't be here.'

Roya smiled and replied, 'But Mother, being here is much sweeter.'

Roya was calm and firm at all times, even under the most severe pressure. I never saw her crying or upset except once, when her mother was very distressed and said to Roya through her tears, 'I fear only one thing in prison – if it happens to you, I am afraid I wouldn't be able to bear it, and just the thought of it makes me tremble.' 'Izzat had every right to be concerned; the political prisoners had told of assaults and rapes, in stories we could hardly bear to listen to.

That was the only time I saw Roya with tears running down her face. 'Mama, I don't want you even to think about that, but you must know even in that situation I would surrender to whatever was ordained for me.' Luckily, since we Bahá'ís were regarded as unclean by the guards, that test never arose for us.

At last we were told we could receive visitors. After over three weeks without any news of Rosita, 'Izzat and Roya were so excited they counted the minutes to visiting time. Rosita was the first to enter, rushing into the room as soon as the door opened, her face lit up with a lovely smile. Before we were connected on the telephones she had gestured to Roya that she hadn't seen their father, and asked how he was. Roya gestured back that she shouldn't worry and he was fine. Then the connection was turned on and we all talked.

Rosita had to make the long journey by bus from the city to the prison twice a week for the visiting days, each time bringing two plastic bags full of fresh fruit and clean clothes, and some money for their needs in prison. Every time we saw her she was as cheerful and charming as ever. One day, Roya wrote a small note for her sister and cleverly sewed it into the sleeve of a shirt she was sending out. On the note she wrote: 'Rosita, don't wait for Mother and Father's freedom, nor mine. You are alone now. Marry the man you love and start your own family.' She gave the clothes to the guard to give to Rosita, and during the visit that day, pointed to her sleeve to let Rosita know that there was a message hidden in it.

Rosita also used her visits to pass messages between her mother and sister, and her father. The second time she came to visit 'Izzat and Roya, she said, 'Last week I saw Dad. He was strong and firm. He asked how you were!'

Her mother replied, 'Next time you see him, tell him that I miss him very much.' Although the Ishráqís were under investigation in the same room every day, they hadn't seen or spoken to each other since the night they were arrested, because in the trial room we were not allowed even to look at each other.

One day Roya said to the investigator, 'Today is the thirtieth day that my parents and I have been in prison. In all this time I haven't seen my father once. I would be very grateful if you would let me turn my head and glance at him, just to see his face.'

The investigator paused for a moment, then evidently touched by her request, took Roya and her father to the adjoining room together; then he gave 'Izzat a chance to be with her husband for five minutes. As soon as Roya saw her father she held him in her arms and kissed him and said, 'Father, I love you very much. Please stay strong.' She looked at her father's pale and tired face and asked, 'Father, why is your beard so long?'

He explained that they were not allowed to shave in prison. Lovingly she kissed her father over and over again. The investigator took advantage of this moment and said to Roya, 'Isn't it a shame! Even though you love your father so much, by refusing to say one word you deprive yourselves of the chance of being together. By simply saying that you are not Bahá'ís you could free yourselves from all of this. I would even unfreeze your family's assets and restore your father's pension.'

Roya smiled at him and firmly replied, 'Your honour, my love for my parents is only natural; my love for Bahá'u'lláh, however, is much greater. Perhaps you should stop and think about what kind of truth this must be that makes a young girl like me refuse to exchange this love even for the love of my parents, even for the whole world.'

The investigator was often lost for words with Roya. He became increasingly frustrated by the courage of the Ishráqí family, and tried every trick he could think of to weaken their resolve. One day when they had taken us out for fresh air, a guard came outside and called Roya over. Immediately they blindfolded her and took her away. I was walking with 'Izzat at the time and when I saw they were taking Roya away, my legs started to shake. I felt all my strength seep out of me as my mind filled with agonized questions. 'Where are they taking her? She has been on trial with all of us every day, so why would they call her back on her own? Are they taking her to torture her? Are they going to execute her? And what is poor 'Izzat going through now? They are taking away her daughter in front of her eyes, and she can't say or do anything about it.'

I was afraid even to look 'Izzat in the face. When we were back in the cell, I went and sat in a corner on the floor without saying a word, hoping she wouldn't see my distress. But she was strong and firm. She kept pacing up and down in front of me chanting the prayer, 'O Lord, my God and my haven in my distress! My shield and my shelter in my woes! . . .' An hour later, they called 'Izzat and took her away too.

Three hours later they called Shírín, Mahshíd, Mítrá and me. As they blindfolded us I heard the investigator's voice saying, 'I have finished with Roya. Oil her back and feet well; we whipped her hard.'

They took us to the trial room and an hour later they brought in Roya and 'Izzat. They hadn't whipped Roya – they were just trying to frighten us.

The investigator tried everything to break 'Izzat's spirit. To torment her, he asked me in front of her, 'Roohizadegan, do you know Rosita Ishráqí? We have plans for her. We are going to bring her here too.' I kept quiet and didn't reply because I didn't want to cause any complications, but he persisted, 'I am talking about Roya's sister, don't you know her?'

'Your honour,' 'Izzat interrupted, 'I know Rosita. She is my daughter. It doesn't matter if you want to bring her here and show her your affection in the same way you have shown it to us. Didn't you bring my husband, my daughter and me here and put us through all this hardship? Bringing Rosita here too won't help you break our spirit or stamp out our faith, I assure you.' When he realized his trick hadn't worked the investigator got even more angry, but he didn't know what else to do so he started shouting at us again.

It was a difficult and bitter day, full of tension and anguish. When we got back to the cell that night, I asked 'Izzat and Roya what had happened after they were called away. Roya said, 'When they called me, they took me to a room and kept me there blindfolded for four hours. Over and over again the investigator came in and said that my parents had recanted and they were waiting for me to recant so the three of us could go home together. I told him that I was a Bahá'í and I wouldn't recant my faith no matter what. He threatened to whip me, and he also demanded the names of the other members of the Youth Committee.'

'Izzat's experience was similar.

They kept me blindfolded in a room for three hours and said if I didn't recant they would torture Roya. I told them I had given my daughter to Bahá'u'lláh, and I wouldn't recant. Then the investigator said, 'You are proven guilty because you were on the Counselling Committee and you helped solve problems between husbands and wives. If you hadn't done so, they would have sought help from the Revolutionary Court and then we would have made them accept Islam.'

I replied, 'The government of the Islamic Republic doesn't recognize Bahá'ís as citizens of this country, so we have to solve our problems ourselves. Therefore, as a friend, I helped some people solve their marriage problems. Is that a crime to you?'

I can still hear 'Izzat and Roya's voices clearly in my head, and see 'Ináyat's calm dignity as he quietly answered the investigator's questions. He and 'Izzat both openly admitted that they had been to the Holy Land on pilgrimage, and to the investigator this was evidence of their guilt: they must be spies for Israel.

Even so, the interrogators continued to torment this brave family, subjecting them to particularly intense and lengthy trials. They tried everything they could think of to increase the pressure on the Ishráqís and break their spirit. One of their favourite forms of harassment was to insult and swear at them in front of one another. Poor 'Ináyat had to suffer hearing his wife constantly belittled and ridiculed, while he was unable to utter a word. 'Izzat, although very strong in spirit, had lost her physical strength. Several times she told the investigator that she didn't have the strength to write any more, but he never paid any attention. The guards seemed to make a particular point of mocking her. Normally they called everyone by their first names, but in her case – she was fifty-six – they spitefully referred to her in front of the other prisoners as 'old 'Izzat' or 'old woman'. Nevertheless, they were all determined not to succumb to the pressure.

In Adelabad, they called a few Bahá'ís every day to the Revolutionary Court for their last interrogation by the Public Prosecutor or the final verdict from the Religious Magistrate.

On 16 January 1983, at 8.30 in the evening, they announced on the public address system that 'Izzat and Roya would be taken to court the next morning at 5 a.m.

The next day they awoke at four. After saying their prayers and kissing their friends calmly and confidently, they left with a few guards for the Revolutionary Court in Sepah. They came back at eight o'clock that evening. As they came in, looking relaxed and cheerful, I asked about the trial. 'Izzat told me:

They wouldn't leave us alone. They kept asking the same questions over and over again. After several hours of this, they asked Roya and me to recant. We told them not to waste their time.

Then they brought 'Ináyat in. The sight of his pale and drawn face upset me so much that without meaning to, I said, 'I wish I could die rather than see you under so much pressure.'

They read out the list of accusations against us: 'Ináyat was charged with being a Bahá'í, membership of the Local Spiritual Assembly of Shíráz, serving as an assistant, pilgrimage to the Holy Land and other Bahá'í activities. I was accused of being a member of the Marriage and Counselling Committee, giving shelter to homeless Bahá'ís, and pilgrimage to the Holy Land. Roya's crime was being a member of the Youth Committee, a teacher of Bahá'í children's classes, and being unmarried. We were all sentenced to death.

The Public Prosecutor, whose name, ironically, was also Ishráqí, asked for 1,000,000 tuman in cash or a security bond on property in exchange for 'Ináyat's release, 900,000 tuman for my release and 600,000 for Roya's.

My husband told him, 'We only have one house. Will you accept it as security for all three of us?'

'Izzat laughed. 'I never knew I was worth 900,000 tuman. Now I am a 900,000-tuman woman!'

'Would you be prepared to give the prosecutor what he asked for and free yourselves?' I asked her.

'It's far too much!' she replied. 'If we offered that much for our freedom it would only encourage them to demand the same from others, and it wouldn't be fair on the ones who couldn't come up with this kind of money.'

The next day they took me for my final trial. It proved to be a long, difficult day full of frustrations, delays and confusion. After arriving at the Revolutionary Court at 5.30 a.m., I and several Muslim women were locked in the washroom for two and a half hours while guards stood at the door. When I was eventually called before the prosecutor, much to my surprise, I found 'Ináyat in the same room. A few minutes later 'Izzat's sister-in-law came in holding the ownership deed to a house, and told the prosecutor, 'Here is the security bond you asked for in return for Mr Ishráqí's release.' He had apparently told 'Ináyat that if he provided one security bond he would be released and could then bring in two more for his wife and daughter.

But the prosecutor said, 'Yesterday I agreed to release them for three security bonds or cash, but today I have changed my mind. Their crimes are too great. He has admitted to being a member of the Local Spiritual Assembly and also to being an assistant. I must send his file to the Religious Magistrate to give the final verdict.'

The prosecutor turned to me. He was polite to me but kept asking the same questions I had been answering all along, and repeatedly asked if I was willing to become a Muslim.

After several hours of this, I asked if I could go to the washroom. He refused to let me go. When I repeated my request for the third time an hour later, he agreed but insisted on coming along with me to stand at the door. As he escorted me back to the office, I was stunned to see my husband and little Payam in the crowd of people milling about the corridors. The families of prisoners came to the court regularly to try to get information about their loved ones. Morad and Payam didn't recognize me, since I was muffled up in my regulation chador, so when we came close to them I asked the prosecutor if I could just say hello to them. He turned and shouted at me for making such a request, thus attracting Morad's attention. Morad brought Payam closer to me, but the prosecutor shouted even more and pushed me into the office.

After more of the same questions and answers, he suddenly left the room and returned a moment later with Payam in his arms. The child looked shocked and frightened, but as soon as he recognized me through my veil, he began to cry and beg me to come home with him, promising never to be a bad boy again. I held him close, but couldn't find any words to comfort him.

Again the prosecutor said, 'Your punishment is execution. Your only alternative is to recant.'

'I am a Bahá'í,' I replied, 'and a member of the Bahá'í community. I hope I can find the strength to remain firm in my faith to my dying breath.'

'Won't you take pity on your child? Don't you love him?' he challenged me.

'Yes, I love him very much,' I said, hugging Payam closer. 'But I will never recant my faith.'

The prosecutor abruptly wrote across my file in red ink, 'Sentenced to death. To be hanged.' He looked up and, keeping his eyes on me to gauge my reaction, he told me calmly, 'In refusing to recant your faith you have thrown away your only chance for release, and you will be hanged. Let me make your choices quite clear: either accept Islam or face the hangman.'

Poor Payam had no idea what the prosecutor was saying, but he registered the angry tone of voice and was frightened. He sat quietly on my lap in that cold room, his eyes never leaving my face. And in those eyes I could sense him pleading with me to come home. Of course he had no idea how serious my predicament was at that moment, and as the prosecutor reeled off the catalogue of my crimes and the hanging that awaited me, Payam slipped his hand into his pocket and pulled out a hazelnut saying, 'Mama, can you crack this nut for me?'

In my state of mind at that moment I did not know how to gather up enough energy to deal with the hazelnut. I looked uncertainly at the prosecutor, trying to assess his reaction, but his face was impassive. I decided to please Payam and quickly cracked the nut with my teeth and gave it to him.

Seeing this, the prosecutor thought the moment was right for driving home the choices that confronted me. 'Right now', he began coldly, 'we will take you to be hanged. This is your last chance. If you truly love your child and want to go back to your home and your family, just write two words on this paper, "*Bahá'í nistam* – I am not a Bahá'í", and that you have become a Muslim. This is just on paper – it means nothing.'

Holding the hazelnut shells tightly in my hand I replied, 'I can't tell such a lie – I would rather be hanged. I will never recant!'

The prosecutor was losing his patience with me. 'You will be hanged this minute,' he snapped, and tried to prise Payam away from me. Payam, however, clung to me for all he was worth and started to scream and cry. The prosecutor told me to go to the door and give Payam to my husband. I quickly popped the nutshells into my scarf and tied it into a knot – they would be a small memento of Payam after he had gone. Then I kissed him on his tear-stained cheek, gave him a hug, and put him, struggling, into his father's arms. I will never forget the look of anguish on Payam's face at that moment; I felt like I was being torn apart – my life and my loved ones pulled me one way, my determination to keep my faith the other.

Then the most unexpected thing happened. As Payam was sobbing, 'No, no, I want Mama,' and trying to reach out to me, the prosecutor went red in the face, looked down, and then said to me, 'If you give me a security bond, I will release you.'

Hardly knowing what I was saying, I replied, 'But if you are releasing me because I am innocent, why do you need a security bond?'

'You have been a member of a misleading sect, and of its administration, and you must be watched.'

'Sir,' Morad intervened politely, 'it should be enough for you to accept our promise. Isn't it the case that when your men come into our homes at odd hours of the day or night to take away our wives and children, we innocently submit to your demands? A security bond is unnecessary.'

'Innocently?' The prosecutor turned on Morad. 'What innocence? You are all guilty!'

Morad asked his permission to speak, then began, 'Your honour, I am a retired manager from the NIOC. A few days ago, I saw one of my old employees in the street. He came up to me cheerfully, embraced me and said, "In the office we often

talk about you, remembering the good times when we worked
with you." I was his boss for many years, but I could foresee
then that the days of a fancy office and impressive title would
not last forever. If I had taken advantage of my position then,
and instead of respecting him as a human being had treated him
as a person lower than myself, he would have turned his face
away today. It's the same for you, Mr Prosecutor, and I assure
you your position of power will not last forever. I implore you to
think about tomorrow, and about the next world.'

I could see the prosecutor was beginning to shake with
anger, so I jumped into the conversation and said, 'Your
honour, please don't upset yourself. My husband is assuming
we're not happy in your prison, or that we're badly treated here,
but you always show us your Islamic kindness and respect.'

This calmed him down a little, and my husband left the
room with Payam, promising to bring a security bond in the
morning.

But my trial continued for a while longer, and together with
'Ináyat I was asked more of the same old questions about
Zionism and political groups. I wrote down the answers at
length in my file for my final defence.

I am a Bahá'í and do not belong to any political group,
and I have never taken part in any political activities in
my life. May all the judges of the Revolutionary Court
understand that the Bahá'í Faith is a purely religious
organization, and not a political one. If you are accus-
ing me of being a member of the Bahá'í community,
then yes, I confess that I am, because each and every
Bahá'í child who goes to a Bahá'í class is a member of
the community, let alone the adults. If you have anything against our meetings, you should ban them. I
assure you that if you did, and if you broadcast the ban,
all Bahá'ís would obey the order, since one of the teachings of Bahá'u'lláh is that all Bahá'ís must be obedient
to the government of their country.

Then, for about three pages, I wrote about Bahá'u'lláh's teachings.

When he read this over, the prosecutor said, 'You think you're so clever. Do you really imagine that we would talk about you Bahá'ís on the TV or radio? If we did, the world would soon know about you, and you would have, in effect, international recognition.'

Once again he wrote in my file that I was sentenced to death. I was now to be hanged twice, my crime was so heinous!

It was about 3.30, and he turned to 'Ináyat and said, 'It's no good talking to you two. Neither of you will recant your faith.' Then he called a guard and told him to take me back to the washroom. I don't know what happened to 'Ináyat after that, but before we were finally separated he looked at me resolutely and said, 'Tell my wife not to expect my release, Olya, because the prosecutor has changed his mind and I don't know what will happen now.'

I was taken back to that dirty washroom. After a while a guard brought me some so-called food: a piece of dried-up bread, two bits of bone and a few peas, and a glass of water. I had to stay there until 8 p.m., when they put me in a bus and took me back to Adelabad.

As soon as I got back to my cell that night, all my friends gathered around, asking me about the interrogation and trial and my final sentence. They also noticed my knotted scarf and I showed them the hazelnut shells I had saved. We all laughed together about my little souvenir of Payam. I told 'Izzat everything that had happened that day with regard to her husband's release, and I also told her about the possibility of being released myself, since Morad had been told to bring a security bond or our house deeds to the court the next day.

'Izzat was very excited about the possibility of my being set free. As for herself and her family, she had totally surrendered to God's will. She said to me, 'When you get out of here, please wait for a few days and see if Roya is also released. If she is, would you take her with you out of Iran, to her brother in America?'

Roya, however, was living in a different world. She simply smiled at the suggestion.

PART III

ESCAPE

Release

CHAPTER 14

I hardly slept that night. One by one, so as not to attract the attention of the guards, each of my friends crept down the corridor to my cell to say a personal goodbye. None of us knew what tomorrow would bring.

Would I be released? Others had been promised before – the I<u>sh</u>ráqís' release orders had been cancelled only that morning. Would I still be here, in this cell, tomorrow night, such a small, cramped, uncomfortable place, yet whose every nook and cranny was filled with so many sweet memories of my dear friends? How could I leave them? We'd been through so much together, it was as if an invisible umbilical cord connected us all, heart to heart. But perhaps yet another fate awaited me.

I will never forget that night. Quietly the women slipped into my cell and whispered their last messages to me. 'Olya, you were a witness to our trials, our sufferings, you can tell our families.'

There was so little they could say to their relatives in the short, weekly visits, especially with the guards listening to their every word, and they were always anxious not to upset their families with sad news. This was their chance to speak freely about everything, just in case another opportunity never arose. And late into the night they came to give me messages of love and hope to take to their families.

Nusrat was the first. She came to me and hugged me, and asked me to send her love to her husband, who had already been released, and to her children. She also wanted me to tell the <u>Sh</u>íráz assembly about the files she had seen during her trials. They included detailed information on more than fifty

Bahá'ís, including members of the national and local assemblies, and she knew the authorities were planning another wave of arrests. Could I warn them so they could save themselves? I promised that I would.

Ṭáhirih came into my cell and gave me a bear-hug. She was happy, and her face was radiant; her only concern was for Jamshíd. He had suffered so much, and the pressure on him was getting more intense by the day, so all her thoughts were directed towards him. She knew they had compiled a thick file on me and had ordered my execution, so she was very pleased that I might be released. 'I am so glad for you. Now that you have your release order, by the grace of God, I hope you will soon be free. If you do get out, please do something for Jamshíd. If they ever decide to release him on a security bond, please go and ask Amín, his cousin, for it. He is a very conscientious person, and I am sure he will arrange something for him. Don't worry about me, my freedom is not important – but try to help Jamshíd get out.'

I can still hear the loneliness in her voice. She kept saying, 'Olya, I wish you every happiness. You know how painful it is to be in here – you have experienced it yourself. Go and tell the Local Spiritual Assembly and the National Spiritual Assembly – even the Universal House of Justice. Let them know what we went through and what these heartless people have done to us. Tell Bahá'ís to live simply, and not to become distracted by this material life. Tell them to spend their time serving others.'

'Izzat came to me and, as she embraced me, tears of both happiness and sorrow filled her eyes. How sad it was to say goodbye to this lovely woman who had become so dear to me in that dreadful place, who had patiently endured long trials full of spite and ridicule, who had showered me with so much love and affection. At every turn she had helped and supported me, always waiting by the showers to hold my towel and clothes, and today keeping back her supper for me so that when I returned from my trial, she could share it with me. How could I bear to leave this wonderful friend?

Together we discussed, as we had done many times, the possibility of my escape from Iran. We had all agreed that it was our only chance. If I could somehow get out, I could tell the whole story to anybody who would listen, and once the conscience of the world was pricked, international pressure on Iran might force the authorities to free the Bahá'ís. This was our hope.

'But how can you get out of Iran?' 'Izzat asked anxiously. We all knew that Bahá'ís could not get exit visas, so simply catching an international flight was out of the question, and the war with Iraq had closed all sea routes. The overland routes to Turkey or Pakistan were the only possibilities. Of these, the route to Pakistan was considered to be the less dangerous.

'Even if I have to crawl on my stomach I will get out,' I replied confidently, imagining that the border between Iran and Pakistan was a barbed wire fence and that I would have to crawl underneath.

Just as Ṭáhirih hoped I would be able to escape so that Jamshíd's pain and suffering might be brought to an end, so 'Izzat's only concern was for Roya. She desperately wanted freedom for her daughter, hoping one day she might be able to pick up the threads of her life, get married and have children.

'You are lucky, you know, Olya,' she laughed quietly as she slipped out. 'If you are released, you won't have to eat beans for lunch tomorrow!'

At 10.30 p.m. the lights were turned off as usual, and the cell doors were closed. Mítrá and I were left alone together. We said some prayers and talked until after midnight when one of the guards came round and told us angrily to go to sleep.

Mítrá was so happy and excited for me. 'Oh Olya, I hope they free you tomorrow,' she said. 'You can see my mother and my sister and give them both my love!' Her own release order had been cancelled only four days ago, but she was so delighted for me, it almost made up for her own bitter disappointment.

'Tomorrow you might be free at last, Olya. How do you feel?' she asked.

My emotions were confused and troubled. 'It's so difficult,' I told her. 'If I *am* released tomorrow – and it might not happen, they might only be playing with me – but if I am released, how can I just leave? After all we've been through together, how can I simply walk out of that door?'

'Perhaps God has a plan for you,' she said thoughtfully. 'You have witnessed so much. You were here with us, you saw everything with your own eyes.'

'The only thing that consoles me when I think of leaving you all is that I might be able to save you. Perhaps, God willing, I can.'

'But if you *are* released,' she teased, 'then tomorrow you won't have to share a cell with me! You can sleep in your own bed, and have a nice lunch. What heaven! And you can cuddle Payam and kiss your parents. You are very lucky, you know.'

I don't think I slept more than an hour that night. All my memories kept flooding back, as people say happens just before you die. I relived the time with my parents, my childhood in Jahrum, my life with my own family and then with all my friends in prison. It was a magical night.

The next morning at 10.30, my name was announced over the loudspeaker. This was the moment we had all been waiting for, and everyone rushed out of their cells to say goodbye. I still wasn't sure I would be released, especially since I had two death sentences scrawled across my file. None of my friends could really believe they would just let me go like that. It wouldn't be the first time a prisoner had been called for release, only to find herself back in the interrogation room in Sepah. This might be just another cruel charade, another empty promise.

But it was terribly hard for me to say my goodbyes. They all hugged me in turn and each repeated the messages they wanted me to take to their loved ones, and thought of last minute requests. 'Kiss this person for me, tell that person . . .' All of them asked me to go to the ruins of the House of the Báb and pray for them, and I promised it would be the first thing I did when I was released – *if* I was released.

'Take this with you,' said Ṭáhirih, pressing a bar of soap into my hand. 'If you *are* released, give it to the guard and tell him it belongs to me. They will announce my name and then we will know you were allowed to go. If we don't hear anything . . .'

'Then you can be sure I am dead,' I finished for her. I looked round at my friends, at their dear, familiar faces. They were all so happy I was being released – it was as if they were being set free themselves. So much love and unity had blossomed in such a terrible place.

I heard my name being called again. Nusrat threw her arms around me. 'Oh Olya! If only I could sneak into your pocket and come with you,' she cried, tears streaming down her face.

She was still hugging me and weeping when my name was announced for a third time. If you didn't present yourself after the third call, your release order was cancelled. Fakhrí Imámí rushed out of the cell opposite and gently loosened Nusrat's hold. 'Quickly, let her go! Olya will be too late for her release,' she urged.

Fakhrí practically bundled me down the stairs. I don't know if I could have found the strength to move without her help. Going down I kept turning to look back, and wondered if I would ever see my friends again – Nusrat, Túbá, 'Izzat, Roya, Zarrín, Símín, Mahshíd, Akhtar, Ṭáhirih, Shírín, Mona and of course my dear cell-mate Mítrá. They were all waving me on. Only the thought that someone must get out to tell the world their story – our story – dragged me away from them.

I hesitated a moment longer, trying to imprint their faces on my memory one last time. 'Run,' they implored me, 'before it's too late!' And I turned and fled down to the ground floor.

When I got there I couldn't find the female guard who did the body search, or the guard who was supposed to take me to the prison office. Brother 'Asgapúr, however, was the guard on duty and he immediately tried to speed up the formalities I had to go through to get out of there. For some reason he seemed very concerned about me. He called one of the female guards and told her, 'This prisoner's old father has been waiting for her since five o'clock this morning. Please do me a favour and search her so she can go home.'

'But I'll get into trouble if they find out,' she replied, 'and anyway, the guard who is in charge of taking her to the office isn't here either.'

I waited. An hour passed and neither of them showed up. Brother 'Asgapúr seemed very worried. Finally, after much begging on his part, the female guard agreed to do the body search. As I turned to go I put the bar of soap into her hand and explained that it belonged to Ṭáhirih. As Brother 'Asgapúr escorted me to the office where Morad was waiting, I heard them announce Ṭáhirih's name over the loudspeaker.

On the way, the guard said to me, 'Sister, do you know why I was so worried? Because there are no rules or regulations around here. They could easily have cancelled your release order, especially since you are a Bahá'í. Weren't you on trial yesterday?' he asked. I told him I had been. 'And you admitted that you were a Bahá'í?'

'Of course,' I replied.

He was shocked and said, 'You must be a very lucky woman.' Then he hinted that my release would not be permanent, and that I should not take my freedom for granted. 'The Revolutionary Court has plans for you Bahá'ís.'

The prison office was near the entrance gate, and there we found my husband anxiously waiting. He was extremely relieved to see me. Before we could leave, however, one of the guards at the office presented me with a piece of paper on which he had written some absurd questions of his own, telling me I had to answer them and sign it. On the paper it said, 'I hereby guarantee that from now on I will not be a member of a cult and will not do anything in opposition to the government of the Islamic Republic. I guarantee that I will no longer be a part of a misleading sect. I promise that I will never again take part in the Bahá'í Zionist administration', and so on.

I returned the piece of paper to him without signing it and said, 'Sir, I was on trial yesterday in the Revolutionary Court. I confirmed in my file that I am a Bahá'í and that Bahá'ís are not involved in politics. I have never been a member of a cult and so I don't see any reason for promising that I won't be one in future.'

He insisted I sign, and Morad and I spent a whole hour arguing with him. In the end I didn't sign the paper, but I wrote a text of my own, and surprisingly he accepted it. I was free to go.

It was a rainy day, but my mother, my sister Laqá and little Payam were waiting outside for me with armfuls of flowers. I kissed and hugged them all. Then we went straight to the ruins of the House of the Báb to say prayers, just as I had promised my friends only a few hours before.

Morad went to arrange some lunch, and as we sat there, silently, in front of the House of the Báb eating kebab wrapped in Persian bread, I thought of 'Izzat's remark the night before. I held Payam close on my lap, and wondered how I could eat delicious kebab for lunch when my friends were behind bars, eating beans again.

Payam was very agitated when we arrived home, and seemed afraid that the guards would burst into the house again to take me away. So we packed a bag and spent that first night in the relative safety of my parents' house. All evening our friends, Bahá'í and Muslim, came round to visit, even members of the Shíráz assembly who were in hiding. I was able to give them information about the women in prison, and pass on Nusrat's message.

As I prepared for bed that night, I thought back over my first day of freedom. It had been a very long, emotional day, full of the joy of reunions mixed with the sadness of reliving painful experiences for others to share. My mind was still full of so many vivid, sharply focused memories of my dearest friends – although I was physically free, my thoughts were still in that prison with them.

When you have suffered so much in company with other people, shared everything with them, and then you alone are released, the separation is almost unbearable. Everyone loves freedom, but you can never forget that your friends are still in prison, still suffering. Mítrá and I shared the same plate and even shared our food, but that evening I had eaten my own supper from my own plate, and she was still in that cell. Every day we had taken our meagre food to the Ishráqís' cell so that we could eat with 'Izzat and Roya. How could I enjoy my dinner with my family and friends all around me, knowing where those three women were, what they were eating?

I remembered Mítrá's words to me as we talked in our cell the night before, and I couldn't bring myself to sleep on the soft, comfortable bed my mother had prepared for me. For two years after that, in fact, I slept on the floor, unable to forget the hardships my friends were enduring. Every time I ate, every time I lay down to sleep, or hugged my children, and especially when I walked in the park in the wonderful fresh air, in my heart I was crying because I was free, but they were not.

In the morning, Morad and I went to the Revolutionary Court in Sepah. According to the law, we could now reclaim the belongings that the guards confiscated when I was arrested.

Morad went up to the front desk and, without giving my name, gave the official my prison identity number and said we were there to reclaim our belongings. The man was polite and friendly, checking through all his files for released prisoners, but he couldn't find my file. He asked when the prisoner had been released, and Morad told him it was only yesterday.

'Perhaps the file is still in Áyatu'lláh Qazá'í's office,' he said with a smile. 'I'll go upstairs and see if I can find it.'

A moment later he came back flushed with anger, all traces of politeness gone. 'Are you a liar?' he shouted. 'You claimed your prisoner has been released! That's impossible. The file is still sitting on Áyatu'lláh Qazá'í's desk. The prisoner is still in prison and has been condemned to death!'

Morad was about to defend himself and insist, 'I am not a liar. Look, here is my wife!' but I put my hand on his arm to stop him and we made a hasty exit.

Six other Bahá'ís had been released at about the same time as me, but I was convinced our release was only temporary, especially when we found my file had not been closed. The next day we went to visit Dr Ahmad Mazlúm who, with his father-in-law Ahmad Khádim, had also just been released. I wanted to find out about the male Bahá'í prisoners and their prison conditions. Dr Mazlúm had been severely tortured in prison, and two months later his back was still bruised and swollen.

'I have a feeling', I said, 'that we have only been released for a short time, so they can follow us to discover the whereabouts of other Bahá'ís.'

He laughed and said, 'I don't think so. I think we are free now.' Then he added, 'I would like to show my back to one of the committees of the United Nations, so they will know what these people are doing to the Bahá'ís.' But a few days later, some of those who had been released were called to the court once again, including Dr Mazlúm and Mr Khádim. They were called back to the court yet again a week later, and this time they were rearrested.

A week after my release I made a trip to Tehran to meet the National Spiritual Assembly, as I had promised, to report on the situation in Adelabad and to pass on the messages that my fellow prisoners had given me. While we were there the secretary of the National Spiritual Assembly mentioned that although individual Bahá'ís are free to make their own decisions, they advised any Bahá'ís who had been ordered to turn themselves in to obey the order. Since I had not yet been recalled by the court, Morad and I decided to go straight back to Shíráz.

On the way back we stopped the car by the roadside in a quiet place and got out to stretch our legs. It was so beautiful in the desert. I breathed in the wonderful fresh air and began to feel, for the first time, how marvellous it was to be free, and how precious freedom was. Back in Adelabad, we had no fresh air and all the windows were painted over so we couldn't see out. But on one small window at the end of a corridor we had scratched some of the paint off with our nails, and when the guards were not around we would climb onto a ledge to get a tiny glimpse, through the scratched paint, of the sky. Although I was so sad my friends were not with me on that desert road, it was a very special moment. As I drank in the beauty of that spot the reality of my freedom sank in.

It was late when we got back to Shíráz, so we spent the night at my parents', and we didn't go back to our own house until 8 p.m. the next day. I don't know why, but whenever we went back to that house, I felt nervous. I had the feeling I was being watched, but I decided to ignore it and didn't even mention it to Morad.

He sat down and started writing a letter to our two sons in England, and I asked him not to say anything about my having been in prison, since at any moment the guards might rush into our house and arrest me again.

'But if they wanted to keep you, why did they set you free in the first place?' he asked. 'Besides, you never signed anything undertaking to turn yourself in if they asked you to. There is nothing to worry about.'

Payam was ill with a very high temperature, and I put him to bed. Then I busied myself doing the laundry. All of a sudden,

I remembered a picture of 'Abdu'l-Bahá that had been hidden in one of cupboards. I wondered whether the guards had found it when they searched the house the night of my arrest. I had often thought about that picture while I had been in prison. I went straight to the cupboard where it was hidden and, to my surprise, I found that it was the only cupboard in the house that the guards hadn't searched. Suddenly the telephone rang, making me jump.

My husband answered it and then abruptly shouted, 'Olya, turn off all the lights. We have to leave the house at once.' The call had been from our neighbour, informing us that the guards had been to our door several times that day looking for me. She warned us that they would probably come back soon, so we should decide quickly whether to leave or stay.

This neighbour was a very religious Muslim and a supporter of the Islamic regime. She had attended every demonstration against the Shah and for Áyatu'lláh Khomeini. Yet she had been the one who had organized the writing of the letter protesting at my arrest, and it was she who, as soon as she noticed that we were back home, called us to warn us about the guards.

Taking the picture of 'Abdu'l-Bahá in one hand, I just paused long enough to grab the stockings Táhirih had given me in prison, and then picked up the feverish Payam. It was a very difficult moment. It was so hard to leave that house, with all its memories; it meant having to leave not just <u>Sh</u>íráz, but the country. I couldn't gather my thoughts. I had made a promise to my friends, but I loved Iran and couldn't bear to think of leaving it. 'Hurry, hurry,' Morad shouted. 'Why are you waiting? Do you want the guards to arrest you? Think of your child.' And I raced to the car with Payam. I saw my husband run to the orange tree that he had planted in the garden and pick some oranges, saying, 'Let me at least taste some of its fruit.' Then we bundled poor Payam into the car and left our beloved home for the last time.

Not knowing what else to do, we headed straight to my parents'. As soon as we approached their house, I saw my mother standing at the door, looking pale and worried. 'Where have you been?' she said. 'Your neighbours have been calling all day to warn you against returning home. The guards are waiting to rearrest you.'

I was sure that if I was arrested again, they would torture me to try and get the names of the members of the National Spiritual Assembly whom I had contacted in Tehran. There was nothing for it but to leave Shíráz that very evening, and we set out for Tehran once more.

On the way to Tehran our car, just like everyone else's, was stopped and searched by the guards several times, but we arrived safely. We had nowhere to live in Tehran, no money, no plans for the future, and a small child to care for. Since Bahá'ís had no identity cards, we could not even get any food coupons. The only thing we had left was the car we were driving.

However, when some of our friends heard about our situation, they immediately welcomed us into their home, and we were to stay in Tehran for two long months. We had decided that if we received a letter from the Revolutionary Court ordering me to return to Shíráz, or if my name appeared in the papers, we would go back at once, but it never happened.

Morad and I both knew by now that we should leave Iran to join our sons in England, but we also knew it was impossible for a Bahá'í to leave Iran by air. To obtain an exit visa we would have to fill in an application form stating our religion, and no Bahá'ís were being granted such visas. In any case, it was very unlikely that they would allow a former prisoner to leave the country. Therefore, we had to find someone to guide us overland across the border to Pakistan or Turkey.

We knew there were people who, for a large cash payment, would take you over the border by car or motor cycle, on a camel or a horse, but not all of them could be trusted and anyway they could never promise to get you to the neighbouring country safely. There had been many cases when, after getting the money, the guide either never showed up, or just abandoned people in the mountains where they were found by the guards. But we had no alternative, so reluctantly we set about finding a reliable guide.

We went to see a Bahá'í in Tehran we knew quite well, and told her we needed to leave the country and were looking for a guide. Did she know of anyone? She told us she knew a man from Baluchistan, a region that straddles the Iranian–Pakistani border, who had helped some of the relatives of the assembly members who had been killed in Hamadán two years before. 'He is very honest,' she assured us, and promised to arrange an introduction.

A week later she rang to say the meeting was arranged, and we sold our only remaining possession, our car, and took the money to her house. There we met a good-looking young man in his early twenties, a soldier in the army who had two months' leave coming up. His name was Khudáyár and, in common with most Baluchis, he was a Sunni Muslim, unlike the majority of Iranians who were Shi'a.

We explained our situation to him and he agreed to act as a guide across the border to Pakistan. He was a very kind man and he was clearly moved by our story, especially by the fact that I was the mother of a young child. It wasn't so much the money that seemed important to him, but to save my life for Payam's sake. Rúhíyyih Jahánpúr and her mother and sister had told us that they wanted to come too, and Khudáyár agreed to take us all. The money was handed over and we settled down to wait for his call.

Of course we didn't get any kind of receipt for that money, and neither did we have a contact address or even a date when we were supposed to leave. We were only told that we would be contacted when the time was right.

Days and then weeks passed with no word from our guide. Those were the most difficult days of our lives, since we had no more money to pay another guide if things didn't work out, and we knew that, even if all turned out well, we had a long and hazardous trip ahead of us. Having heard nothing for more than a month, we decided to return by bus to Shíráz for a day to see my family and find out if anything had happened to the Bahá'ís in prison.

It was 13 March 1983, and we arrived back in Shíráz just after the news had reached the Bahá'ís that Rahmat Vafá'í, Yadu'lláh Mahmúdnizhád and dear Túbá Zá'irpúr had been hanged the day before. Despite the difficult times, everyone went to visit the families of those who had been killed, carrying bouquets of flowers and wearing smiles on their faces. We went too, but the Bahá'ís urged us to go back to Tehran as it was far too dangerous for us to stay in Shíráz.

I desperately wanted to go to Adelabad to say goodbye to my friends and reassure them that we would escape, but it wasn't possible. Instead we said a final goodbye to the rest of our friends and relatives, and without telling them of our plans we left by bus for Tehran.

As soon as we got there, Rúḥíyyih Jahánpúr rang to say that Khudáyár had telephoned them but no one had known where we were. The trip had had to be postponed. Her mother was very worried that that would be the last we would hear from him, but ten days later he got in touch again and told us to stay in Tehran. He would call again when all was set, and we must be ready to leave at a moment's notice. Despite our suspicions, Khudáyár turned out to be an honest man after all.

The following week the telephone rang. 'Tomorrow, at two o'clock, you must catch the bus to Záhidán,' Khudáyár told us. 'Go to the bus station now and buy five tickets. Don't give your real names, but use a common name like Rawhání, because guards often travel on the bus in plain clothes and your names might be on their list.'

Morad went to the bus station that afternoon to get the tickets. The ticket clerk told him that they didn't have any left for that bus – they had all been sold and the bus was full. Morad pleaded with him. In Iran the clerks often keep some tickets back so that they can give them out as a favour if they wish, and eventually Morad convinced the man of the urgency of our trip without giving too much away. He arrived back with the five tickets and immediately telephoned the Jahánpúrs to tell them to meet us at the bus station the next day in time to catch the 2 p.m. bus to Záhidán.

Farewell to My Country

CHAPTER 15

We spent our last night at Morad's sister's house in Tehran. None of us got much sleep. Ever since the traumatic events of the night of my arrest, Payam had been anxious and insecure. He suffered from nightmares, crying out in his sleep and even sleep-walking. After I got out of prison, he insisted on sleeping with me, and when he woke I would reassure him I was still there. This lasted for a whole year. That night, he woke up screaming several times. I could not sleep, and lay next to him, thinking about what was in store for us and crying.

My friends were still in prison and I had not been able to see them since my release, and my parents didn't even know we were planning to leave Iran in the morning. It was too risky to tell anyone, but especially my parents who were still in <u>Sh</u>íráz. If they didn't know anything, then they could say truthfully, if asked, that they had no idea where we were. We also wanted to save them anxiety, because they would have worried dreadfully had they known what we were about to undertake. The overland route to Pakistan was very dangerous. There were many stories of people dying from dehydration or exposure on the way, especially the old and the very young, and of others being shot by border guards. How could we tell our relatives what we were going to do? In the end, only some very close friends, a Muslim family, were told. Even my sister-in-law and her family were completely unaware that when we left their house that morning, we would not be coming back.

I stood by the window looking out over the city that night, weeping quietly, steeling myself for the emotional wrench of leaving my homeland. On the one hand, I knew in my heart that my friends' only chance of freedom lay in my escaping Iran and taking their story with me – we had discussed it so many times in prison. On the other, I knew that once we left I wouldn't get any news from them or be able to find out what was happening to them in Adelabad. After so long together, I couldn't bear the thought of being so far away.

The next day was the thirteenth day after Naw Rúz, the Persian New Year, and we had all been invited to go on a picnic with a large group of Bahá'ís. Morad's sister was ill that morning, so I quickly cooked a Persian rice dish for the rest of the family to take with them, and explained that unfortunately something had come up and we would not be able to go with them as planned.

As soon as they left the house, we quickly tidied our things and slipped out. Khudáyár had told us not to bring anything with us in case we had to run, so all I brought with me was a small carrier bag containing the stockings Ṭáhirih had given me in prison, the photo of 'Abdu'l-Bahá which the guards had left behind in our house, a camera and some food for the journey.

We got to the bus station just before 2 p.m. and saw the Jahánpúr family waiting by the bus stop. We didn't greet each other. Shortly afterwards the bus arrived and we climbed aboard. I sat with Morad and Payam on one double seat, and the other three sat a few seats behind. We pretended not to know each other. Surprisingly, the bus left on time, and we settled down for a long journey.

Záhidán is about 900 miles from Tehran, almost twenty-four hours away by bus. Payam was tired and although he dozed off occasionally, he found the journey very difficult. We were desperate not to attract attention to ourselves, and tried to keep him quiet with chocolate, but it is hard to persuade a three-year-old to sit still for such a long time in the cramped confines of a bus. A lot of people were sick on the bus that afternoon, but the bus driver refused to stop for them. However, when Morad begged him to stop so he could take Payam to the toilet, he reluctantly pulled over and they quickly got off.

In the early evening the bus driver stopped at a roadside café and everyone got out to stretch their legs and have something to eat. We found a table and some chairs outside and sat down to eat the cutlet (the Iranian equivalent of a hamburger) and bágálí polo, a risotto of broad beans flavoured with dill, that I had brought with us from Tehran. Morad went inside and reappeared with some small glasses of black, sweet tea, and soon it was time to get back on the bus.

At four o'clock in the morning the bus bumped over the gravel verge and ground to a halt, waking me from a fitful sleep. It was time for prayers. Everyone clambered off and some shuffled into the nearby café while others went over to join some men who were already standing in the yard in congregational prayer. It was still quite dark, and the air seemed beautifully crisp and cool after the stuffiness of the bus. Even after two months of freedom it still gave me a rush of excitement to feel the fresh air on my face.

We went inside for a simple breakfast of bread, butter, jam, cheese and fried egg, washed down with the hot black tea that is traditionally sipped slowly through sugar lumps.

At 11.30 a.m. we arrived at last at the bus station in Záhidán. We spotted Khudáyár standing beside a white Toyota van on the other side of the road. He was dressed in the traditional Baluchi *qamís-shalvár*, a simple cotton shirt over baggy cotton trousers, which would help to pass him off as a local over the border in Pakistan. He gestured to us and we all hurried over. Morad and I were asked to get into the front seat with Payam, while Mrs Jahánpúr and her two daughters were directed to the back of the van. I was worried the women might be offended at being sent to the back, so I clambered in after them and we set off.

Khudáyár drove to the other side of the town and dropped us off at a kiosk where an extraordinary man was waiting for us – he was a dwarf, dressed in a cream-coloured *qamís-shalvár* and cream turban. Khudáyár introduced him as Hassan and told us that he would be accompanying us on the next stage of our journey. We should buy a bus ticket from Záhidán to Khásh, a small town on the Pakistani border about 100 miles away, and he warned us that on no account should we talk to Hassan on the way. We were to watch him carefully, and as soon as he got off the bus we were to do the same.

About half an hour later a minibus drove up and we all got on. It was clear from their clothes that all the other passengers on the bus were natives of Baluchistan, and we felt very conspicuous. Khudáyár followed the bus in his van. About three miles out of Záhidán, some Revolutionary Guards stopped the bus and rushed on board, holding pictures in their hands and looking at each passenger's face.

We tried to stay cool, but I was worried Payam would react badly. Ever since my arrest he had been terrified of the guards, and always cried out if he saw any in the street or on television. He was sitting on my lap and I hugged him closer as the guards slowly worked their way down the bus. Our hearts were pounding as they reached the back of the bus where we were sitting, but after a cursory glance they left without saying a word, and waved the driver on his way.

We drove on for two hours, Khudáyár sometimes overtaking the bus, sometimes dropping back. All of a sudden Hassan jumped up and asked the driver to stop. We were in an area of rocky desert with small hills either side of the road, about fifty miles from Záhidán. Hassan had been watching the white van carefully and had seen it pull off the road and turn onto a dirt track leading into the hills. As soon as the startled driver stopped the bus, Hassan jumped out. We hurriedly followed him, watched by a busload of surprised passengers.

Hassan was already sprinting over the stony ground towards the van and we all rushed to keep up with him. There was no time to look back at the bus to see the driver's reaction.

'*Zúd básh! Zúd básh*! – Quickly! Quickly!' Khudáyár shouted and we all jumped into the van. With a shower of stones he drove away from the main road as fast as possible and was soon speeding around the nearest hill. In this part of Iran there are very few roads, and the mountainous desert is crisscrossed with rough paths and tracks that only the Baluchi people know.

Khudáyár drove like a madman. We were all sitting on the hard metal floor in the back, and we were soon bruised and aching as the van swerved and bounced over the stony track. It was especially hard for Payam, and he began to cry loudly. Khudáyár shouted at us to try to keep him quiet as there were guards everywhere, and no one must hear us. Quickly we explained to Payam that we were trying to escape, and that if he cried the guards would find us and kill us. Did he want us to be taken back to prison? He seemed to understand the danger and immediately fell silent.

The sun went down and soon it was pitch black in the desert. Just as we were beginning to wonder how long we would have to endure this new torment, the van headlights fell on three black tents looming up out of the darkness. We had arrived at our resting place for the night.

It was 8 p.m. as we drove slowly up to the tents, the head-lights turned off and the engine purring quietly. This was the home of Khudáyár's family, we discovered, and they came out of one of the tents to greet us. They welcomed us warmly to their home. As we lifted the tent flap we were enveloped by a wonderful smell. Khudáyár had made arrangements with his mother and brother-in-law to kill a lamb for us and supper was all prepared when we arrived. There, on a carpet on the ground, they had laid out steaming plates of shísh kebab with home-made Persian flat bread cooked on the embers of the fire that was still glowing red in the middle of the tent.

We sat round the fire and ate supper, served attentively by Khudáyár's mother. The tent was surprisingly large and roomy inside, and already half full with the family's sheep. Khudáyár explained that if the guards came, the sheep would act as cover for us. His sister came to visit us after supper, speaking Farsí with a strong Baluchi accent. She had three children herself, and asked me about Payam and my sons in England. We drank the customary sweet, black tea, and then Khudáyár went out, taking Hassan with him. They would be sleeping in his sister's tent next door, he explained, and we should go to bed as we had a very early start in the morning.

His mother brought us some blankets and we settled down to sleep, the sheep on one side of the tent, us on the other. I wrapped myself in one of the blankets and lay down next to Payam, his small hand clutching mine as he tossed and turned in his dreams. Each time he woke up he reached out for my hand again to make sure I was still there beside him, the fear of my leaving him never far from his mind, even in sleep.

Just after four o'clock I woke up to the sounds of K̲h̲udáyár's mother moving quietly round the tent preparing breakfast. The sheep had disappeared, the fire was already lit and she was pouring water from a goatskin bag into the heavy kettle hanging over the flames. The tea would soon be ready. Payam stirred beside me, and I quickly took him outside to go to the toilet. When we went back into the tent, breakfast was already laid out and we sat down to eat newly baked bread and boiled eggs with some delicious white cheese made from the milk of the sheep, our noisy bedfellows of the night before.

While we were still eating breakfast, K̲h̲udáyár came in to tell us he was going on ahead to check the area and if it was safe, he would come back to get us. He introduced two friends, Muḥammad and Ja'far, who would be accompanying us all the way to Pakistan on a motor cycle, and together they set off to check the road ahead.

Meanwhile, it was getting light and we had to hide inside the tent because it wasn't safe to be seen outside. We waited and waited. At last K̲h̲udáyár returned, with the news that it was not a good time to go yet. Muḥammad and Ja'far had already been up to the border with Pakistan and had signalled to friends on the other side, who had warned them to wait. K̲h̲udáyár then left us again.

At 9 a.m. we all heard the sound of a helicopter in the distance getting nearer and nearer. K̲h̲udáyár's mother became very nervous. She told us that border guards had come only a few days before to search their tents, and seemed to suspect that K̲h̲udáyár was involved in smuggling Iranians across the border.

Curiosity got the better of me, and I peeped out of the door to see a grey helicopter heading in our direction. K̲h̲udáyár's mother quickly pulled me back inside the tent. 'Oh my God,' she cried, 'if the helicopter lands and the guards come here, they will arrest you all. What will become of your poor child if you are sent back to prison?' She was really worried for us, and especially for little Payam, as well as for her own son.

The helicopter circled overhead. Inside the tent, the noise was deafening and the sides and roof were blown about violently under the downblast from the propeller blades. Our hearts were beating hard and K̲h̲udáyár's mother was by now beside herself with fear. I tried to reassure her that the power that had kept us safe until then would, God willing, keep us safe now; nothing would go wrong if God wanted us to cross the border.

The helicopter continued to hover low over the tent, as if about to land. Then, in a matter of seconds, it changed direction and flew away. Everyone relaxed and began to laugh, especially that sweet woman who had risked so much for us. Theirs was a very simple life and their home was humble to say the least, but to us it seemed like heaven because of their wonderful kindness. Khudáyár had explained our situation to his family, and they showered us and the Jahánpúrs with such love and concern, not – I am sure – simply for the money, but because of the genuine sympathy they felt for us. They were lovely people and we felt cherished in their care.

An hour later, we heard a car driving at speed up to the tent. It skidded to a halt on the loose stones, and Khudáyár rushed in. It was no longer safe to stay there and we had to leave immediately, he said. We all ran outside and were told to get into a light blue truck driven by yet another guide, Alláhyár. Hassan sat in front, and the rest of us had to lie on the floor of the truck and keep our heads down. Then the convoy set off down the track, first the motor cycle, then us, then Khudáyár bringing up the rear in his van. The motor cyclists raced on ahead, checking the hills with their binoculars and signalling back to Alláhyár, our driver, that all was well.

We went on like that for several hours until in mid-afternoon Alláhyár suddenly pulled the truck off the road and came to a stop behind a hill. The white van had disappeared, and we hadn't seen any sign of the motor cycle for some time. He told us that we had better hide ourselves, since the others might have been caught by the guards. We waited. After an hour or so, Khudáyár reappeared, explaining that the motor cycle had got a flat tyre, and that in his opinion the road was not safe for us and we should not continue our journey. We couldn't go on and we couldn't go back, and he was clearly very worried.

He decided to take the motor cycle in his van to a nearby village for repairs and asked Alláhyár to go and get some food for us, leaving us with Hassan, the dwarf. By then it was around five o'clock and we hadn't had anything to eat since breakfast over twelve hours before. Khudáyár's mother had pressed two or three loaves of flat bread into my hand just as we were leaving, saying 'These are for Payam!' So we shared them out as we waited in that cold, deserted place.

Time passed and it was soon dark. Night-time in the mountains was very cold – it was still only April – and we had no blankets to help protect us from the bitter wind. We sat huddled close together behind a small hill, but the wind blew over the top and we were soon covered in dust. I wrapped Payam tightly in my arms to try to keep him warm, while Morad paced up and down, beside himself with worry. Mrs Jahánpúr, too, became very anxious, but her daughters calmed her. Several times Morad asked Hassan where all our guides had gone, and Hassan told him that they'd gone to the village to get blankets and food, and would be back soon. But as time went on, still with no word from the others, Hassan began to get frightened himself.

Morad questioned Hassan closely as to what he thought might have happened to Khudáyár, and Hassan replied that perhaps he had been arrested by the guards. Then Morad asked him what we should do, but by now Hassan was as cold and frightened as we were, and was beginning to think perhaps he might be arrested too. He clearly didn't know what to do, and sat there in the dark shivering miserably. When Morad realized that Hassan, who was supposed to be a local man and our guide, was terrified and helpless too, he started to worry even more; but his biggest fear was that if Hassan disappeared or got caught by the guards, we would be left stranded on our own in the middle of nowhere, at the mercy of wild animals or even Revolutionary Guards.

Compared to prison, however, this was paradise. 'Look,' I said to Morad. 'I had to endure much worse in prison. I would rather be killed by wild animals here in the mountains, than by the guards in prison. At least animals are swift, and they only kill once. The guards kill people a thousand times.'

By now the little food we had had was gone, the cold was creeping into our bones, and we were getting desperate. Before he had left, Khudáyár had warned us not to light a fire in case it attracted the attention of passing guards and they found our hiding place, but poor little Payam was shivering uncontrollably. We began to search around in the dark for firewood, but we didn't have any matches. Morad tried clumsily to rub two sticks together, but Hassan rushed up and told him to stop. I don't think it would have worked anyway, but we were desperate enough to try anything.

In the early hours of the morning, we heard a car approaching us. It had its lights turned off, and stopped a short distance away. We were terrified. All of a sudden we heard Khudáyár's voice whispering, 'Are you still there?' He was as relieved to see us as we were to see him. When he had left us, he said, he was followed by the guards and it took him six hours to get rid of them, driving on the mountain paths with his lights off. He said he had prayed to God for our safety as he drove, and he would sacrifice a sheep in gratitude. He had brought blankets and a little bread with him, and we wrapped ourselves up and waited till dawn.

Alláhyár reappeared with his truck as it was beginning to get light, shortly followed by Muhammad and Ja'far on the now repaired motor cycle. The Jahánpúrs climbed into the back of Khudáyár's van, we clambered in after them, and the strange convoy set off once more towards the border. After a few hours we passed the last village in Iran, and shortly afterwards entered Pakistan.

We had come to a high pass through the mountains and Khudáyár stopped the van at the side of the road. 'This is your last chance to see Iran,' he told us. 'We've just crossed the border.'

We all got out and stood together on that deserted road looking back at our homeland. I looked across at Morad and noticed a tear slip down his cheek. I too felt very sad to be leaving, but I could also feel my goal edging closer towards me. Soon I would be able to fulfil the promise I had made to my friends.

About fifteen miles inside Pakistan the convoy came to a halt behind a small hill. Khudáyár asked us to wait there while he drove to a nearby village to rent a Pakistani vehicle. When he returned about an hour later, Muhammad and Ja'far, Alláhyár and Hassan came up to say goodbye. We all shook hands and the men slapped Morad heartily on the back. They were so happy and proud they had managed to help us escape, and we felt so close to them after the experiences we had been through together. Our lives had been completely in their hands, and they had risked theirs to help us to safety.

'Thank you. God bless you.' It was so hard to express the depth of our gratitude.

'Remember us,' they said with bashful smiles.

'I will tell my children how you saved their mother,' I promised.

It was 9 a.m. when Muhammad and Ja'far got back on their motor cycle, Alláhyár and Hassan climbed into the blue truck, and they all drove back down the track to Iran. We got into the Pakistani van that Khudáyár had managed to rent, complete with driver, and drove on into Pakistan. We drove all day through the desert and into the evening. At about seven o'clock we came to a small village and were taken into a family's home where a wonderful dinner had been prepared for us.

It was our first proper meal since breakfast in Khudáyár's tent over thirty-six hours ago, and it was also, of course, our first meal outside Iran. We were given chicken in a mild curry sauce with local bread, and a huge plate of oranges, mandarins and bananas – the latter were such a rarity in Iran that hardly anyone could afford to buy them, and Payam wolfed his down in no time at all.

We were staying in a very simple village house. There was no furniture at all, not even tables and chairs, but it was clean and tidy. There was a rustic Persian *gilím* rug on the floor, and the food was placed on a plastic table cloth on top. After we had eaten, everything was cleared away and the woman of the house laid out thin mattresses and *laháfs*, thick Persian quilts like eiderdowns. We all settled down to sleep, exhausted after our long journey and the sleepless night we had had in the mountains.

Early the next morning I took Payam to the toilet in a small shed on the other side of the yard. As we were walking back, I noticed a gold ring in the dust. I promptly picked it up

and handed it to Khudáyár and told him where I had found it.
He went to our hostess and said, 'You see how honest this
woman is. She could have slipped it into her pocket and kept
it for herself, but she didn't.' It wasn't the woman's own ring,
and everyone decided it must have belonged to an earlier
refugee. Khudáyár insisted our hostess keep it, and she was
very grateful.

We had a simple breakfast of bread, cheese and black tea
and prepared to leave. Khudáyár had arranged the night before
for an old man from the village to come with us. The idea was
that if we were stopped by the Pakistani police the old man
could say I was his daughter-in-law. As soon as he arrived we
set off, Khudáyár in the front next to the driver and the rest of
us lying down and keeping as low as we could so it would look
as if Khudáyár and the driver were travelling alone.

After a few hours, the driver suddenly put his foot down hard.
He raced past two police checkpoints at breakneck speed, ignor-
ing the guards' attempts to flag him down. At the third there were
rocks in the middle of the road, but he just managed to squeeze
through the gap. He was an excellent driver and though he drove
so fast down the winding road that the van skidded on the loose
gravel, he never lost control and we sped on.

A few miles further on, we suddenly found the road ahead
blocked by a police car. Two Pakistani policemen were standing
in front of the car pointing guns at us, and we had no choice
but to stop. One policeman got into the front seat beside
Khudáyár to check his papers and ask questions. The other
came round to the back of the van. He could see immediately
from our clothes that we were not from Pakistan.

He asked the old man in Urdu who we were. Our compan-
ion was clearly terrified, and with his eye on the gun pointing
menacingly in his direction, he denied any knowledge of us.
The policeman strode round to the front of the van and
shouted at Khudáyár, 'You said the old man was that woman's
father-in-law but he says he doesn't know these people!'

We didn't really understand what was going on exactly, and
sat in the back miserably waiting for our fate to be decided
without us. Meanwhile, Khudáyár sat in the front arguing heat-
edly with the two policemen. After what seemed like hours, he

came to the back and explained that they wanted to arrest us and escort us back to the border. He had offered them money, but they wanted more and he didn't have enough. We would have to go with them. The first policeman sat in the front with K͟hudáyár and the other drove the police car. We set off back towards Iran.

K͟hudáyár continued trying to negotiate with them for the price of our freedom, but two hours passed and we were still heading back the way we had come. The Iranian border was getting ever closer and with it the frightening prospect of finding ourselves back in Iran in the hands of the Revolutionary Guards.

Suddenly the van ground to a halt. K͟hudáyár came to the back of the van and called to me, 'Olya, bring your child and talk to them. Maybe you will be able to persuade them to let us go.'

I protested that I couldn't speak a word of Urdu, but he said it didn't matter, he would translate. So I climbed out of the van and Morad held Payam out to me. 'Tell them everything about your situation,' K͟hudáyár instructed me quietly. 'He wants a lot of money. I have already offered what I have but he wants more and I can't change his mind. Perhaps you can.'

The other policeman had come up, and I told them, 'You have the power to decide our fate. The choice is yours: you can deliver us back to Iran into the hands of the guards, and they will kill us, or you can help to save our lives.' I gestured to Payam. 'I am the mother of a three-year-old child. I haven't done anything wrong. My only crime, and the only reason I was put in prison, is that I'm a Bahá'í. There are only two ways to leave Iran right now. I can't leave by plane unless I recant my religion. That only leaves this way. And if you send me back and they kill me, how will you answer to my little boy? You want money? This man has already offered you whatever he has and is telling you the truth.'

The police were moved, or perhaps they decided that K͟hudáyár might be telling the truth about the money after all. In any event, they called him over and said, '*Bashih* – OK. Give us the money.' K͟hudáyár handed over the cash, Payam and I climbed back in the van and we were waved on our way. K͟hudáyár didn't stop till we reached our destination.

It was 1 a.m. on 7 April when we arrived at the outskirts of
Karachi. Despite the hour, everything was lit up and music was
playing. Bazaars were still open, children ran in the street, rick-
shaws weaved in and out between the cars and the city buzzed
with life and colour. The van drew up outside a luxury hotel.
Khudáyár paid the bill for us in advance and treated us with
incredible kindness and consideration. The Jahánpúrs had one
room and we had another, and we all went straight to bed. It
had been a long, exhausting journey.

The next morning, while we were eating breakfast,
Khudáyár got in touch with one of the members of the
National Spiritual Assembly of Pakistan, Parvíz Rawhání, and
told him that he had brought some Bahá'ís with him from Iran
who needed help. Mr Rawhání came round to the hotel immediately, and we spent some time introducing ourselves and
explaining our situation to him. He promised to come back in
an hour, so Khudáyár whisked us off to lunch. He took us for a
chelo kebab, and I thought of poor Shírín still waiting patiently
for a chance to go to her favourite restaurant in Tehran.

It was hard to say goodbye to Khudáyár. This wonderful, kind
man had endangered his own life to save ours, and arranged
everything with a care and attention that money could never
buy. We said an emotional farewell and he returned to Iran.

Parvíz returned to take us to the Karachi Bahá'í Centre
where, at last, I was able to give a detailed account of the persecution of the Bahá'ís in Iran and especially the experiences of
the women in Adelabad. They had put so much faith in me,
and were depending on my testimony to speed up their release.

The next day, we went to the United Nations Office to register for refugee status and to make another official report on
the Bahá'í situation in Iran. First we were taken to a flat, and
later a Christian family, who had themselves been refugees at
the time of the partition of India and Pakistan, offered all six of
us a room in their home. We stayed with these wonderful
people for many months while our application for international
refugee status was processed by the United Nations.

We had no contact with Iran. No news ever reached us of our
friends in prison, and we didn't know what had happened to

them. Being so far from them, from our relatives, and from our country was very painful. But one night, just over two months after our arrival in Pakistan, I had a very vivid dream. I dreamt that Nusrat Yaldá'í had come to me and stood in the doorway of my room. She was smiling happily, her arms open wide, and she was laughing.

'Dear Olya,' she cried, 'don't be sad and don't worry about us. Look at me, I am free like you now, and I've come to see you.' In the dream I was filled with happiness too. I was about to embrace her when I woke up.

I immediately burst into tears. Morad tried to comfort me: 'Oh Olya, it was only a dream. I'm sure it didn't mean anything, and they're all fine.' But I cried and cried.

It was 19 June 1983. I was filled with a dreadful sense of foreboding, and was disturbed all day. At about 6 p.m. we were listening to Radio Israel, which occasionally reported news from Iran, when the announcer began a news flash: 'Yesterday in Iran,' he began, 'ten women were executed in Shíráz. Their crime was to be Bahá'ís. Two days earlier, six men were hanged on the same charge . . .'

I screamed and dashed straight out of the house to the Bahá'í Centre to find out if it was true, and if so to discover the names of the victims. They were already on the telephone to the National Spiritual Assembly of the United States. One by one, the names were read out to me: Jamshíd Síyávushí, 'Ináyat Ishráqí, Bahrám Yaldá'í, Bahrám Afnán, Kúrush Haqbín and Qulám Husayn Azádí. And then the women, Nusrat Yaldá'í, 'Izzat Ishráqí, Roya Ishráqí, Ṭáhirih Síyávushí, Mahshíd Nírúmand, Símín Sábirí, Akhtar Sabet, Zarrín Muqímí, Shírín Dálvand and Mona Maḥmúdnizhád.

Epilogue

My friends were dead, taken to the hangman's noose before the full force of international outrage had begun to impress itself on the leaders of the Iranian government. Indeed, their deaths were to a large extent the cause of that outrage.

As news began to reach me in Pakistan from their relatives, I started to collect accounts of what had happened, as a moving memorial to these brave women.

Rosita Ishráqí was one of the first to share her experiences with me. This is taken from her diary:

Our last visit with my father was on Wednesday, 15 June. That day my fiancé and I told him the date of our engagement. He was very happy, and his eyes filled with tears. 'Please don't be sad', he said, 'that we are not there for the celebrations, because our love will be with you. You can be certain of that.' He sent his regards to all and said he was thinking of everyone and that he was obedient to what God had ordained for him.

Visiting time was longer than usual, and he left us looking full of excitement and happiness. The next day, as we were preparing happily for our engagement ceremony, at around four o'clock in the afternoon they called my father and five other Bahá'í men and told them that they were taking them to court. They all knew that there was no court on Thursdays and that they were being taken for execution.

We received the news on Saturday morning, 18 June. Some Bahá'í friends came to the house looking distressed, and I knew straight away that something had happened. They told us that my father and five other men had been killed two days ago. I could not take it in. I kept repeating, 'My father, my dear father.' I leaned against the wall and slowly slipped to the floor, sobbing.

We went to the morgue in the hope of getting permission to bury my father, but this basic right was denied to us. They wouldn't even let us see the bodies at first, but finally, because we begged one of the guards on duty whom we had known for years, they allowed the close family to see the corpses for just a few minutes.

They opened the door and I saw seven bodies lying on the floor. I recognized them all, except the seventh person who was not a Bahá'í. I saw my father straight away from a distance. I was very nervous and didn't know what to do, since I had never seen a dead body before. As I was walking towards Dad I couldn't take my eyes off him; I tripped over one of the bodies and fell on the floor.

As I edged my way over to him, I kept repeating, 'Oh God, is this my father?' And I couldn't stop crying.

I kissed his face; he was cold and his skin was hard. I sat beside him. His whole body had swollen so much that I couldn't see the rope marks on his neck. His arms were resting at his sides and he looked composed, with a beautiful smile on his face. I was shivering uncontrollably when I left the room.

My fiancé drove me home. All the way I was weeping, saying, 'Now, how am I going to tell Mama and Roya?' But he reassured me that I would be able to do it when the time came.

It was Saturday afternoon and we were going to visit Roya and Mama soon. I was afraid that my mother would never be able to bear such tragic news.

On our prison visits, we could usually tell from a distance how the prisoners were feeling. At first glance, I knew Roya and Mama were happy. I was trying to control myself but I couldn't, and burst into tears again. Roya pointed to my new engagement ring and said,

'Wear it with joy.' I started to cry even harder. She asked, 'What is it, Rosy?' Before they had even connected us by telephone I had made her understand that our father had been hanged.

She was shocked. 'Are you sure?' she asked. I nodded. Her eyes filled with tears, but a beautiful smile lit up her face and she put her hands to her heart, saying, 'Thank God.' I was astonished.

Mother asked her what was going on, and Roya put her arm around her and explained. Mama said, 'O God, I hope to die.' Then Roya said something I didn't catch, and Mama looked at me and said, 'Don't you worry. It's all right.'

I was astounded at their strength and firmness. I kept thinking, is this my mother? She asked, 'When did it happen?'

'Thursday night.'

'I knew it. I have done my crying. I had a dream in which we were together – we are going soon, any day now, maybe today or tomorrow! I want you to be strong and happy and get on with your life. I wish you all the happiness in the world and I leave you in God's protection.' I was crying, but my tears were for myself because she wasn't sad at all. She didn't shed a single tear.

I told Roya that I had seen Dad's body, and that he was smiling. We promised one another to be strong and to keep smiling, just like him.

Roya told me, 'One time they took Mama for execution and I thought Dad was with her as well. I detached myself from both of them at that time and said my goodbyes then in my heart.'

Roya kept giving me courage and hope. In the last moments of our visit she said, 'Rosy, bring your hand up and let us see your ring. We all want to look at it.'

When the visit was over everyone said, 'Take a good look at them. It might be the last time.' Tears were running down my face and Roya was smiling, saying, 'Don't cry. You promised me.' Her eyes were shining in a way I had never seen before in my life.

They were leaving with such dignity and courage. What patience! They were so close to God. What was it that they saw and felt that made them so joyful to leave this world and everything in it, and everyone they cared for?

Farkhundih Mahmúdnizhád, who had just been released from prison when the ten women, including her daughter Mona, were taken to be hanged, and Taránih, Mona's elder sister, both wrote to me about those momentous days. Farkhundih wrote:

One day in early June, not long before the anniversary of the passing of the Báb, Mona woke up in the morning and said, 'I don't want to eat anything any more.' For thirty hours she fasted, refusing to eat or drink. After that she brought some bread, cheese and a piece of watermelon and before she ate she told me, 'I was connected.' I didn't ask her any questions. The day of commemoration was getting close. We decided that we would all gather in one cell and say prayers at twelve o'clock sharp. Mona wanted to be alone, but I asked her to join us. She didn't say anything. After prayers we had lunch and scattered to do what we had to do, such as cleaning the cells and washing dishes. Because it was Ramadan they were reading the Qur'án over the loud-speakers, and it was very noisy.

Mona came to my side and said, 'Mama, I really wanted to be alone and commemorate the last anniversary of the passing of the Báb on my own.'

I didn't understand why she said the 'last' anniversary, but I assumed she meant the last one in prison. Now I realize she meant the last anniversary for her in this world. I said to her, 'You should have told me that; I wouldn't have kept you from being alone. You shouldn't just do as I say all the time.'

'But Mama,' she replied calmly, 'you had the right to ask me.' Then she went for a walk in the corridor. A few minutes later she returned and said, 'Mama, I want to talk to you. I want to tell you something. Please come with me.'

I went along with her. The corridor was so narrow that the two of us could hardly walk side by side. We walked a little way and then she stopped. I stopped beside her, and waited for her to speak. She looked into my eyes and said, 'Mama, do you know that they are going to execute me?'

Suddenly my whole being seemed to be on fire. I didn't want to believe her. I said, 'No, my dear daughter, they are going to let you go. You will get married and have children. My greatest wish is to see your children. No, don't even think that.' I was completely oblivious to the world she was living in.

She got upset and said, 'Mama, I swear to God that I don't have such hopes, and I don't want you to have them for me either. I know I will be killed. I just want to tell you what I am planning to do. If you don't let me tell you now, you will lose this chance for ever, and then you will be sorry that you didn't let me talk. Now do you want me to tell you or not?'

Haltingly I agreed, 'OK, tell me.'

Mona held my elbow and started to walk. 'You know, Mama, the place where they are going to hang us is probably going to be higher than the ground, so they can put the rope around our necks. I will first get permission to kiss the hands of whoever puts the rope around my neck. You know, Mama, I think they will definitely let me do that. I will then explain that we Bahá'ís are not allowed to kiss anyone's hand except the hands of our murderer. That hand must be kissed, because it will speed up our journey towards our Beloved. Then I will kiss the rope I am to be hanged with. Then I will ask their permission again, and say this prayer.' As she was standing in front of me she closed her eyes, crossed her hands on her chest and, in a very spiritual manner, like a lover singing a song for her beloved, she chanted a prayer. Then she opened her eyes and said, 'And then I will pray for the true happiness of all humankind and I will say goodbye to this mortal life and leave, to go to my adored one.'

I looked at her but I couldn't see her. I heard her but I couldn't comprehend what she was saying. On the one hand my emotional attachment to her was frightening me, on the other hand she had taken me to a beautiful spiritual world. But somehow I couldn't believe it, and said, 'It was a beautiful story.'

Mona looked at me, tears in her eyes, and said softly, 'It wasn't a story, Mama. Why can't you accept it?' Then she left me and for a long time continued to pace up and down the corridor. My beautiful Mona knew that she was going. She knew how she was going, and I couldn't believe her. Ten days later she was killed. It was five days after my release.

The day I received the news was such a difficult day. I kept going over in my mind what Mona had told me that day in the prison. I was numb. People were talking to me and I couldn't hear. I thought to myself, 'My God, how can I bear this?' But God gave me the strength.

I remembered that when the Bahá'í prisoners were told they had four chances to recant or they would be hanged, Mona had had a dream. She had dreamed that as she was standing in the cell saying her obligatory prayer, 'Abdu'l-Bahá had entered the cell and sat on the bed where I was sleeping, and put his hand on my head. Ṭáhirih was also sleeping by the bed. 'Abdu'l-Bahá raised his other hand towards Mona. Mona thought to herself that if she continued with the obligatory prayer he might leave, so she stopped praying and sat on her knees before him, and held his hand in hers. 'Abdu'l-Bahá asked her, 'Mona what do you want?' and she answered, 'Perseverance.'

He asked again, 'What do you want from me?'

She replied, 'Perseverance for all the Bahá'ís.'

'Abdu'l-Bahá asked her for the third time, 'Mona, what do you want for yourself from me?'

Mona said again, 'Perseverance.' 'Abdu'l-Bahá then repeated, 'It is granted, it is granted.'

The next morning she had told everyone about her dream. Zarrín hugged Mona and said, 'Oh Mona, what a wonderful wish you asked for from 'Abdu'l-Bahá. You know it will be a tragedy for the Bahá'ís if they execute us all, but I am sure they will be firm. You could have requested freedom for yourself and your mother – even freedom for all of us – but you asked for the most wonderful thing and he granted it.'

I was released on 13 June. 'Izzat Ishráqí asked me to attend Rosita's wedding on her behalf and take a red carnation on behalf of each prisoner. Everyone asked me to do something for them on the outside. My beloved Mona was the last person to say goodbye. She kissed me and as she was holding my hand in hers, said to me, 'Mama, you supported everyone and warmed all the hearts here. Continue to do the same for the ones outside; encourage them to be firm and strong.'

I kissed her again and said goodbye, but it wasn't the last time that I kissed her lovely face. The last time was in the morgue where I kissed her beautiful, cold cheeks and returned that treasure to its original owner. On the last visiting day Mona had said to me, 'Mother, we will be guests of Bahá'u'lláh tomorrow.' Next day I heard the news of their execution.

This is Taránih's description of those momentous days.

On Friday, the day after those brave men were hanged, there was uproar in Shíráz. Once again the Bahá'ís were visiting the families of the martyrs with huge bouquets of flowers, tears in their eyes and smiles on their faces. They were rushing in groups to the houses of the martyrs to visit their families, and despite all the oppression their houses were packed with people.

Saturday came and we went to visit the prisoners in the afternoon. My mother, who had just been released five days previously, and I went to see Mona, taking my baby daughter with us. We had bought a watermelon for

Mona and I had made a new headcover and bought a new towel for her.

I couldn't wait to see her. I only had the chance to see her once a week and for a very short period of time, but it made me very happy. I didn't know that this was to be our last meeting.

Before we went in to see the prisoners, all the Bahá'ís gathered in the prison yard, consulting on whether we should tell them about the martyrdom of the six men. My mother said, 'I know how it is in prison.' She kept insisting that we must be honest with them, because 'I know if we don't tell them, the guards will, and they will do it in a very harsh manner, just to hurt them. It is much better if we tell them ourselves.'

The time came for our visit. We all sat in the small booths and when the connections were turned on we started to talk. First my mother talked to Mona. I was impatient because I was afraid that we wouldn't have much time, so I grabbed the phone from Mama and started to talk. Mona always inquired about everyone's well-being in her usual cheerful way, and would tell me, 'I would like to hug you and squeeze you.' She laughed and said, 'You must be very happy now that Mother is with you!'

I quickly answered her questions and then, without a preliminary, I said, 'Mona, I have news.'

'What? Tell me.'

'Six of our men were executed.'

I wish I could describe her reaction to you. Her beautiful green eyes were suddenly filled with tears. She put her hand on her heart and softly said, 'Who were they?'

She was crying as I named them. Táhirih Síyávushí was in the next booth talking to her father. I pointed to her and said, 'Táhirih's husband, Jamshíd,' and then I named the rest.

Every time I named one there were more tears in her eyes and she pressed her hand harder to her heart. She said, 'Good for him, good for him.' I named Mr

Ishráqí last and I saw tears rolling down her beautiful cheeks. 'Good for all of them,' she said. 'Taránih, I swear to God these are not tears of sadness or grief. They are tears of happiness.'

'Mona, you will go soon,' I said.

'I know, I know,' she replied. 'Taránih, I have a favour to ask. I want you to pray that we go to the execution ground dancing and singing.'

I promised her that I would. I said, 'Whatever God has ordained will happen.'

'I have another favour to ask too, and that is for you to pray that God will forgive my sins before I'm executed.'

I looked at her and said, 'What sin have you committed, that you want to be forgiven?'

I tried so hard not to cry and not to talk so I could watch her and hear her beautiful voice. I told her, 'My dear Mona, now I will let you talk to Mama,' and I handed the receiver to my mother.

While my mother and Mona were talking, Táhirih's father was kind enough to let me speak to her. She said, 'Tell your mother not to worry about Mona, she is as strong as ever and we take care of her.'

Time was limited and we couldn't afford to lose a second. Impatient to speak to Mona again, I grabbed the receiver from my mother and said, 'You were together for months, now it is my turn to speak to her.'

Mona laughed and said, 'You know what makes me so happy? To know that we are Bahá'u'lláh's chosen ones.'

I just looked at her. What could I add to that? Then she said, 'My dear Taránih, send my regards to all our relatives and friends. Kiss everyone for me.' Then she indicated my baby daughter Nora and said, 'I want you to bring her up just like Father.'

In my heart I said, 'I want to bring her up just like you.' But I wanted her to talk so I didn't say anything.

Then we were disconnected and that was the end of our visit. For the last time we kissed our fingertips and put our hands to the glass. Mona and all the other prisoners left one after the other.

Every time I think about that day I remember my beloved sister's beautiful face and how she kissed her fingers and placed her hand on the glass. Even though there was an inch of glass separating our hands, the warmth of our love was felt in our hearts and nothing could have prevented that.

It was late afternoon on 18 June when the prison visit was over. Shortly afterwards the guards called the ten women and ordered them to board a bus. They were Mona, Roya and her mother 'Izzat, S͟hírín, Zarrín, Mah͟shíd, Símín, A͟khtar, Ṭáhirih and Nusrat.

The bus driver who transferred them from Adelabad to the execution site was greatly affected by the bravery and strength of the women, and he recalled that moment as follows: 'I thought they were going to be released until we came up to the gate for the security check. That was where we found out that the ladies were going to be executed. All the way they were chanting; they were all cheerful and proud.'

Another witness was one of the executioners who put the rope around their necks. He told the mother of one of the girls, 'We gave them the opportunity to recant up to the last minute. First we hanged the older women, and then it was the turn of the young girls, one by one in front of the rest. The youngest was last. We thought they would be so frightened that they would recant. We said to them, "Just say once that you are not a Bahá'í and we will let you go." But none of them did. They all preferred to die.'

At 10 p.m. the bodies were taken to the morgue.

The next morning, when the families of the six brave men who had been executed two days previously went to the morgue to try once more to collect the bodies, they found out that the ten women had been hanged the night before. The news spread like wildfire and profoundly affected everyone in S͟híráz.

Rosita Is͟hráqí's husband wrote:

Sunday morning we went to the morgue to try to collect the bodies of the Bahá'í men. We heard rumours that

some Bahá'í women had also been martyred the night
before. Two Bahá'ís were walking towards us as we
approached the morgue. One was hitting himself about
the head and repeating, 'Mass murder, mass murder.'
Rosita asked, 'What is it?'

He replied, 'They have just brought in ten women.'

'Is my family there?' she asked quickly.

He replied hesitantly, 'I saw Roya, but I do not
know about your mother.'

Rosy became very distressed. I had a feeling that it
was mostly because she was afraid her mother would be
left all alone in prison. She couldn't bear the thought of
such a great test for her mother. While she cried, I
myself felt just about ready to explode. We drove back
home.

The house was full of visitors and everyone was
debating about how to give Rosy the news that she
already knew. Half an hour later, we received a phone
call confirming that Mrs Ishráqí was one of the ten
women, and this calmed Rosita.

We went back to the morgue, and Rosita and a few
other people were allowed to go in and see the bodies.

Rosita described what happened next.

The guard had been punished the previous day for
letting us in, but he still opened the gate for us knowing
full well he would be punished again. On the gate there
was a sign reading, 'No Admittance in any Circumstances'.

It was cold and quiet in the morgue. The first body
I saw was Roya's. The sight of the ten of them was
frightening but glorious. Their faces were completely
transformed. I only recognized Roya by what she was
wearing: white and red striped trousers and a navy blue
tunic. One of her socks had fallen down to her ankle,
and her left hand was resting on her forehead as if she
was asleep. The blindfold that they had put on each of
the women before hanging them was still on her fore-

head. Her face was slightly swollen and purple, and the rope marks were visible on her neck. There were traces of dried blood on her hands. Her body was cold but the skin was still soft. I kissed her face and repeated, 'Thank you Sister, thank you Sister.'

Then I got up and looked for Mama. The more I looked, the less I could recognize any of them. They were all so transformed.

I saw an old lady lying beside a young girl. Her chador had been removed, revealing almost white hair. I thought to myself, who could this be? I didn't know anyone like her. Then my eyes were drawn to the scarf knotted around her neck. My God, it was my mother, and that was the scarf I had bought for her! I sat beside her and kissed her face. I put my hands on her shoulders and said, 'Thank you Mother, thank you Mother.'

I touched her hands. Her veins were visible through her pale skin, indicating the hardships she had endured over the years. She was very cold.

All of the women looked innocent, yet strong. I looked carefully at all of them so I would never forget their faces. As I was kissing Mama again, the guard came up to me and asked, 'What is your relation to her?'

'She is my mother,' I said. 'Come with me and I will show you my sister.'

I took him over to where Roya was resting. He knew I had been there to see my father the day before. His eyes filled with tears and he said, 'Why are you standing here? Go out! Go out!' We all left.

It was around noon when all sixteen bodies were put in ambulances and transferred to the Bahá'í cemetery by the guards. They buried all the bodies with their clothes on and without coffins, in previously prepared graves. They covered them with dirt and then destroyed the boundaries between the graves so we wouldn't be able to tell who was buried where. But that didn't make any difference. They were all pure love, they were all light and they all returned to the same source.

Soon after their death I received a gift from 'Izzat I<u>sh</u>ráqí. She had remembered a chance remark I made in prison, and when her execution was approaching she had arranged for someone to send me a set of teapot covers, which were forwarded to me in Pakistan. Her gift demonstrated what a loving heart she had, which showed itself in the smallest things as well as the greatest.

Zarrín Muqímí's mother also wrote about her experiences on the day the news of the hangings broke.

> Early Sunday morning I was given the tragic news that ten women had been executed the previous night. I rushed to a friend's house to see if they had the list of names, but they didn't, so I ran out of the house to enquire elsewhere. In the street I saw three Bahá'ís crying. They showed me a list, and I saw Zarrín's name on it.
>
> Weeping, I ran towards Adelabad. This was the place around which our lives had revolved for the past eight months. They let me go into the morgue.
>
> I never thought I would be able to carry on living after that moment. What I saw in that room and what I went through that day are indescribable. When I went in, Oh my God, I saw ten angels sleeping motionless next to each other. I knew all of them; I had been in the same prison with them. There were mother and daughter, 'Izzat and Roya I<u>sh</u>ráqí, lying there. What strength kept me breathing and on my feet I don't know.
>
> I visited all ten angels. I found Zarrín, embraced her cold body and put my cheek against her delicate and cold face. I kissed the mark of the rope on her beloved neck on behalf of all of her family. Her face looked natural and tranquil.
>
> Zarrín had told her friends and relations that after her martyrdom no one was to wear black or to cry out loud, except me, her mother, who was permitted to cry just a little.

Finally, here are Taránih Ma<u>h</u>múdni<u>zh</u>ád's words about how she received the tragic news.

The pain I felt that day was the same as when I heard the news of my father's martyrdom. Knowing Mona, I had been certain that she would never give in. Besides, I had never even asked Bahá'u'lláh for her freedom, because I did not want anything other than His will. But several times I had thought to myself, if they kill Mona, how am I going to endure the sight of her dead body? I thought I would go mad. The prospect was so painful that psychologically I refused to accept it. Instead, I imagined the day when she would return home; her footsteps, her laughter, her lovely voice; I imagined embracing and kissing my beautiful sister. I wanted to share the pain of my father's martyrdom with her, and I needed to talk to her about the painful days when they were all in prison. I wanted her to share with me the sufferings she had gone through. I had plans for us to be together and support our mother.

But the divine plan was different from what I had hoped for, and there can be no other way but resignation. So many thoughts rushed through my head in the moment when I heard the tragic news of the martyrdoms. I hoped that someone would come in and say it wasn't true. But when my mother and I managed to get into the morgue, with great difficulty, and saw their motionless bodies, I stopped hoping. As my mother said after kissing each and every one of them on the cheek, 'I wish I had the eyes of all the world, to show them how the love for Bahá'u'lláh and the truth has blossomed in these beloved souls.'

Mother went back to the body of Shírín Dálvand a second time. 'Shírín, my dear,' she said, 'I shall give you two more kisses, on behalf of your parents in England – one from your mother, and one from your father. Accept these kisses from me.'

I was still kneeling beside Mona. It was a bitter experience seeing my sister for the last time without a glass partition to separate us. I kissed her cold cheek and said goodbye to her. With all my heart, I wished she would open her eyes and let me see her smile one last time. But I knew she was observing us from above with an eternal smile, and one teardrop would break her heart.

Thus, my beautiful Mona, I smile for the love you had for Bahá'u'lláh and humankind. May the world discover why you sacrificed your life.

Postscript

My husband, Payam and I spent eleven months in Pakistan applying for asylum to England, Australia and Canada. We were refused by all three countries. While waiting in Pakistan I trained as a beautician and hairdresser and obtained my diploma there. Eventually, the United Nations intervened on our behalf and, because our children had been studying in England for several years, we were granted a visa to join them there on 6 March 1984.

One of my aims in speaking out about what I had witnessed was to help alleviate the extreme pressure on the Bahá'í community in Iran, and to bring their plight to the attention of the people of the world, as I had promised to the ten women. In 1984, 850 Bahá'ís were imprisoned in Iran solely for their religion and the persecution of the Bahá'í community there was still increasing daily.

My testimony in Pakistan was not effective in saving the lives of my friends in Adelabad. However, on my arrival in England I had a meeting with a representative of the United Nations Human Rights Commission and an interview with *Newsweek* magazine, which was printed on 18 June 1984, exactly one year after the hanging of the ten Bahá'í women in Shíráz.

Further interviews followed with national and local media such as *The Guardian*, BBC World Service, BBC 2 *Newsnight* programme (broadcast on 4 February 1985), Anglia TV News and many of the major international newspapers such as *Le Monde*, *The New York Times* and *The Washington Post*.

On 28 November 1985, I was invited to attend the hearing of the European Parliament in Brussels on the human rights situation in Iran, to testify as a witness to the persecution of the Bahá'ís. Soon after this the European Parliament passed a resolution condemning the persecution of the Bahá'í community in Iran, and requesting the Iranian government to extend basic human rights to the Bahá'ís.

As a result of this resolution, together with the mounting pressure exerted by the United Nations through various resolutions against Iran's persecution of the Bahá'í community, the international Bahá'í community's own efforts to bring the plight of their fellow Bahá'ís in Iran to the attention of the people of the world, and the intercession of individual governments around the world with the Islamic Revolutionary Government of Iran, 550 Bahá'í prisoners were freed in a relatively short period of time.

The following year I also went to the United Nations offices in Geneva on 26 November to testify in a full day's hearing on the situation of the Bahá'ís in Iran.

Payam is now a teenager attending a local grammar school. My second son, **Fazlu'lláh**, has a BSc in Physics and an MSc in Optics, and works in telecommunications. My eldest son, **Behnam**, is now married. He is a Chartered Engineer and also has an MBA. My husband, **Morad**, who has been my greatest support and helper both in Iran and since coming to England, is retired and enjoys spending time on his garden, as well as helping our family and friends.

As for me, the experience of imprisonment has given me a heightened sense of freedom, in both thought and action. Prison was the best of universities. My arrest changed me completely, and I see life through new eyes – the daily problems we face seem trivial, and I have a much more positive approach to life's ups and downs. I am happy, and life is beautiful.

Mítrá Íraván was released in 1984 after two years' imprisonment. She moved away from S̲h̲íráz and is now married with two children, still living in Iran.

Mínú Násirí was released on bail of 40,000 tuman. She managed to escape with her husband to Pakistan before she could be rearrested. She now lives in Florida, USA and has a beautiful daughter called Maryam.

Rúḥíyyih Jahánpúr left Pakistan for Canada with her mother and sister, where they still live.

Rosita Isḥráqí was married soon after the execution of her father, mother and sister. Her husband was imprisoned shortly afterwards and later released. She is now living in Iṣfahán with her husband and two children.

Farkhundih Maḥmúdniẕhád, whose husband was hanged on 12 March 1983, was released on 13 June 1983, five days before her daughter Mona was hanged. She has remained strong despite all the hardships she endured, and still lives in Shíráz.

Aḥmad Yaldá'í was released from prison after handing over the deeds of his house as security for his release, some months before the execution of his wife Nusrat and son Bahrám. He is still living in Shíráz.

Farhád Bihmardí was taken from Adelabad to Evin prison in Tehran and then to Qasr Prison, Tehran. Farhád was freed after four years of imprisonment and torture and is still living in Iran. His brother **Faríd Bihmardí**, a member of the National Spiritual Assembly of Iran, was, however, executed after two years of imprisonment and a great deal of torture, on 10 June 1986.

Suhayl Húshmand was executed on 28 June 1983, ten days after the Shíráz women.

Ḥusayn Muqímí, Zarrín's father, was eventually released from prison after about two years.

Firishtih and Muḥammad Anvarí rejoined the Bahá'í community a few years ago. They moved away from Shíráz and are living with their children somewhere in Iran.

Khudáyár, our Baluchi guide, returned to Iran and continued

to help Bahá'ís, and others in danger, to escape. He was arrested
on his way to Záhidán one day while arranging the escape of
sixteen Bahá'ís. All seventeen were arrested, and K̲h̲udáyár was
severely tortured. It is not known whether he is still alive.

Áyatu'lláh Dastg̲h̲ayb, one of those responsible for issuing the
order to destroy the House of the Báb, left his house one Friday
to go to public prayers. He was approached by a Muslim woman
apparently trying to give him a letter. Although initially
stopped by the guards, she insisted on delivering the letter to
him personally. Once allowed through, the woman embraced
the Áyatu'lláh and detonated a bomb strapped to her body.
They were both blown to pieces in a massive explosion. It later
emerged that the woman who had carried out this killing was
from Jahrum, and that her brothers had been executed on the
orders of Áyatu'lláh Dastg̲h̲ayb because of their political activities.

Áyatu'lláh Qazá'í, the Religious Magistrate who gave the order
for the ten women to be executed, was moved from S̲h̲íráz to
Isfahán by the government, and continued his persecution of
the Bahá'í community. He was later arrested by the authorities
accused of some illegal activity, and was himself imprisoned in
Isfahán. He was tortured and lost the sight of one eye.

Mr Is̲h̲ráqí, the Public Prosecutor, is still believed to work in
the Revolutionary Court of S̲h̲íráz.

Áyatu'lláh Khomeini, who came to power in Iran in 1979, died
ten years later in Tehran.

The whereabouts of the first group of members of the **National
Spiritual Assembly** of Iran, who were arrested on 21 August
1980 with two Auxiliary Board Members, is still unknown and
all eleven men and women are presumed dead, buried in an
unmarked grave, somewhere in Iran. Eight members of the
second National Spiritual Assembly were later arrested, and
they were executed on 27 December 1981. The third group of
National Spiritual Assembly members were subsequently arrest-

ed, and four were executed in 1984. A fifth, Faríd Bihmardí, was executed in 1986. In August 1983 the government of Iran finally banned Bahá'í activities and made membership of assemblies a criminal offence. All Bahá'í institutions were disbanded in obedience to the government's order. There has not been a National Spiritual Assembly in Iran since 1983.

Of the nine men and women elected to the **Local Spiritual Assembly of S̲h̲íráz** in 1982, six were arrested, four of whom were executed, and the remaining three were forced into hiding. The second and third reserve groups who bravely took their place to serve the community suffered a similar fate. The assembly was dissolved in 1983.

The Bahá'í community of Iran is still denied constitutional protection: Bahá'ís are, under the law, 'unprotected infidels' and as such they are discriminated against. They do not enjoy the basic human rights granted to other citizens in Iran. Bahá'í marriages and divorces are not recognized, Bahá'ís cannot travel freely outside Iran, and their children are denied access to higher education, although they have now been readmitted to primary and secondary schools.

The economic oppression of Bahá'ís that began in 1979 has continued. More than 10,000 Bahá'ís in government employment were dismissed in the early 1980s, and a large proportion remain unemployed. Of course, they do not receive any state benefits. Pension rights have not been reinstated, Bahá'ís cannot officially open their own businesses and many Bahá'ís have had their homes and farms confiscated.

The fact that the Bahá'í Faith is still not a recognized religion in Iran means that Bahá'ís cannot freely express their religious beliefs, they have no right of assembly and they cannot elect their democratic administrative bodies. They cannot publish and distribute their sacred literature, and are forbidden to organize classes for children.

Bahá'í holy places, historical sites, cemeteries and centres, like the one in S̲h̲íráz, have either been destroyed, damaged or remain confiscated. The site of the House of the Báb has been completely levelled and a road and public square have been built on it. Architectural plans of the structure remain safe in Bahá'í hands. The House of the Báb will be built again.

Tens of thousands of Bahá'ís fled Iran to escape the persecution and 201 were killed by mobs or executed in the years between 1978 and 1992. Although the annual toll has declined since its peak in the 1980s, arbitrary arrests continue, as do sporadic outbursts of mob violence against Bahá'ís. Until the Bahá'í Faith is officially recognized as a minority religion in Iran, its members will remain outside the protection of the law, and their rights to freedom, education, property, work, to the practice of their religion and to life itself, although they are upheld by the Universal Declaration of Human Rights to which Iran is a signatory, will continue to be compromised.